PSYCHOTHERAPY FOR THE OTHER

PSYCHOTHERAPY FOR THE OTHER

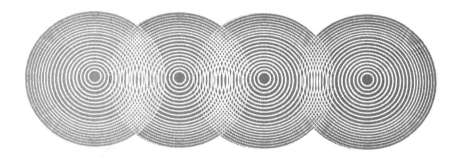

LEVINAS AND THE FACE-TO-FACE RELATIONSHIP

EDITED BY

KEVIN C. KRYCKA, GEORGE KUNZ & GEORGE G. SAYRE

DUQUESNE UNIVERSITY PRESS
Pittsburgh, Pennsylvania

Published in the United States of America by
DUQUESNE UNIVERSITY PRESS
600 Forbes Avenue
Pittsburgh, Pennsylvania 15282

Library of Congress Cataloging-in-Publication Data

Psychotherapy for the other : Levinas and the face-to-face relationship / edited
by Kevin C. Krycka, George Kunz, and George G. Sayre.
    p. ; cm.
  Includes bibliographical references and index.
    ISBN 978-0-8207-0479-1 (paper. : alk. paper)
I. Krycka, Kevin C., 1959– , editor. II. Kunz, George, 1934– , editor.
III. Sayre, George G., editor.
[DNLM: 1. Levinas, Emmanuel. 2. Psychotherapy. 3. Philosophy.
4. Psychoanalysis. WM 420]
RC480.5
616.89'14—dc23

                                                                2014037222

∞ Printed on acid-free paper.

CONTENTS

This is an important book. It offers a new fundamental orientation for psychology and psychologists, for psychiatrists and psychotherapists especially, by appropriating the interpersonal ethics of Emmanuel Levinas. Each author shows in both concrete and theoretical ways, laying out and commenting on specific case studies, a path upon which the healing imperative of psychology is joined to and derives its guidance from an ethical imperative, from selfhood defined no longer by self-interest but by moral responsibility for others. The path to mental health is through goodness.

That psychology and philosophy are put in proximity is no surprise. Aside from the fact that theory and practice are inseparable, even if their conjunction is sometimes only operative implicitly, the modern discipline of psychology from its very origins has always depended upon philosophy, most obviously on a philosophy of science. Their joint history, however, is older than that, for psychology did not emerge in the late nineteenth century ex nihilo.

The works of many philosophers are filled with psychological insights and elaborations, and sometimes these are not merely asides or passing observations. One thinks of Locke and Hume on ratiocination, or Kierkegaard and Nietzsche on alienation. Nietzsche adopted the label "psychologist" in preference to "philosopher." Edmund Husserl first called his new and revolutionary science "descriptive psychology," and later, when distinguishing phenomenology from psychology, he nevertheless emphatically insisted on the "*precise parallel*" between the two.

From the side of modern psychology, it is not only the meta-narratives of a Freud, Jung, Binswanger, Koffka, Fromm, or a Lacan, say, that wax philosophical. The link is deeper. The very structures these and other psychologists attribute to the human psyche —whether mechanical, mythological, existential, Gestalt, social, or linguistic— take up and are predisposed by prior philosophical conceptions of the same. Even more telling are the scientistic presuppositions adopted by and defining today's many behavioral psychologies, philosophical presuppositions all the more efficacious for being hidden by their presumed and thereby unexamined self-evidence.

Psychology cannot be divorced from philosophy. Indeed, no social science, or any science at all, can be divorced by philosophy understood in the broad sense of self-reflection regarding one's own fundamental principles and concepts. The fact that in our day much of psychology would disavow its philosophical roots is itself and paradoxically the product of a particular philosophy, to which we will turn shortly.

First, however, let us think for a moment longer about the differences between philosophy and psychology. No doubt they have different aims. Despite their shared interest in truth, both are ruled by other interests, interests served by their shared truth-interest itself. Philosophy aims not only at true knowledge or science but also at wisdom. As its name tells, it is a "love of wisdom." The term "wisdom" almost seems archaic in our day. But it indicates that cognition or intellection is not enough. Philosophy is also desire: desire guided by reason, desire made reasonable, reasonable desire. The life of wisdom is thus larger than science for it aims not only at the true life but at the good life—life in accord not merely with ideas, even if true, but with values, the highest values. Philosophy is life oriented by the search for and an accord with what is best, by excellence, by virtue, whether achievable or always desirable. True, as Socrates insisted, one must know the good. But one knows the good in the doing of it. Or as Aristotle put the matter in a seeming paradox that is actually no paradox but the starting point of wisdom: to become good one must do as the good person does.

Psychology likewise aims at truth, the truth of the psyche specifically. And it too is not simply true knowledge, research, science, but also therapy, psychiatry and psychotherapy, a healing art, a part of medicine, making well, curing sickness, helping others in psychic pain. It is *episteme* bound to *techne*, knowledge guided by practice, the two inseparable, neither reducible to the Other, neither itself without the Other. Like philosophy guided by virtue, psychology too is guided by a standard, an excellence: health. In seeking and guiding toward mental health lie all the greatness and all the difficulty of psychology, not to mention its intersection with philosophy. What is mental health? What does it mean to have or to be a healthy human psyche?

It is in response to these necessary questions, a response perforce philosophical, that psychology today, in practice and in the academy, has become increasingly problematic. This is because psychology, like so many other areas of contemporary life, has increasingly come under the penumbra of *positivism*. This is the "particular philosophy" referred to above. It is the intellectual conviction that only what can be quantitatively measured is real, and the rest is merely subjective, merely anecdotal, unreliable, opinion, and not truth. While no practicing psychotherapist can in good conscience act on such an outlook, this view nonetheless has tremendous theoretical cache, opening the door to the pharmacy while closing that of philosophy. Obviously such a philosophy—for it is a philosophy—derives from the enormous success of the natural sciences and the application of the outlook of the natural sciences to all things. Opposing the reductions and consequent abstractions of positivism, already in the nineteenth century Wilhelm Dilthey distinguished two types of knowledge: "explanation" and "understanding," the former suitable for object relations and the latter for human relations. Positivism, like a latter-day Pythagoreanism, rejects such a distinction and accepts only explanation, only what can be measured, computed, digitalized. On top of that, it offers soma in place of suffering.

Once again, however, it is a case of success breeding failure. Never has a more powerful—analytic, precise, universal—form of knowledge existed on the planet Earth than physics and chemistry, modeled as they are on mathematics. Their success has rightly swept away the scientific pretensions of mythology, superstition, folklore, scripture, and the like. But positivism goes farther: inebriated by the success of the natural sciences, it is a philosophy greedy for more of the rewards brought by this success, such as industry- and government-sponsored research grants and funding. It would reduce all types of knowing to mathematics, physics, and chemistry to their facsimiles and discard the remainder as nonsense, sweeping them under the rug and looking the other way.

Positivist psychology, then, is simply part of this larger trend. But the humanity of the human is not so easily dispatched, especially in a discipline devoted to mental health. The price of positivism in psychology has been high. What has happened is not that psychology has become truly scientific but, precisely and unfortunately, the reverse.

It is an instance of the famous "return of the repressed": positivist psychology insisting on its scientific credentials has increasingly become unscientific. There are several reasons for this.

First of all, the hard sciences are not hard in the way imagined by positivists. That is to say, their objectivity is neither purely objectivist nor mathematical. The sciences themselves are human products, indeed, social constructs. This doesn't make them "merely" subjective, as positivism fears, but it allows us to see how they are not purely objectivist either. Science, its knowledge, its method, its truths, depends upon social negotiations. Science is an exacting discipline, to be sure, but for all this, it is never exact, never purely mathematical or mechanical, not in establishing the boundaries of disciplines, not in defining their aims, and not in the invention of hypotheses and their testing. Every scientific hypothesis—already a human creation—must be confirmed by other scientists before its truth value is established. The positivist psychologist, trying to imitate what is actually a false image of the natural sciences, ends up like the Wizard of Oz dealing with fantasy not reality, a map and not the terrain.

Further, because a Disney-like image of the real takes precedence over the messier, more intimate and value-laden transactions of human sociality, two things unfortunate and unscientific happen. Attempting, impossibly, to avoid value judgments, a huge value judgment comes to dominate positivist psychology, namely, the defining of mental health as *adjustment.* No doubt psychic illness, like all illness, is a deviation from a norm. But defining mental health as adjustment says nothing about what that norm is. And by taking no stand, it stands for too much. Its alleged value neutrality simply means it supports the status quo, defining mental health as adjustment to whatever social norms are given; making no judgment as to their value, it thereby values their given social estimation all the more. During the communist era in the Soviet Union exactly this same positivism meant adjustment to the ideology of a Stalinist state, so that political dissent was indistinguishable from psychological deviation and political dissidents were locked up in mental asylums for mental illness with the full endorsement of the Soviet psychology establishment.

So, two additional and related problems are generated by positivist psychology. Despite—or really because of—its own claims to objectivity and value-neutrality, it becomes *relativist.* Mental health and sickness are defined in terms of the status quo, the Establishment, the contingent givenness of whatever social norms are contemporary or politically enforced. Thus it also becomes *conformist*, defining health as adjustment to *given* social norms. So in America today, positivist psychiatric practice, like the outcomes of all the positivist social sciences, far from being value-neutral or scientific, translates into the endorsement and enforcement, in the name of mental health, of selfhood playing its cooperative part within a self-interested consumerist worldview.

Because contemporary positivist psychology fails to perceive its own value judgments it has become ideological rather than scientific. Like all ideologies, it is blind to its own prejudices and cannot see far enough to correct them. Here we must recall Socrates' dictum that genuine ignorance is not lack of information but not knowing that one does not know. Such ignorance is not excused by all the rewards it may garner or by the fact that so many other social sciences have succumbed to the same narrow-minded scientism. What should never be overlooked by psychology and psychologists is mental health, the value of and the values inherent in such a determination. And for that one must have a more developed conception of human being than is possible within the strictures of positivism.

Fortunately all is not lost. If not most professional psychologists still many, including the editors and authors of the present volume, are acutely aware of the problems that arise due to the positivist constricting of horizons.

One important nonpositivist school, which I mention because it must be distinguished from the Seattle School owing to its apparent similarity, is Existential psychology. Existential psychology, as the name suggests, obviates positivism by turning to the various notions of human "existence" elaborated by 20th century Existentialist philosophers. What this means, concretely, is an appropriation of Existentialist conceptions of selfhood—including alienation, ennui, meaninglessness, boredom, despair, Angst, being-toward-death, and the like—to aid in understanding and diagnosing certain psychic illnesses. Here one thinks especially of the influence of the philosophy of Martin Heidegger (though he always denied the label "Existentialist") on the "*Dasein* analysis" of the Swiss psychologist Ludwig Binswanger. But there are many such instances, such as Rollo May, Paul Tillich,

Philip Rieff, R. D. Laing (in relation to Sartre especially), and Thomas Szasz, of psychologists/philosophers influenced by Existentialist themes and producing a large professional and popular literature of existentially oriented psychological theory and practice.

Unfortunately, while Existential psychology saw the positivist problem, its turn to existential themes did not prove sufficient as a solution. Grasping that alienation, say, or mortality are not elements of human existence that can be explained away or squashed through chemistry; and that they must be faced with mindfulness, while certainly a step in the right direction toward self-understanding, does not by itself go far enough toward curing persons acutely suffering from alienation or meaninglessness. Existentialist psychology, for all its genuinely corrective insights and sensitivity, remained bound to the standard of adjustment and to the flaws inherent in such a norm, even if that to which therapists now pointed their patients comprised a more accurate description of the human condition.

What remained missing is what Levinas's thought has been able to supply: recognition that human mental health involves human existence, yes, and must thus take account of social existence, yes, but even more fundamentally, that human social existence is from the first an *ethical* relation. What all of Levinas's philosophy teaches is that human subjectivity is neither an object nor a monad, whether altruistic or self-absorbed and self-interested, but rather, that its humanity comes from *ethical responsibility for others.* Being "for-the-Other" comes before being for-oneself. It is this structure—which is not merely a gloss or a second-order explanation or interpretation—of selfhood, its first-person responsibility, a turning toward the Other, individuality singularized because obligated to and for the Other, taking care of the Other, that constitutes the true self. What this means for psychology is that human mental health can no longer be detached from human goodness, from moral kindness toward the Other who faces, and from the call for justice for all that is part of kindness toward the Other.

It is a remarkable indeed a stunning insight, even if at the same time one wants to proclaim its obviousness. It is obvious because morality is not something for the few, for intellectuals, for the cultured. The simplest person, the "idiot" Dostoyevsky might say, like the most sophisticated can attend and ought to attend to moral obligations. A human is not simply an object, to be sure, but neither is a human an existence or an odd type of being, like a fingerprint. Rather, the "humanity of the human," as Levinas calls it, arises as nobility, the nobility of responsibility.

Each and every human being is thus "chosen." Better than caring for objects or things or ideas, even if all three do and must come into play, the human is, rather and most profoundly, a concern for the welfare of the other person as one's innermost and highest directive. The self or the selflessness of self-sacrifice as the true self! Selfhood as "love of the neighbor." Such claims are not empty or merely high-flying rhetoric but indicate the most concrete of relations, one person in relation to another, and the most difficult of tasks, obligations that extend beyond one's circle of intimates, or beyond even one's own generation, or truth be told, beyond the human community altogether to include the community of all sentient being. Mental health, the true singularity of the person, comes through the moral engagement at the root of genuine sociality, relations to others made possible by and originating in moral responsibility for the one who faces and concluding in the unfinished tasks of justice for all others. These are not externals or fancy window dressing, but who we are, who you are, who I am, in our utmost humanity.

To take responsibility for another is to rise to one's most human self. The healthy human being is the one who takes up his or her responsibilities, responsibilities for those who are close, for family and friends, for community, and for those who are far, those who are different, those who are enemies, those who live on the other side of the planet, even as far as other species, as far as all of creation. Goodness, kindness, compassion, humility, love of neighbor... these are not—or ought not to be—demeaned as terms of mere rhetoric. They cut to the heart of the human. Nothing is more pressing, more exigent, more sobering, nor is anything more noble. To help the patient reattach to his or her responsibilities and find meaning in them, this is the responsibility of the therapist and the real aim of psychology.

Such, in any event, are the claims—the claims of a knowing broader, deeper, higher than that of physics or chemistry—made by the authors of the articles that make up this fine collection. Addressing these concerns, forging this new path for psychology, such, so far, have been the hard labors of discovery and recovery and the noble goal of the Seattle School of psychology, to which I wholeheartedly commend the reader.

Richard A. Cohen
Buffalo, New York

Introduction

George Kunz, Kevin C. Krycka, and George G. Sayre

Kunz writes: I carried a copy of *Collected Philosophical Papers* for Emmanuel Levinas to sign when visiting him with my family in Paris in 1987. Levinas wrote an inscription, "Avec tous mes regrets devant une occasion de sympathie active — manqué. Paris le 2 juin 87, E. Levinas," and as he wrote, he asked, "Why would a psychologist be interested in my philosophy?" I tried to explain. The short answer: his description that autonomy (self-directed freedom) follows what he calls heteronomy (other-directed responsibility). Reaching beyond his existential and phenomenological teachers Heidegger and Husserl, he found not freedom but responsibility to be the defining characteristic of the human. He states this quite clearly in *Ethics and Infinity* (1985): "I speak of responsibility as the essential, primary and fundamental structure of subjectivity. I describe subjectivity in ethical terms. Ethics, here, does not supplement a preceding existential base: the very node of the subjective is knotted in ethics understood as responsibility" (95). He ratchets it up in *Otherwise than Being* (1981): "This identity is brought out by responsibility and is at the service of the other. In the form of responsibility, the psyche in the soul is the other in me, a malady of identity, both accused and self, the same for the other, the same by the other. . . . it is a substitution, extraordinary" (69).

My responsibility for the Other comes before my freedom. This reversal allows me to recognize what private freedom is: only freedom. My responsibility releases me of the pretense of defending what my freedom is not: independently autonomous. Isolating myself

1

in my independent freedom leaves me paradoxically not free. The price of recognizing that I am responsible for what I did not initiate, for the Other, is certainly a "malady." The Other traumatizes my ego and shakes me out of my self-deceived identity. This frees me to responsibly serve. The burden of service paradoxically frees me to be more fully human. Again in *Ethics and Infinity* (1985): "I am responsible for him, without even having taken on responsibilities in his regard: his responsibility is incumbent on me. It is responsibility that goes beyond what I do. Usually, one is responsible for what one does oneself. I say, in *Otherwise than Being,* that responsibility is initially a for-the-Other. This means that I am responsible for his very responsibility" (96).

My discovery that I am not the center of myself but find the Other there is a Copernican revolution. I am responsible for this Other, even for what the Other does. This responsibility is not a law of nature. I can disregard, even violate, the Other and, by this, sabotage myself. This responsibility for the Other is commanded as a moral imperative. I do not have a choice in being called; I do have a choice in how I respond. By nature I'm self-interested. But my freedom ought not be capricious, for my and the Other's good. My freedom is not solely mine; it is invested in me by others for others. My freedom is called forth by the needs of others and given to me as responsible. The self can and should enjoy life—but not irresponsibly. Levinas offers the best of how enjoyment and responsibility serve each other.

Levinas certainly challenges relativism that allows freedom to do wherever and however I want. But he is not a moralist telling us what to do and not do. He urges us to look at the Other who commands us to be responsible. He reminds us that freedom is to protect the freedom of others. He is a phenomenologist describing how the face of the Other revealing her/his fundamental dignity and otherness calls us to tasks of ethics: to not kill, to not harm, to not judge, but serve. This revolution allowed our existential-phenomenological psychology (EPP) program to better understand and more forcefully challenge both the determinism of naturalist psychology and the chaos of postmodern individual relativism.

Levinas's philosophy is simultaneously both an individualism and a communitarianism but twists both these "isms" from how they are usually understood. His is an individualism because it is incumbent on me as an individual to be responsible for others. My individuality does not originate from myself—my self-reflection, self-initiative, self-care—but as the individual right here called to provide for the needs of the Other right there. I cannot escape the individual I am. His philosophy is a communitarianism, not because my responsibility is for the collective but, instead, for every individual in the community. He often quoted Dostoyevsky's *The Brothers Karamazov*, for example in *Ethics and Infinity:* "We are all responsible for all and for all men and before all, and I more than all the others" (Levinas 1985, 98, 101). This difficult challenge helped us understand more clearly how ego-centrism is the basis for pathology and ethical responsibility the basis for health.

His phenomenology goes beyond classical phenomenology. It finds the Other on the hither side of the perceived phenomenon. That is, Levinas describes the Other presented by her face as what is "otherwise than being," as not present to observation. He warns, "I do not know if one can speak of a 'phenomenology of the face,' since phenomenology describes what appears.... I think rather that access to the face is straightaway ethical" (1985, 85). I can see her countenance, her eyes, forehead, chin, but this makes her an object presented as a phenomenon. As face she shows herself to be always more than what I can see—and more than what she can reveal. Her real identity escapes me. She reveals herself as beyond me exceeding my powers and as above exceeding my rights, calling me to obligations; she comes first (see Williams, chapter 8). This turnabout may be scandalous (Severson 2011) to those who hold the fundamental characteristic of self-identity to be self-preservation, self-perpetuation, self-development. For our EPP program, this turn was the alternative to the culturally powerful myth of the primacy of self.

We certainly see, both in others and ourselves, the noisy, exhibitionist, me-first, give-in-order-to-get, self-assertive style but always against the quiet, often unnoticeable, background of selfless, nonreciprocated, sacrificial generosity. Pure self-interest does not match experience, nor does it show itself to be in our own best interest. Nor can we be certain of the purity of motivations in service, neither my neighbor's nor my own. While self-interest is necessary for survival, responsibility trumps it. Self-less-ness and generosity haunts us as ideal, better than self-interest. Saints and sinners all admire saintliness (Levinas 1985). We cannot be certain that our service will give what the Other needs, nor that we are the one to serve this particular need. Despite the ambiguities and enigmas about how to respond, we are called to be responsible, to do what we can. Calculating and choosing how to best respond is the beginning and end of reason. Reason comes from the work of obligation (see Pape, chapter 12).

Authors of fiction and observers of historical facts affirm the paradox that the power of self-interest can be its own worst enemy and the weakness of neediness can be powerful, and that obligations are burdensome. This Copernican revolution is not new. Humans have always known themselves to be obligated. We often try to escape the burden but find no way out (Levinas 2003b). Dostoyevsky and all good writers give us a psychology not only more profound but truer to our own experience than modern psychology still committed to the determinism of nature.

Kunz reflects: Home from Paris, I got a good translation of Levinas's inscription, "Avec tous mes regrets devant une occasion de sympathie active—manqué" (With all my regrets on this occasion of active fellow feeling—missed opportunity). I took him to mean: "nice talking to you, too bad we could not discuss the questions you mailed earlier, which I promised in a responding letter for our visit, but missed." My family's visit was short and casual, and my stunted French kept us from the opportunity to talk in our face-to-face meeting about my previous written questions. Over the years, however, reading closer his themes of responsibility, shame, guilt, obligations beyond abilities, first a servant, already late and guilty for being late (1981, 87), I began to understand how his regrets and missed opportunity (manqué) could describe the anguish of therapists called to fulfill what they could never possibly complete. Those we train do insightful, self-sacrificing, and generous work, but the needs of their clients could never be rendered to whatever they as therapists offer.

In 1975 Steen Halling published "The Implications of Emmanuel Levinas's *Totality and Infinity* for Therapy," reprinted here as our first chapter. It was the first paper exploring the implications of Levinas's thought for psychotherapy. The following passage is central to the approach we want to communicate in this text: "The therapy situation may be one place where we can hope for genuine discourse to take place, at least occasionally, and where the hours of rhetoric may be interrupted by moments of conversation. The hope resides not in the wisdom and cleverness of the therapist, but the fact that we are in the presence of someone who may dispossess us of our understanding, our comprehension, and allow us to hear and speak" (Halling 1975, 221). To dispossess rather than confirm our psychological knowledge and skills is at the core of what we understand to be *good* psychotherapy. Only when therapists are brought out of themselves, humbled and hurt, can dialogue begin. Phenomenology gives us a method, one that proposes that without theoretical filters in the way we are better able to observe what clients reveal.

Since Halling published his seminal paper, there has been an increase in scholarship dedicated to the intersection of Levinas with psychology and psychotherapy. In 2002 Edwin Gantt and Richard Williams from Brigham Young University collected ten articles in *Psychology for the Other: Levinas, Ethics, and the Practice of Psychology*. In 1998 Kunz published *The Paradox of Power and Weakness: Levinas and an Alternative Paradigm for Psychology*.

Therapists often tell us they remember their academic preparation with disappointment, sometimes with regret. A genuinely therapeutic attitude, they discover later, is developed by sitting receptively with clients more than sitting in class on theory and technique. Clients teach the therapeutic attitude. Once out in practice therapists complain about agencies requiring tasks that reduce both clients and themselves to units (cogs) in an industrial machine: manualized, mass-produced, market-forced, evidence-based techniques (see Krycka, chapter 3). They knew it would be difficult but never thought of it grinding into routine, oppressiveness, and even violence to the dignity of the people they hoped to serve (see Slocum, chapter 13). Contrary to their deep reflection on what makes therapy therapeutic, their work is often drained of meaning. They are not quite sure why forces outside their clients' revealing themselves and making choices hijacked their noble intentions. Many therapists burn out and leave or unhappily stay. Their honorable service has become detached from what they anticipated would be helpful to people developing their own honorable self-respect and concern for others.

Don't misread us. Most therapists like helping clients even when the chores of managing therapy seem more like matching spreadsheet-outcomes with contracted-treatment-plans than helping folks manage their life-worlds. They often find ways around these constrictions in order to protect their clients, preserve the therapeutic attitude, and help. Their efforts continue to be generous when, using Levinas's poetic language, they "stare with straightforwardness devoid of trickery or evasion, into his [their client's] unguarded eyes" (Levinas 1990a, 293). They respond with genuine care and concern. They do good work with individuals and contribute to the common good by helping desperate and sometimes disruptive people calm their fears, angers, confusions and become responsible to families and others (see Grimesey-Szarka, chapter 6). Despite realizing that they do not know enough about pathology nor will ever fully understand their clients, they continue to listen carefully to strange and haunting stories of trauma and pain. Despite being humbled by their inability to change lives, they help folks struggle with better choices. Despite not feeling adequately empathic, they suffer because they cannot quite reach across this isolating separation from the suffering of their clients. They suffer because their clients, who do not deserve to suffer, do suffer (see McNabb, chapter 5). They blame themselves for not being good enough for the kind of success expected. They confess inadequacies to supervisors and consultation groups but continue to serve simply, humbly, and compassionately. With their simplicity, humility, and patient compassion, they keep on keeping on and elevate this noble profession (see LeBeau, chapter 11).

Faced with psychologically frustrating and psychologically demanding work, therapists need to brace themselves with self-care—not self-pampering but self-grounding care, with continual rigorous but reassuring reflection on what psychotherapy is all about. The authors of these chapters have found that the epi-phenomenological insights of Levinas keep them going by setting aside burdensome theories and clunky techniques in order to be ethically present to the meanings revealed by clients. Refusing to search for clear and distinct (self-reassuring) explanations, they find that straightforward-facing clients dispossess them of self-attention, to be more useful than searching for objective (mythical) causes. They see hope in relational psychoanalysis replacing overanalyzed, too complex, and weighty systems of depth analysis. They are encouraged by the practice-based-evidence approach among cognitive/behavioral therapists whose evidence-based-practice is over-technologized and bogged down in calculations according to standardized treatment plans from research.

Practice-based evidence relies on the therapist being awake to the revelations of their clients as therapy proceeds, as opposed to evidence-based practice based on evidence from independently gained data in controlled situations. Evidence directly from the client has been the approach of phenomenology. After a while all perceptive and compassionate therapists become ethical phenomenologists: facing clients whose faces ask them to hold back their abstractions and practiced methods and listen for the meanings that appeal for help revealed in stories told.

This *Psychotherapy for the Other: Levinas and the Face-to-Face Relationship* is certainly not a how-to book, no six easy steps to successful healing—there's no such thing. Over time individual therapists develop styles to engage clients. Nonetheless their accustomed habits, as good as they might be, are continually called into question by each client asking for an individual and personal encounter. Every psychotherapeutic approach and method has a set of assumed beliefs about the nature of the human condition, about hurting, and about healing. Too often these beliefs have not been sufficiently reflected upon. This neglect comes from either giving up under the pressure from supervisors or funders cutting services or insisting on particular practices or from not being rigorously thoughtful for self-questioning. They work on shaky ground but it's the only ground they have. We all need reflective renewal on the presuppositions that guide what we are all about. This need to be better therapists originates from the vulnerability and dignity of clients.

Disturbed by what is asked of them, therapists struggle with ethical questions. Genuinely caring people cannot help but wonder about the moral ground of their work and find it not in abstract principles and commissioned rules but in the goodness and call for responsibility from the Other sitting across from them (see Macdonald, chapter 7). Therapists need both a philosophical foundation to ground their complaints about what failed or their gratitude for what happily surprised them and a philosophy of responsibility to continue committed to their enigmatic clients. They find the basis of this philosophy in face-to-face facing. Putting this into inspiring language, Levinas, in "On the Usefulness of Insomnia" (an interview with Bertrand Revillon first published in 1987 [Robbins 2001]), tells us what philosophy ought to be:

> Philosophy permits man to interrogate himself about what he says and about what one says to oneself in thinking. No longer to let oneself be swayed or intoxicated by the rhythm of words and the generality that they designate, but to open oneself to the uniqueness of the unique in the real, that is to say, to the uniqueness of the other, ...to love...to be awakened, for a new sobering, more profound, philosophy.... The encounter with the other is the great experience, the grand event. The encounter with the other is awakening. Philosophy as insomnia, as a new awakening at the heart of the self-evident. (234)

It is the encounter with clients who call therapists to philosophize, to interrogate themselves, to be awakened, to sober up to the "grand event" they undergo in each session (see Goodman and Becker, chapter 9). The authors of this collection have thought deeply and questioningly about what is human about being human, what is pathological about pathology, and what is therapeutic about therapy.

Our chapters are invitations to fellow psychotherapists to enter this kind of philosophical territory, perhaps unfamiliar with its challenging language and seeming impractical "head stuff," knowing their colleagues want an approach for thoughtful reflection and will be relieved to find one here. They have wanted an alternative to egology (self-focus) with its explicit or implicit primacy of self-interest. Levinas's heteronomy (other-focused alterology) has inspired their search for an approach to depose their egoic self and replaces it with the Other to help clients break out of their lonely isolation. Therapists find themselves as the one "right here" in "the grand event" called to be responsible for the Other "right there," to be present with simplicity, humility, and patience.

Levinas does not offer a theory about the structure of the human psyche nor even an organized philosophical treatise. His philosophy is not a logical discourse but, rather, more like inspirational poetry to evoke awe, respect, and service. The basis for these authors' therapeutic practice is not rational understanding but ethical standing-under. Therapy is not primarily knowledge of clients but responsibility for them. Knowledge can get in the way if it is not solidly founded on the desire for the good of the client. These therapists do not construct classification systems for pathology and therapy from his philosophy. Their intention is to develop a way to be with clients. Some point out the gaps in Levinas for understanding pathology and the practice of therapy and add what they see missing. He is not a psychologist but offers the best for finding ethics as the basis for psychological interaction. He is not an authority but an inspiration. Their job is to work out the therapeutic implications of this radically ethical-centered desire for the good of the Other.

To state their discovery directly: it is the ethical that makes therapy therapeutic. Listening with simple ethical openness—without presupposed totalizing knowledge of the client—is therapeutic. Working with humble ethical obedience, without techniques driven by a "prescribed agenda," is therapeutic. Desiring the client with ethical compassion because he suffers the terrifying horror of the raw *there is* of isolating existence makes therapy healing. Levinas describes the *there is*...as the inescapable given-ness of being trapped in who the self is at this time and in this place when she would like to escape her troubled embodied presence. Therapy shows the possibility of transcending to a better existence with others. Therapists are grateful for the exasperating gift of the singularity (Bozga 2009) of the client, his saying that he is singularly hurting, and his capacity for healing himself. Atterton (2010) shows how Levinas's distinction between the (oracular) said (*dit*) and the ethical saying (*dire*) can make talk in therapy be revealing and attending more than merely storytelling.

• • •

What does Levinas offer these authors?

(1) A rich description of enjoyment (*jouissance*), not only of ordinary "good soup" (Levinas 1969, 110) but of everything consumed, and relished before consumption. For a philosopher who is known for describing difficult ethical responsibility, his description of enjoyment is richer and, as the beginning of ethics, more sensual than that of other philosopher. Enjoyment is not contrary to responsible sacrifice for the Other but serves as part of its foundation. Only the one who experiences the enjoyable materialization of matter through the eyes, on the tongue, in the nose, the ears, or the hand can be ethically responsible and use these body parts to serve the material enjoyment and needs of others. Levinas tells us, "In enjoyment matter carries on, 'does its job' of being matter. Matter materializes in the satisfaction of it. Before matter fills an emptiness, it delights a hunger" (Levinas 1981, 73). Objects can only become materially objective, fully separated from the subjectivity of the subject's knowledge and possession when given to another by naming in conversation and by use in the Other's actions and enjoyment.

(2) The distinctive uniqueness of every singular person. The exasperating gift of singularity of each client demands that therapists face that client as an individual searching for identity by enjoying happiness and struggling against the suffering of his or her unique pain. Phenomenologists have always urged calling into question presuppositions. But Levinas inspires in us an ethical obligation to self-question and *be* the one called to respond to others with radical openness.

(3) A radically deeper ethics, one neither based in the self choosing to be good nor located in the abstract principles of philosophy, religion, law, customs, habits. Ethics shows itself in the unfathomable face-to-face relationship. There is something excessive about responsibility in Levinas's account: its depth is limitless, I am never done

with my responsibilities (1981). From a negative ethics—"thou shalt not kill" (1981)—therapists know a variety of ways to kill, sometimes by an expression, a look, or a word and even with a good conscience: the common killing in all innocence. More than a "being toward its own death" (Heidegger 1962), the human is a "being responsible for the death of others." And from a positive ethics—"thou shalt serve" (Levinas 1981)—his most powerful metaphor is of the maternal psyche: "gestation of the other in the same. . . . the groaning of the wounded entrails by those it will bear or has borne. Maternity, which is bearing par excellence, bears even responsibility for the persecuting by the persecutor" (75). It is a tearing away of bread from the mouth that tastes it to give it to the Other (64) (see Cohen's marvelous article, "Maternal Psyche" (Cohen 2002). His is radical phenomenology, a phenomenology beyond ontology and epistemology, beyond being and knowing; it is an ethical phenomenology.

(4) A broader reach for ethics. All behavior and relationships are fundamentally ethical. All are included between a simple act of courtesy—"after you, sir"—and total self-sacrifice—"I'll give my life." Behavior does not become ethical by the virtuous disposition and initiative of the doer. Nor is ethics spread on top of relationships making them better like butter on toast. To be human is to be ethical. The authors of this collection have found that every act alone or as a response to another's needs is ethical. We are really never alone; others are never far away, always "in our psyche" even when somewhere else. There is no escape from responsibility.

(5) The basis for understanding the talking part of the "talking cure" with Levinas's distinctions between language in its instrumental function, the said, and language as a relation with another, saying (Atterton 2010) (see Severson, chapter 2). We could call therapy the "saying cure" to show how it is the expression of the client saying, "Here I am before you painfully revealing my suffering and naked neediness, asking you to be present to really listen and help." It could also be called the "saying cure" from the expression of the therapist saying, "I am here for you with deep respect for your worthiness and infinite otherness, listening to you revealing yourself." These sayings are the primal expression carrying what is said between them, the content of their dialogue, their questions, disclosures, suggestions, and expressions of concern.

What do these chapters contain? We asked the authors to include the following characteristics. Their articles were to be (1) inspired by Levinas's philosophy; (2) clinical, containing case studies; (3) without a lot of philosophical or psychological technical language making them inaccessible to lay-folks; and (4) associated with our existential-phenomenological approach at Seattle University. To this end, we have divided the text into two sections: a theoretical part, focused mainly on broad questions regarding the intersection of Levinas and psychotherapy, and an applications part, where the authors explore in detail the clinical importance of Levinas's thought.

We begin with an update of Steen Halling's 1975 paper, "Levinas's *Totality and Infinity* for Therapy," which describes his humbling experience of being dispossessed by the otherness of clients in three cases and finds inspiration from Levinas to understand that the good therapist is the person who remains willing to let the other person reveal himself. Eric R. Severson's "Levinas, Psychology, and Language," is the most philosophically challenging chapter, digging deeply into a key tool of therapy: talking. Severson unpacks Levinas's description of what comes before or after or beyond talking about things, what he calls the said. The saying, before the said, is the revealing by the face of the other person whose suffering summons from before words and themes. Severson uses the term "deēsis," a quasi-religious term almost like prayer. At this register, which Severson calls the "dialect of the Other," language is more like supplication, an election to indicate that the Other first calls the self to be responsible. He offers a critique of hermeneutics (diagnosis and understanding of the client) as an incomplete epistemology that doesn't always ethically attend to the deeper layer of language and discourse. The encounter with the suffering Other is diachronic, always other: the therapist cannot synchronize the client's temporal existence with her own. Kevin C. Krycka's "Asymmetry in Psychotherapy" questions the preference for symmetry found in notions of balance, harmony, equality, fairness, power, diversity, and even justice. Holding too firmly to the comforts of symmetry—the gentle hum brought to consciousness from the constant erosion of fresh thinking that relies upon exteriority—therapists tend to refuse to honor the significance of the asymmetrical nature of dialogue, relationship, and performance. Unlike Levinas, they honor sameness over otherness. They should be open to the asymmetrical. Alexandra Adame closes out this theoretical section with the chapter "Martin Buber and Emmanuel Levinas." Here, Adame draws together Buber's anthropology and Levinas's ethics of responsibility in order to explore the interrelated concepts of authenticity and community.

In the applications section, we collected chapters with very concrete cases. Marie McNabb's chapter, "The Aftermath of Murder," describes working with a young man orphaned by the murder of his parents and suffering post-traumatic stress disorder (PTSD) as well as McNabb's own vicarious trauma. Using Levinas's distinction between the said and saying, McNabb asks if there is a face-to-face saying when one person kills another, if there is an encounter. She rejects the common thinking that the killer reduces the victim to an object and suggests that the murderer encounters the face of the Other and is unsettled by the victim's subjectivity looking back from a disturbing depth. The murderer sees something that evades naming and attempts to be bigger than the infinity he encounters. As murder is the inability to stand in awe revealed in the face, so therapy must be to stand under to revive in clients another possible outcome. Murder and therapy are situations of saying without the said within an ethical act, without either participant fully knowing what is happening.

Jackie Grimesey-Szarka's "The Tragedy of Domestic Violence" uses Levinas's distinctions between need and desire, between love and desire, between separation and the illusion of independence, between care and control, between patience and becoming a victim in order to help define how the home can turn to danger, imprisonment, violence, and abuse from the one who says he or she loves. She offers an alternative. Heather Macdonald, in "Levinas in the Hood," describes herself as a clinician working with African American adolescents in foster care. For her, ethics is not only the first philosophy but also that seeing the face of the Other becomes a daily imperative for survival and not a philosophical abstraction. What happens when frameworks for perceiving, comprehending, and communicating have changed under our feet, when the signifier and the signified no longer reference one another?

Richard Williams's "Levinas and Psychoanalysis" describes Levinas's view of the human condition, his place in contemporary thought in psychology, and how this radical turn outward from oneself and up to the Other can help for understanding self-betraying emotions. David Goodman and Brian Becker's chapter, "Trauma as Violent Awakening," advances Levinas's notion of trauma as it relates to the complacent self and the disturbing face of the Other. The authors consider how the presence of the therapist can either push the client deeper into self-protection or invite him out of hiding to be awakened to responsibility, from the "lesser freedom" of autonomy to the "greater freedom" of giving oneself to others. From case material, they ask how the therapist can avoid perpetuating a trauma response. They wonder whether we can develop from Levinas a process to move from slumber to safety and familiarity, and finally, then, to the freedom and aliveness of responsibility. George G. Sayre's "Toward a Therapy for the Other" exposes the paradox that, while therapy is intended for the well-being of the client, it is other-centered for the therapist and often self-centered for the client. He urges therapy for the good of the client by helping her or him be ethically good for others, making de-centering both the means and the ends of therapy.

Three very fine chapters with haunting cases round out the book. Claire Steele LeBeau's "Therapeutic Impasse and the Call to Keep Looking" asks what happens in therapy when understanding occurs out of moments of apparent impasse. How do therapists experience moments when they have missed something vital in their being with their client, so that the client must then come to teach the therapist? She explores these two questions in a clinical example with a severely depressed person who called her to fully engage the impasse and to keep looking for the client beyond it. In moments of profound frustration in being "stuck" with the client in wastelands of despair, Levinas's words came to instruct and inspire the author to keep looking for the client by fully questioning her own "counter-resistance." She held on to her tethers of hope for his "enjoyment" and "happiness of living." In order to move through impasse, she was called into a paradoxical surrender of her own tethering in order to join him in his despair. Kathleen Pape's "Face of the Other in Motherhood"—using her personal account of initial revulsion, being called to respond to her infant's vulnerability, and her visceral response—explicates the transcendent nature of responding to the radical Other within the mother-child relationship and the developmental process inherent in that role.

Trevor Slocum's "When Therapy Wounds" uses Levinas to face a persistent social problem. He describes how psychotherapy both reflects and reproduces its cultural context, which includes the moral traditions embedded in political structure and how to maintain a responsible approach to not pathologize homosexuality. Gay men won a significant battle when homosexuality was removed from the *Diagnostic and Statistical Manual* (*DSM*). But there lingers those who insist on treatment to "help" homosexuals become "normal." Levinas's phenomenology helps maintain a responsible approach to this issue.

We close with George Kunz's "Weak Enough," returning attention to the graduate program at Seattle University. He describes the paradox that the power of the therapist—her knowledge, skill, and neutrality—can sabotage therapy, whereas allowing herself to be "weakened" (opened) by the infinite otherness of the client, his absolute dignity and separateness, can be the foundation for therapy. Furthermore the goal of the program is not only to help therapists become radically open but for them to help clients develop an ethical "weakness" (openness) in the forms of the paradoxical strength of simplicity, humility, and patience.

In closing we want to offer another interpretation of Levinas's inscription in Kunz's copy of his book about regrets and manqué (missed opportunity). We regret that psychology has missed the fundamental characteristic of the human, that is, to be ethically responsible. We urge a shift from a self-centered to an other-centered paradigm. As Severson says, we not only regret, we lament our ignorance, our clumsiness, our apathy. But we have this paradoxical weakness of power to offer as a gift to help heal the Other.

PART ONE

THEORY

ONE

Levinas's *Totality and Infinity* for Therapy

Steen Halling

> There is a man who calls me wife
> Who knows me but does not know my life
> And my two sons who call me mother
> See me not as any other
> Yet if the fabric of my day
> Should be unwound and fall away
> What colored skeins would carelessly
> Unwind where I live secretly?
> — Miriam Waddington, in *Call Them Canadians*

INTRODUCTION

The central intention, the direction of Levinas's thought remains consistent throughout *Totality and Infinity* (1969). At the beginning of this book he says, "The moral consciousness can sustain the mocking gaze of the political man only if the certitude of peace dominates the evidence of war" (22). The certitude of peace, for Levinas, would come from the primordial reality of the face-to-face relationship that is already presupposed in war, since war is precisely the disputing,

Reprinted with permission. Originally published as S. Halling, "The Implications of Emmanuel Levinas' *Totality and Infinity* for Therapy," in *Phenomenological Psychology*, vol. 3, ed. A. Giorgi, C. Fischer, and E. Murray, 206–23 (Pittsburgh: Duquesne University Press, 1975).

and the attempt to deny the radical otherness of the Other by imposing our will on him. It is this awareness of otherness that is the basis
for speech and for the objectification of the world. One of the basic
objectives of Levinas's work is to demonstrate that the face-to-face
relationship is the source of ethics, teachings, and speech and is foundational for other types of relationships (79). Because of the importance of the personal, immediate relationship in the understanding
and in the vision of Emmanuel Levinas, his thought has important
implications for therapy. His writing can be characterized as presenting a philosophy of intersubjectivity and of ethics directed to our
encounters with concrete others in our daily world (173, 216).

We are living in an age where "professional help" is recommended
or sought almost as a matter of course when one experiences problems in interpersonal relations. In popular thinking, the therapy situation is seen as aiming for directness, honesty, and helpfulness to a
degree surpassing ordinary social situations. This view is supported
by a number of professional therapists. For example, in writing of
the "rules" of therapy, one psychiatrist says, "We could never formulate or describe one single sentence as to the therapeutically desirable response of the therapist to a given behavior of a given patient
because no formulation can guarantee that when the therapist would
make this response under the given circumstances to the given patient
that it would be a therapeutically spontaneous and genuine expression of the therapist's mind" (Kaiser 1965, 161). Indeed, within the
context of therapy, the patient or client is allegedly given an opportunity to work out interpersonal problems, problems of dis-ease in
the face of the Other, issues of sexuality, intimacy, openness, and
discourse. Additionally, since the one person—the therapist—takes
it upon himself to "maneuver" and to "intervene" for the benefit of
the Other, the client, the notion of ethics is already implicitly present.
And it is of ethics that Levinas speaks so powerfully.

But it should be made clear that Levinas, who approaches these
issues as a phenomenological philosopher, is not just speaking in an
empirical manner. As Gaston Bachelard (1969, 4) puts it: "Empirical
description involves enslavement to the object by decreeing passivity
on the part of the subject. The psychologist's description can doubt-
less add documentation, but the phenomenologist must intervene to
set this documentation on the axis of intentionality." That is, he is

not just describing our everyday experience but is appealing to the reader in light of his experience to follow the direction of his vision. He wants us to see that within our experience there resides not only actuality but also ideality and potentiality. In this paper, then, the psychological documentation will be in the form of descriptions of therapy sessions. These descriptions, although fictional (strictly speaking), are drawn from actual therapeutic experience.

Levinas makes it very clear that our access to others is through our already existing first-person point of view. In his discussion of what he calls psychism, enjoyment, and egoism, he points out that it is our rooted, finite, and separate existence which makes it possible that I meet the Other as Other—"our relations are never reversible" (Levinas 1969, 101). Again, this fundamental reality precedes all considerations of therapist-patient, the therapeutic and the nontherapeutic. This means I cannot "empathically," "imaginatively," or in any other way place myself in the Other's position or take a genuinely exterior point of view on myself and on my interaction with the Other. Consequently, the viewpoint of this chapter is, throughout, that of myself as the therapist.

BEYOND/BENEATH PSYCHOLOGY

The Other as the Absolutely Other

> The Other remains infinitely transcendent, infinitely foreign; his face in which his epiphany is produced and which appeals to me breaks with the world that can be common to us, whose virtualities are inscribed in our nature and developed by our existence. Speech proceeds from absolute difference.
>
> — Emmanuel Levinas, *Totality and Infinity*

There is nothing striking about this man sitting across from my desk, his shoulders hunched forward, his face lined with discouragement and weariness. His family, I know already, is a large one, and he himself is the sixth of eleven children. This is the type of man who by middle age feels worn down by years of hard work. Sensing the end of his powers he then makes a late, too late, attempt to escape from the limitations of his own religious tradition, and the confines of his life situation by starting an affair, which is from the beginning doomed to an abrupt end. His own sense of guilt apprehends him in what he thought would be the moment of liberation. I can almost visualize his wife, though I have never met her—robust, strict in her principles, dedicated to her family, and counting her boredom as the inevitable price one pays for being righteous. As the man sits there, barely giving any sense of life, I nonetheless know more or less what his concerns are. Weighed down by his own burden of guilt he has taken the whole world on his shoulders, he feels responsible for everything and everyone and remains closed to any assurance that he takes his mistake too seriously. After all, within the next day or so his wife will undoubtedly come to visit him at the hospital, self-sacrificingly offer him forgiveness and the promise of a welcome once he recovers from his depression.

This man is quite typical in terms of the type of behavior pattern he shows. In another culture, less dominated by Protestant notions of duty, obligation, and the life of virtue, this man's existence might have run a happier course. As it is, it is my task, my job, to help this man feel less depressed and to recover sufficiently to return to his home. I have to be the understanding, yet firm therapist, who by means of his skill can get this individual to take more initiative.

In a sense, this is a rather boring situation to be in; it is far too familiar, too trite, and the sequence of events that is going to follow is predictable, to a large extent. The course of this man's improvement—for he will improve, of that I have no doubt—follows a gradual, coherent pattern with the risk of suicide coming at a certain stage, that is, when his depression starts to lift to the extent that he is no longer so immobile and passive.

With some slowness, some difficulty, this man starts to speak, and as I patiently ask questions and listen to him, the pieces of his life fall into place for me. I come to see his sense of loss. His oldest daughter is about to leave home, and at the same time he is forced to sell part of the farm to cover expenses that were unforeseen, yet not so unforeseen. There is also his own sense of a lack of worth, of never really having achieved anything that he could be proud of. As he speaks I nod understandingly, an outline already forming in my mind for the report I have to write about him at the end of the session.

Of course, my own plan of attack, so to speak, also spontaneously becomes available to me — "Surely," I will tell him, "surely bringing up a family is no mean achievement, indeed you are being too hard on yourself." Having decided on this approach, I feel more relaxed and glance rather casually at the man again, noting almost with surprise that he is still speaking and moreover that he is looking directly at me in a way I do not understand.

For the first time I really recognize that I have never seen this man before, this is the first time he has been in my office and we have spoken together. Where is that man who sat silently a moment ago, that large, hunched-forward figure with the immobile features? He is practically sobbing now, speaking of how much his wife means to him. I feel a little taken aback as I would not have expected so much display of emotion so early in his depression. But then, of course, he must be feeling lonely here in this hospital, and however much a burden his wife's nagging must have been to him when he was at home, here in unfamiliar surroundings, that bit of the familiar would be welcome. Of course, this is understandable. Given the same situation, if I was in jail, for example, I might well feel the same way.

"It is not so much that I miss her, but that she has a difficult time being alone with the children, especially the oldest." This man looks at me with such naïve confidence, and I am taken aback. Surely he cannot be so different from me, although of course his background is one to which I have had very little exposure.

I try again, "Oh, you mean that you feel guilty leaving your wife alone with all that responsibility."

"No, it is just that it is very hard for her." What is it that I missed? Where did I miscomprehend this person? Somehow I must have missed a clue that was obvious, but which in my attempt to make sense just escaped my attention.

Not being quite sure what else to do, I ask him to do a psychological test, the Draw-a-Person test. As he obediently follows my instructions and bends over the paper, holding his pencil tightly, I watch him carefully, taking note of both his approach and the figure he draws. It is a young woman, done with care but missing one hand, strangely enough. I ask him about that, seeing that even in his carefulness he cannot disguise what he wants, and what he feels he cannot get—the young woman is not going to reach out to welcome him. He blushes a bit and answers with some visible embarrassment that he must have been thinking of his daughter who had an accident a few years back. There is no believing or disbelieving this statement. I simply respond with "I'm sorry."

The Limits of Interpretation

What then can I say about this episode, about this experience of discovery, of being called into the presence of another? First, the situation is initially understood dialectically—I am the therapist, he is the patient. Together we form a situation, the therapeutic situation. Levinas would not maintain that such viewpoints ought not to be held or that we do not frequently see reality in such terms. However, he would want to bring us to a recognition of a more fundamental level of awareness, which he describes in the following manner: "The alterity of the Other is in him, and is not relative to me; it *reveals* itself. But I have access to it proceeding from myself, and not through a comparison of myself with the other" (1969, 121). As the therapist in the above description, I come to recognize that the fundamental reality I am called to is that of being in the presence of another person, a person who reveals himself as he speaks, who is his own witness to himself, and who therefore cannot be understood in terms of preconceived categories. It is only when I respond to the Other as an integral person that I am face-to-face with him. What becomes apparent to me is that the meaning of this man's life cannot be taken from him through interpretation—or through ruse, as Levinas puts it (1969, 70). Even though my interpretation might be correct, in the sense that he affirmed it as true, his very affirmation would be a "shattering" of the grasp constituted by my understanding of him. That is, his expression of agreement with me would again be his witness to himself in my presence as opposed to my explaining to myself the type of person he was.

The Separateness of the Other

But how are we to understand concretely the rather striking and almost offensive way in which Levinas refers to the Other as the absolute Other? I believe he is here referring to human separateness and independence. Although the response of the Other is a response to what I say to him, it is not necessarily given as either determined or predictable. While we follow the demands of the roles that we take on much of the time and may speak in a stereotypic, habituated fashion more often than not, this does not mean that speech is always like that. The Other who is separate from me, other than me, may well surprise me. However, when Levinas speaks of the Other, being infinitely foreign, he is not suggesting that the Other is strange, or peculiar, or in some dramatic way unlike me in terms of his "psychological traits" (Levinas 1969, 215). He makes it very explicit that he is not speaking of the face-to-face relation as a meeting with the wondrous, the awful, nor is he referring to an experience of ecstasy (203). Quite the contrary. When I as the therapist respond to the Other, it is not in fear and trembling but, as we shall see later, in response-ability.

The experience of the genuine face-to-face occurs not in a moment of need, such as when I want to be the helpful one, and the Other must therefore be the one who is going to be helped by me. Within the situation of need, we are within a totality, a dialectical structure where I do not let the Other be. Instead, "The alleged scandal of alterity presupposes the tranquil identity of the same, a freedom sure of itself which is exercised without scruples" (Levinas 1969, 203). So in a manner of speaking, it is in a moment of un-concern that I as therapist can be concerned about the Other. It is as I am secure in my identity that I can genuinely move toward the Other in what Levinas calls desire. Desire is animated by the Other, it is a pull from without, and since it does not have the intention of "feeding an appetite," it is insatiable because one never fully reaches, one never quite grasps the Other. In that sense, he is absolutely Other. In that sense, when I turn my attention to the Other, or more accurately, when he calls forth my attention, I am genuinely in a face-to-face relationship. I can move toward that Other—who is not an extension of myself or someone I have a fixed view of in relation to a need that I have, as an agent, bearing witness to myself in my words, no longer the "product" of a psychological chain of events or the captive of a particular social role.

In conversation I find myself where I *never* was before, speaking to someone who is exterior to me (Levinas 1969, 73). How can anyone be prepared for this? What training can give the therapist the experience and the understanding necessary to deal with such a situation? As has been already suggested at least implicitly, and as will hopefully become clearer, the issue of preparedness is not a concern from within this experience.

Ethics, the Other as Master, Teacher

> My freedom does not have the last word; I am not alone.
> — Emmanuel Levinas, *Totality and Infinity*

It is about our tenth session together. This woman is quite attractive, much more attractive than most patients in a state hospital. We seem to have made considerable progress; she is speaking less often now of her inabilities and occasionally shows a sense of humor, which temporarily allows her to look relaxed and joyful. Generally I feel good toward her, confident in my ability to help, and allowing her to learn from what I know. Today she starts to speak again of her own ineptitude and paints a very critical picture of her unsuccessful efforts during the day. I start to speak to her of how she should allow herself some peace, and as I judge from her face that she is listening appreciatively, I go on to talk about the need for acceptance of self. As I speak, I can almost feel my momentum increasing, words come to me more easily, her presence to me is not quite as vivid as before. Her lips tremble somewhat, but I pay scant attention.

Then she raises her eyes, says hesitatingly, "I'm not sure I follow you." She hesitates, looks away, and adds, "I feel sort of alone."

There is a silence that is almost like a clearing of the air. Although I am not sure what to say or do, I feel less rushed, the blood no longer seems to race through my body. There is a moment when we look at each other. How long would I have gone on talking had she not spoken? Probably quite a while. In a way I'm surprised that I just stopped rather than address myself at length to her comment, explaining what I meant. But I do feel relieved somehow. What was I trying to prove anyway? When I speak again it is as though just a second has passed. I make a comment, half-humorously, to the effect that under the circumstances it is not surprising she feels lonely. She too seems relieved and starts to speak about the lack of closeness she experiences with her mother. As she starts to speak, I remember vaguely in the back of my mind reading about her relationship with her mother in a social history. She leans forward a bit and describes an incident, a very everyday incident, about a little girl going shopping with her mother. The purpose of the shopping trip was to find a party dress for her, the little girl. Finally she finds a dress that she just adores and turns to her mother enthusiastically, holding the dress up for her to see. She finds herself looking into her mother's impassive, almost vacant face, and in a half-irritated, half-hurried voice her mother says, "No, no, that won't do at all." As they rush through the store, mother and daughter hand in hand, she feels as alone in the world as if she were the last person on earth.

Surely, this is a moment of togetherness and of sharing. Yet even as I am deeply moved by what she says, I sense the distance between us as intraversable. She has "bared her soul," and yet experientially that does not fit at all. The feeling I am left with is one more of respect than of intimacy, of being in the presence of someone who is destitute, who is calling upon me to respond. But I feel inadequate to the demand, and I say something, each moment sensing a hunger in her that I could never fill, sensing that I move out from myself and yet do not quite touch her. It becomes almost an effort for me, a strain. She leans back, glances at me, and speaks of being at peace with this aloneness, of having accepted it. I am somewhat puzzled. Was she indeed not feeling destitute? Surely I did not alleviate that. But she is speaking to me more lightheartedly, talking about her children, how she will go out with them in the park when she goes home.

The Initiative of the Other

"It is not the insufficiency of the I that prevents totalization, but the Infinity of the Other" (Levinas 1969, 80). In this situation, it is the other person who brings me to question my freedom, my project as I am speaking so easily about life. The Other is for the moment the recipient of my thoughts and ideas, and in that way there is a totalizing moment. I speak and she listens, and there is for me a getting caught up in my own freedom. The radical critique that Levinas presents of contemporary notions of freedom consists in pointing out that our real concern should not be with the development of a society in which each person is allowed full freedom. Instead he suggests that the real issue is ethics, the questioning of arbitrary freedom (83). How is it that I come to question my freedom? How does the Other lead me to become aware of my responsibility in a situation? "The 'resistance' of the other does not do violence to me, does not act negatively; it has a positive structure: ethical. The first revelation of the other, presupposed in all the relations with him, does not consist in grasping him in his negative resistance, and in circumventing him by ruse. I do not struggle with a faceless god, but I respond to his expression, to his revelation" (197).

The beginning of conscience is not my act of questioning my own freedom spontaneously, nor does it begin with my self-disciplined restraint. For Levinas it does not start with the power of the Other opposing my freedom, telling me in so many words that I am guilty or wrong or that if I continue he will no longer approve of me, as in the Freudian viewpoint. When the young woman looks at me and speaks about her loneliness, I am in a way brought to myself, I am responding to her expression, her revelation. As I look at her, my arbitrary freedom is brought into question, not in an act of reflection, not in a stepping back from the relationship in which I find myself. On the contrary, I find myself in the face-to-face relationship, and I find my freedom brought into question. "There is here a relation not with a very great resistance, but with something absolutely other; the resistance of what has no resistance—the ethical resistance" (Levinas 1969, 199).

Rhetoric and Power

Why does Levinas speak of what has no resistance? Can this be anything other than poetry? If we bring in the contrast with rhetoric, this expression becomes more understandable. Rhetoric is the attempt through speech to control and to persuade the Other. In speaking rhetorically to the Other, the Other is for me the one who is going to be persuaded, not the one who is allowed to speak to me or even to listen to me on his own terms. The relationship is then defined from my point of view in terms of this specific intention that *I* have with respect to the Other. It is a relationship of exercise of power. Power, however, implies a grasp, a hold on what is to be controlled. I cannot exercise power over what or who is beyond my reach and my grasp.

The truly Other is exterior to me, he is absolutely other. Therefore Levinas can speak of the Other as the Stranger—we do not share a common citizenship, we are not bound together by common loyalties or by principles or laws that exist separate from us and make us a moment in a totality. Again, Levinas is not suggesting that the Other is an alien being in a negative sense; if that were the case we could not even speak to each other. What he is emphasizing is the fundamental reality that I am I, and the first person's position that I occupy is not interchangeable with the position of the Other, the you that I am addressing myself to. Also, that "you" is an active, constituting agent, not just the recipient of my action or of environmental forces.

As the therapist I am surprised that I stop speaking, that I do not try to convince my client or clarify what I meant to tell her. I was not forced to stop, but I did. I became more restrained and respectful. Later, as the woman talks about the relationship with her mother and describes the particular incident, which is a very personal one, there is again for a moment the apparent but then obviously illusory possibility of fusion with the Other. She "bares her soul." But the distance remains, not the distance of impersonality, or of schizoid presence, but of separateness. The Other "escapes my grasp by an essential dimension.... He is not wholly in my site" (Levinas 1969, 39).

Response-ability

This is not the beginning of paralysis or the end of my ability to express myself, nor is it a freedom harnessed for the sake of ethics. It is the beginning of response-ability, of my responding to the Other, of freedom within the face-to-face relationship. Then who is it I am responding to? First, we need to remember that the coming into question of one's own freedom is simultaneously the welcoming of the Other, the Other over whom I can have no power "because he overflows absolutely every *idea* I can have of Him" (Levinas 1969, 87). Then the Other is the Master—not in the sense of domination but in the sense of presenting an appeal that may dissolve my power.

The person I am speaking to as therapist calls out in me the desire to respond, to care, to show respect, or even to be angry. As I understand him, Levinas is not saying that, in the face of the Other, the Same becomes meek, tame, or subdued. These three adjectives are still within the notion of a power relationship where the Other controls and dominates. Admittedly, a response such as anger may be the attempt of the same to dominate the Other. Anger can be used in the service of rhetoric, in the service of need and possession. I can become angry at the client who does not understand what I am trying to say to him or her, who is defying my intention. But anger may also take place within the context of the recognition of the Other as other, and as exterior to myself.

The Situatedness of the "I"

One might easily come to believe through a hasty reading of Levinas that he is suggesting it is the Other who is always in some way morally justified and it is the Same who is always caught in the act of exercising his capricious freedom. This is not what he means. In some way I know that I am the Other of the Other. But this does not change the fact that it is the Other who is looking at me, I do not see myself looking at him, nor could I possibly. Even my pretense of being a spectator to my relationship with the Other—possibly in the form of analyzing a therapeutic interview after the fact in terms of what the two people must have felt and thought, that is, looking at myself and the Other from a third-person point of view—only illustrates that I cannot escape my existential position. If I were to trace back my intentions that led me to engage in this type of analysis from the third-person point of view, I would find myself reconstituting my identity as the Same, just as I am always this ongoing reconstituting identity. My very attempt to escape from myself is an affirmation of my self-identity, not just logically but also existentially. What Levinas wants to emphasize is that ethics is a relationship with someone exterior to me. In other words, ethics arises in a genuine relationship, not in a pseudo-relationship where there is a meeting of two parts already belonging to a larger whole, where I meet my own image or reflection. Within such a "relationship," one could not speak of freedom because of the way the two parts always mutually implicate each other; one could only speak of reactions back and forth, stimulus and response.

Now I want to come back to anger. First, it is a genuine affirmation of the freedom of the same insofar as it is responsive to the

Other. Mature anger is not blind rage directed at an object one fantasizes about, but rather, it is directed toward a person that one sees. It is speaking to another, calling for his response, not an attempt to annihilate his capacity for responding, as in rage. It is an appeal in an attitude of at least some openness. I would suggest then that anger can be a movement of Desire, a movement toward the Other rather than a movement based on need with the goal of assimilating the Other.

The Other as Teacher

What is also at least implicit in this description of me with this particular woman is that the Other is the teacher. Previously, I referred to the fact that in a genuine face-to-face situation I find myself where I never was before. Levinas points out that only the absolutely foreign can instruct us (1969, 73). That is, learning means coming to meet the new, not the already known. What is new, however, is not the content of what someone tells me. What I learned from this woman was not that incidents in early childhood are significant for the course of personality development, nor did I learn a specific fact about this person's life. While this is how we speak in our everyday lives, it is already too abstract, in the sense of abstracted from our experience. It is at the level of a psychological understanding, bypassing the reality of the Other, that psychological theory nonetheless already presupposes in addressing itself to a listener or an audience. After this interview, very likely I would have thought about what happened in terms of the new understanding this experience had given me, I could make notes on what this woman revealed to me about herself. However, that approach would only have captured a limited aspect of the experience since:

> Attention is attention to something because it is attention to someone. The exteriority of its point of departure is essential to it: it is the very tension of the I. The school, without which no thought is explicit, conditions science. It is there that is affirmed the exteriority that accomplishes freedom and does not offend it: the exteriority of the Master. Thought can become explicit only among two; explicitation is not limited to finding what one already possessed. But the first

teaching of the teacher is his very presence as teacher from which representation comes. (Levinas 1969, 99–101)

Levinas suggests here that the first given and precondition for learning is the presence of the Other as teacher. I meet the reality of the exterior point of view, which is not given as constituted by me. This does not mean that what the Other says or does is unrelated to me but that his exteriority is not dependent on me. Meeting the Other as teacher also implies the uprootedness of the I from history. For instance, if I approach the patient with the attitude that I am the therapist listening to this already known type of patient, doing the preconceived kind of therapy, there is no room for the new. The Other conceived as the end-point of a certain developmental history really has nothing to teach me. I know already who she is, all she can do is give me the specific coloration of her particular life, and so we go through the motions together. She and I are then both playing the roles in a drama—the Jungian, the Freudian, or the Christian drama. I am not the author of the drama, and I do not fully understand the meaning of each line nor the movement toward the final conclusion that is going to reveal the real meaning of the events I was witness to (1969, 52). Such is not the relationship of the I to the Other as Teacher.

When I am listening to this young woman as she describes this childhood incident, I am in the presence of the new. This new given is meaningful in the moment because its narrator presents her meaning to me in that moment. It is not for me, later, to understand *really* what the meaning of the incident was. What I perhaps recognize after the interview, sitting in my office, is that I have been somewhere new and have returned to myself. At the time of the conversation, I was not sitting as judge and jury, having the final power to decide what she was telling me. I respond to her in some way and she tells me what she means. When I speak to her, I do not know beforehand what I will say in responding to her, and in that way our dialogue is creative. Even in speaking to myself, the anchorage point again is the presupposed Other, the Other who can listen and understand, the Other who responds and for whom I thematize my world and my thoughts.

Therapy as the Call to Responsibility

There is another dimension to the ethical relationship, which Levinas touches upon briefly but which strikes me as being extremely important. Often the criticism is made of individual therapy that it operates in the service of ego-gratification and political stagnation. Thus Herbert Marcuse (1962) in *Eros and Civilization* criticizes the use, or rather the misuse, of psychoanalysis as a tool of repression. He is referring to the whole ideology of mental health within which the function of therapy is to help the individual to "adjust" to his situation no matter how abusive it may be. Political rebels, within that ideology, are necessarily seen as people who are maladjusted, and the prescribed course of action is to change them rather than to consider the justice of the criticisms they make of certain political realities (6). Another criticism is that individual therapy amounts to an undue concern with the development of one individual, and for that reason it is socially irresponsible. My point here is not to deny that both or one of these criticisms may be very valid. Rather, I want again to examine these issues in terms of implications drawn from *Totality and Infinity*. Levinas speaks quite directly to these considerations when he says: "Language as the presence of the face does not invite complicity with the preferred being, the self-sufficient 'I-Thou' forgetful of the universe...the epiphany of the face qua face opens humanity.... The presence of the face, the infinity of the Other is a destituteness, a presence of the third party (that is, of the whole of humanity which looks at us), and a command that commands commanding" (Levinas 1969, 213).

Expressing the meaning of this quote very crudely, I would say that meeting the Other is not of the order of a "peak" experience that one can indulge in without the rest of one's life being implicated. It does not invite me to bask in the sunlight of some benign, vaguely mysterious other, but on the contrary it is a call back to responsibility, to life with concrete others. The therapy situation might then not just be a protective environment where one is relieved of distress, but a place where one is called from unreal obligation and false guilt to real responsibility and genuine guilt in the face of the Other. It is not just a situation in which I as the therapist am simply involved in divesting someone of fantasy preoccupations, maladaptive behavior, or in which I am the dispenser of "insight." More fundamentally, it is a situation in which the Other calls upon me to be responsive.

Speech, Giving, Community

> Objectivity results from language, which permits the putting into question of possession. This disengagement has a positive meaning: the entry of the thing into the sphere of the other. The thing becomes a theme. To thematize is to offer the world to the Other in speech.
>
> — Emmanuel Levinas, *Totality and Infinity*

It has taken me a good while to get used to being with this particular person. She has appeared distant, sometimes cold, and often suspicious. Her features were frequently almost immobile although there were signs of life in her eyes. Initially when I was with her, I had felt rather alone and had fumbled as I tried to speak to her, hoping to get a response from her and seldom getting more than a rather obscure or satirical comment. How does one do therapy in this type of situation? This was a question I posed to myself incessantly for several weeks until I decided that it was really quite hopeless. Having decided that, however, I found it much easier to be with her, to really not expect anything specific either from myself or from her. Eventually I got to the point where I could sit silently with her for periods up to half an hour and it would not be uncomfortable for me. One particular day she asked me in a tone that was mildly sarcastic, and yet kind, what made my life worth living. Since I was a therapist surely I knew about these things!

The question surprised me and at first I did not know how to respond. First of all, with her I had stopped thinking of myself as a therapist, and second, I had to reflect a while to recall what the content of my life was, so to speak. There was an initial doubt in my mind whether I really ought to answer that question, but looking at her I felt she had simply invited me to speak. As I started to talk about my family, my work, and my education, I had the experience of almost handing all this over to her, it was no longer just mine, no longer my "secret" possession, but something she could comment on or criticize if she wanted to. At the same time in speaking about the content of my life, I recognized that all these things were not me, I existed apart from them, although in some way I also knew I would go back to them. Her response though, was such that it just seemed proper that I reveal my life to her, not in the manner of a confession of secrets, but more in a spirit of giving.

As I spoke, it also seemed that the horizons of my life were spread before me and came to stand out for me almost as a panoramic view. Yet when she asked me a few more things, I felt her questions were addressed to me rather than being impersonal requests for information about some topic. Then she started to tell me about her work. I already knew something about that, but this was the first time that she told me what it meant to her. We ended up talking about loss and injustice, the difficulties of coping with the world. The world seemed out there and yet also between us. Our words seemed so futile, after all we were just talking and what earthly good can that do? We ended the session and went our separate ways. As I walked toward my car and as I drove back home, I was somehow more aware of the humanness of the world. It is the world that I share with others and that I come to be aware of through others.

Speech as Generosity and Presence

While the above description is fiction, strictly speaking, in another sense it is not, insofar as I drew from my own experience and write about what is alive for me. In recent years "verbal" therapy has been described as being wasteful, unproductive, and remote in content from the lives of the people participating in it. I do not want to make the counter argument on behalf of this type of therapy, if it can even be spoken of as a "type" of therapy. However, what Levinas says about the origins of objectivity and the meaning of language strikes beneath the separation between so-called verbal and nonverbal approaches to therapy. Again, he wants to remind us of the more basic issues.

Levinas deals at some length with speech as dispossession in the face of the Other's appeal to my freedom and his judgment of my unrestrained action. Within the realm of the notions of egoism and enjoyment and totality, I exist for myself incorporating things into my own identity. The Other's call to me allows me to be generous, to present my world to him, thematizing it in speech. From a situation of contentment I was able to respond to the plea or request of the woman in therapy and be generous of myself with her to some extent. As I speak about my own life I am no longer immersed in it, and thus I distance myself from it. This distancing is at the same time the beginning of the sharing. Yet the meaning of the sharing is not just determined by my giving and my speaking. I expose myself to the judgment of the Other, but that exposure is not a betrayal of the self. "That of which I speak is not me"—there is already a distance—but in my speaking and in her answering there is the beginning of community (Levinas 1969, 98). This is true—concretely, in the above situation, but also more generally and fundamentally insofar as objectivity and language arise in relationship with others. Whilst speech can be at the level of impersonal communication, this does not mean that this is what it is most basically. To speak within relationship—and not from a position standing outside of—is to be present to the Other in what one says. Since Levinas affirms the importance of things and of enjoyment, these then are matters that we can speak about and whose meaning is transformed for us in conversation just as intelligibility arises in that context. If speaking were simply a matter of expressing in words ideas that one already possessed, then speaking would be both impersonal and uncreative. The minute I have described for someone the content of my life then my life is no longer quite the same. When we say after a good conversation, "Now I have a clearer idea of where I stand," we do not mean that we just had an opportunity to correct our misconceptions or that we acquired information we could equally have obtained from a book, a radio, or any source whatever.

The therapy situation may be one place where we can hope for a genuine discourse to take place, at least occasionally, and where the hours of rhetoric may be interrupted by moments of conversation. The hope resides not in the wisdom and cleverness of the therapist but the fact that we are in the presence of someone who may dispossess us of our understanding, our comprehension, and allow us to hear and speak.

CONCLUSION

I have spoken about some of the implications of Levinas *Totality and Infinity* for therapy. Through the imaginary descriptions, I have attempted in a less abstract way to present these implications and to suggest that he is referring to a fundamental human experience, and that it is indeed this level of experience that makes all theory and philosophizing possible.

Levinas as Visionary

What then are some of the implications and some of the problematics of the implications already laid out? First of all, if we can speak in these terms at all, in what sense can we now speak of the therapy situation and of the therapist and client? Is not what Levinas addresses so fundamental that it becomes erroneous, superficial to speak of therapy? Here we have to remember that therapy and theories of therapy are grounded in visions of man that go beyond the empirical and have metaphysical and ethical implications. Even to suggest that the remedial process for someone who is disturbed involves his or her entering a certain type of relationship with another person is already to express a very basic belief about the priorities of human life. The primacy of the face-to-face relationship is affirmed. What is striking about Levinas is that he affirms this primacy more fully and much more deeply than do most psychotherapists. For many psychiatrists and psychologists, theoretical considerations seem to have overshadowed considerations about the Other, and the emphasis is placed on comprehension and expertise rather than on attentiveness. Levinas has pointed out that the concept of totality dominates Western philosophy, and assuredly it permeates all of our culture. People approach a therapist and ask him what they are really like, what their problem really is, or what the deeper significance of their behavior might be. They are requesting, most often, not a personal response to themselves but an opinion from someone who understands how, in the final analysis, they fit into the framework of the world, what part they have in a larger totality.

Is Levinas then a prophet or a visionary who hands us a theory of Infinity, of the Same and the Other, in order that by following his instructions we might escape the wilderness of totalities and total-izing ways of acting and speaking? I believe he is a visionary at least in the sense that he speaks and thinks very well about certain themes that most of us see only dimly. But in speaking of these themes, he is not setting up pathways or guidelines for us. He is radical in calling us back to our roots and the face of the Other. It is from our roots that we can move out. "The metaphysical desire tends towards something entirely, toward the absolutely other" (Levinas 1969, 33). This desire implies transcendence, response-ability, openness, and acceptance of oneself. It implies the end of egotism rather than self-effacement or self-denial. The Other calls me forth and if I respond, it is to him that I respond.

Significance for Therapy

What then does all this mean with reference to everyday interaction with others, be they in the context of therapy or not? We find quite typically that the other person appears to be much like ourselves. We see people in terms of likeness and difference, we act in terms of needs and move toward possession, and we listen more or less inattentively and unresponsively to many of the people we meet. Is the person who is a therapist now going to strive to be open, is he going to curtail his theoretical thinking during the therapy sessions in order that he may hear his client more fully? These are questions that come to us quite naturally, but they belong within an objectivistic, pragmatic attitude, and this is precisely what Levinas is speaking against. The world is not just made up of implements and objects that we use and that which we look at in curiosity. We can neither study what Levinas writes as another interesting theory nor use his ideas as guidelines for a better life for all! He is asking us to listen, and in listening we may come to meet the new and we may take warning against trends that permeate our lives. Levinas provides us with an excellent critique of contempo-rary ethics, which may leave us to question ourselves. He brings into question, in a thematic way, the meaning and value of psychological understanding.

I believe it is especially here that we need to take him seriously. We can easily succumb to the belief that in terms of interpersonal rela-tions the psychologist has the last word. The direction Levinas moves in is not to suggest that it really should be the philosopher who has the last word. If either were the case then, in some sense, we would be playing roles in a drama not of our own making whose inner secret way is revealed only to the chosen few. Instead Levinas reminds us that it is the Other who speaks to us and tells us what he means.

Maybe the "good therapist" is the person who remains willing to let the other person reveal himself to him. If that is the case, then separation is affirmed and relationship is possible. One of the greatest problems in therapy is the tendency for the person who sees himself as therapist to end up not being responsive to the client or patient but feeling responsible for him. This is a movement toward totalizing and possessive modes of action and thinking. However, if we grant that the Other is acting on his own behalf and is his own witness to himself, then this type of fusion is not possible. But more accurately it is a question of being open to a reality already given, not a question of granting. In his very speaking, the Other is already present to me as separate, and every attempt on my part to deny this is at the same time an affirmation of it.

Therapy, then, is in some sense possible, but it is possible only because everything does not depend on the therapist, because there is another whom each of us can meet.

Two

Levinas, Psychology, and Language

Eric R. Severson

There is a fascinating, legendary tale from the early pages of the Jewish and Christian sacred texts referring to the tower of Babel (Gen. 11:1–9). The tale is partly about the hubris of human beings who attempt to build a tower to the heavens. The story is fascinating on a number of levels, none more intriguing than the divine solution to the problem created by these overly ambitious prehistoric people. Their pride is addressed by way of a peculiar curse: they are rendered multilingual. The technological and political cohesion that had made their ambitious project possible was totally unraveled by their inability to understand one another. They could hear only babbling, which leads to misunderstanding, miscommunication, and even violence. This story provides an early and intriguing attempt to cope with the fallibility of language and the curse of misunderstanding. The narrative mirrors, in many ways, the story of Adam and Eve, whose hubris robs them of paradise. The people of Babel had a different kind of paradise, a purity of communication that allowed for massive technological and political advances. With this curse comes a loss perhaps more crippling than the loss of Eden.

If philosophy can be of any service to the discipline of psychology, and I certainly hope it can, such assistance may be most obvious on the problem of language and communication. This is not to say, of course, that communication is confined to language or even that philosophy and psychology are principally concerned with language. I open with the story of Babel because the fragmentation of language plays a critical role in resolving the problem of human pride and overinflated ambition. In the Talmud, the rabbis offer one possible reason for such drastic measures (Ginzberg 2010, 88, 91–94). It is said that the workers on the tower were required to keep careful count of every fallen or damaged brick, but that they took no notice at all if a worker fell from the heights to his or her death. According to the Talmud, the slippage of meaning in our discourse is instituted to prevent us from allowing technology and production to stand between our faces. The fragmentation of language is a safeguard; linguistic synchrony is too intoxicating and blinds us to the suffering of others as well as to our own unique existence. The closer we draw to the purity of apparently seamless communication, the more perilous our discourse becomes. In this chapter I utilize the work of philosopher Emmanuel Levinas to explore the possibility that philosophy has done a disservice to psychology by failing to identify a serious gap in its pursuit of understanding and language. Levinas suggests in some of his later works that a more original and exigent layer of language is masked by Babel's synchrony.

Turning to Levinas

Aligning the work of Emmanuel Levinas with the discipline of psychology will forever be a complicated endeavor. His language and focus at times resonate deeply with concerns at the heart of psychoanalysis and psychotherapy. This resonance has led to many efforts to create a convergence of Levinasian themes with these disciplines. In other moments, Levinas deals a harsh blow against the fundamental disposition of psychology.[1] We should bear in mind that Levinas's wariness concerning the field of psychology is complex. Some of his reluctance to engage this field is the product of misunderstanding—or legitimate concern for the way psychology has sometimes dressed itself as a totalizing discourse aimed at "knowledge" or "understanding" of the other person. As such, psychology has sometimes tended toward the reductive, situating the analyst in a position that transcends the analysand. Psychotherapy, for its part, has sometimes been inclined toward the diagnosis and treatment of identifiable pathologies. While there are certainly exceptions to these trends, the contemporary pressures regarding insurance and payment seem to accentuate the imperative to align the disciplines of psychology with medical and scientific models.

Levinas, for his part, rarely directed rigorous attention to psychology. Furthermore, his philosophical career pre-dates many intriguing developments in psychology, which have transformed the landscape of this discipline. His concerns, nevertheless, continue to haunt the studies and practices familiar to the psychologist. In this chapter I wager that this haunting is a healthy one and that closer examination of Levinas's later work promises to enliven the disciplines of both psychology and Levinasian philosophy.

There is a wide diversity in modern psychology. I write as one aware that my gestures and forays over the line of philosophy and into other fields are hazardous moves, and I hope to make them with reverence. I have much admiration for the intense and precarious discipline of psychotherapy. My hope is to engender lively and helpful discourse by presenting some of Levinas's ideas about language and the encounter with the other person. I present these as a devoted reader of Levinas, though not a perfect one. His work may or may not be relevant to the concerns of psychologists. I seek only to present Levinas's work, particularly the less celebrated labors near the end of his career, with an eye toward potential convergences with the concerns of psychology.

Despite the chasm that sometimes separates these disciplines, a great many common terms and concepts unify philosophy and psychology. In this chapter, my principle focus will be on the function of language. The related concepts of language and time take center stage in the later work of Levinas, and his unique interpretation of language remains one of the most fertile ideas for further exploration and research. His innovative concepts of the Saying and the Said continue to baffle readers of his final great work, *Otherwise than Being, or Beyond Essence* (Levinas 1981), and yet they remain critical for rethinking the dynamics of human communication.

Michael visits my office weekly and emails much more often.[2] He is in his mid-twenties and reeling from childhood sexual abuse that seems repeatedly to twist his life into knots of physiological and psychological trauma. He was once my student, and his visits to me are only supplementary to regular appearances at the offices of a psychiatrist and a psychotherapist. In our first meetings he stated a staunch refusal to visit anyone associated with the mental health professions. I have minimal training in professional therapy, so it quickly became unwise for him to continue seeing only me. The intensity of his flashbacks and the claims he made about his mental states and behaviors almost instantly exceeded my expertise. He simply stonewalled my repeated insistence that these would be safer and more constructive conversations if they were held with a psychotherapist. After a few sessions, I refused to schedule another appointment with him unless he would also be seeing a professional.

Eventually, Michael agreed and began therapist shopping, a long adventure of rejecting one office after another for a wide variety of reasons. What fascinates me about conversing with Michael is the way he looks at me when he speaks words about his life, his memories, his condition, and his psychological state. He watches my face for reactions to catch phrases that he works into the conversation. Michael is a bright man, an excellent student, and a college graduate with a major in psychology. At first I was sure he was just toying with me, seeking to meet understandable needs for human contact by stringing me along with signs and symptoms of various mental disorders and syndromes. I felt that his self-analysis was occluded by the jargon he thought I would find meaningful or that would elicit a particular reaction. My meetings with Michael have become, as much as anything else, a quiet struggle for language.

Michael learned, through encounters either with me or with other people like me, that certain keywords inevitably elicit responses. He talked of self-mutilation, fantasized in great detail about suicide, and suggested that he might be a danger to other people around him, especially children. These are surely not surprising patterns to psychoanalysts and therapists, and I took great comfort from the fact that Michael was also seeing people accustomed to these phenomena. A noticeable tendency has developed in our discussions. When Michael feels like his emotions and experiences are striking a resonance with me, he is less likely to appeal to the trigger words he knows will incite a visible response. Levinas's philosophy of language provides a subtle but powerful suggestion about the dynamics of dialogue. Michael and I fumble for tools to talk to one another, each reaching back into a complex history of our own experiences, resources, and studies in an attempt to find some spark of connection with the Other. But for Levinas, this way of thinking about language and discourse is derivative of a philosophy of the same, a metaphysics of presence.[3]

Linguistic Foundations and the Floundering of Language

The question is far from settled among philosophers: what is the primary purpose of language? There are several manners of addressing this important question: anthropological, historical, archaeological, and evolutionary, among many others. In the face-to-face relation with someone like Michael, it is not difficult to be aware of multiple linguistic layers. To ask the question of the origin of language as a philosopher, and perhaps also a psychologist, is to inquire about the most important function of language. In this regard, we could discover the first, or perhaps the most common, use of language without getting to the heart of the question. The philosophical quest is to discover how language operates *primarily*. Levinas, for his part, will point to the subtle way in which speaking's primary operation is subsumed, silenced, and ignored by a secondary operation of language that he believes is mostly mistaken for the primary. The heart of human communication, for Levinas, is maddeningly evasive. Rather than undertake the rigorous hunt for the elusive event of language, the Saying, we settle for the much louder and more accessible Said.

The question of language's original and primary purpose has been a key puzzle for philosophy from the beginning. In *The Protagoras*, Plato utilizes the title character to explore the origin and importance of language. We know relatively little about Protagoras, with just a few surviving fragments, legends, and reports. He died when Plato was young and long before Aristotle, but they both remember him as a seminal thinker on the importance of language. Plato's Protagoras suggests that language arises out of the need to overcome the chaotic separation of human beings from one another. In *The Protagoras* he suggests that when Prometheus steals fire from the gods he makes humanity capable of rising above other animals. This ascension is expressed first in the ability to worship the gods, since humanity newly partakes in divinity and a "share in the divine attributes" that comes with the power of flames. And simultaneously, humans gain the power of language and use it to form alliances against the chaos of "dispersed" living. Without language, and the cities and governance that words provide, humanity was "destroyed by the wild beasts, for they were utterly weak in comparison of them" (2009, 40.322b). Language made possible politics and government, which in turn gave rise to justice and equality.

And for Protagoras, this establishes a fundamental ambiguity to language. In his *Rhetoric,* Aristotle remembers him for his extraordinarily rigorous work on the importance of grammar, clear meanings for particular words, and carefully defined terms (Aristotle 1984, 3:5). He gives Protagoras credit for laying down the basic categories of terminology to make clear classifications between objects and ideas. We have in Protagoras a fundamentally ambiguous philosopher, for his championing of linguistic clarity was undermined in part by his participation in the Sophist tradition. Protagoras knows that there is something both arbitrary and potentially manipulative about the act of creating and using language. He made his living, we are told, teaching Athenians how to craft words better and achieve success through the power of language (Guthrie 1971, 267). So his investigation into the mystery of the origin of human language provides him with the basis for a powerful career as one of the most learned Sophists. But at the same time, his legacy is in some sense that of a sly lawyer; he knows that language rests on the shifting sands of human desires, needs, and selfishness. His most famous line comes from Plato's *Theaetetus:* "man is the measure of all things" (1990, 297). There is, for Protagoras, no absolute referent to which human meaning is to be measured. There are only words, and those wise enough to use them to their advantage.

Sophists like Protagoras play frequent roles in the Platonic dialogues, often as foils for Socrates to exploit in the development of his wiser positions. It may be the case that Socrates and Protagoras are not always as far apart as they seem. Yet the battle between the Sophists and Socrates never strays far from the question of relativism, and particularly the challenge of communication and the capacity of human beings to transfer ideas and communicate virtue. Protagoras plays the role Plato is fond of pushing on the Sophists, registering serious doubt about whether virtue can be taught.

Against the backdrop of the skeptic philosophers of pre-Socratic Greece, Plato becomes the principal architect for the future of philosophy. Plato's blueprint for philosophy has many rooms and multiple agendas, but one fundamental aim of Platonic philosophy is a dedication to the accurate transmission of ideas through language. Sophists, fairly or unfairly, are often depicted as two-faced manipulators of language. The most apt modern comparison might be shady lawyers who disregard any concrete truth and focus only on whether and how an argument might be won. Plato takes philosophy in another direction, toward the clearer communication of ideas. He points philosophy toward a common and universal Good. For Plato, the Good is not something utterly foreign to each person but, rather, something that exists in veiled and incomplete manifestations in everyone. For this reason, Socrates is fond of stimulating conversation by appealing to the ancient Greek aphorism "Know thyself."[4]

Words are subject to the same folly as other fleshy objects; they are temporary, conditioned by their surroundings, and deeply fallible. An idea, on the other hand, transcends the language in which it is clothed. Take, for example, the concept of a perfect sphere. There is something beautiful and pristine about the concept of a perfect orb that exceeds in simplicity and exactitude the mathematical language used to describe it. Every point on a sphere is equidistant from the center of the object. It is ironic, and important, that there is no object that achieves this perfection. A sphere is an *idea* that cannot be actualized, even by the finest craftsperson. Socrates teaches in *The Republic:* "We should consider the decorations in the sky to be the most beautiful and most exact of visible things, seeing that they're embroidered on a visible surface. But we should consider their motions to fall far short of the true ones" (Plato 1992, 529c). We can only use the physical world around us as a model for our study of the true ideas, the perfect realities that the universe can only approximate. The nature of a sphere, for Plato, is not something we are taught. To learn about the geometry of a sphere is to become aware of something that one already *knows* but must recover from the fragmentation of ideas that characterizes our ignorance. And the truth, the *eido* (idea) of a sphere, is something common to all people. When in conversation we invoke the concept of a sphere, there is an intersection, a synchrony of understanding. And this is the kind of perfection that all language must pursue.

Fortunately, Plato is well aware of the faultiness of the physical and observable world. Likewise, he was aware that language never achieves its most noble goal of providing perfect synchrony between the one who speaks and the one who listens. There is forever slippage, misunderstanding, missed innuendo, and erroneous assumptions. This has not stopped philosophers and linguists from pursuing a new language that would be more direct in its symbolism, a dialect that would draw closer and closer to a perfect language system in which there could be no misinterpretation of words and symbols. Gottfried Leibniz, for instance, hoped that language could be so chastened that it would become a universal and mathematically perfect instrument for communication.[5]

We wrestle today with a vital question about the capacity of language to achieve the Platonic aim of synchronized understanding. The quest for understanding has, for better or worse, been dominated by the journey that leaves behind the Sophists and aims toward perfect and mutual knowledge. There are many variants and adaptations along the way, but philosophy and linguistics have basically accepted the puzzle of language as it has been posed by Plato. At this register, a conversation with another person is a kind of mutual pursuit of a common goal: synchronized understanding. That goal is at least approximated in geometry, which provides a paradigm for the purpose of language in other discourses. We may have diverse interpretations and experiences associated with the term "breakfast," for example, but we at least commonly associate that term with a meal taken early in the day.

The structure of the relation presumed in such understandings of language is clear: when we relate to another person, we relate to someone who is another instance of what I find myself to be. The Other is another ego with the same basic nature and, most important, the same fundamental reality (for Plato the *real* Real is the one found in the *eidos*). Language addresses the puzzling distance between our shared true nature and our puzzlingly fragmented existence in the materiality of the world. We drift like islands in a sea of diversity and misunderstanding, with no recourse but to create "bridges" to span the chasms between us. Some bridges, such as the shared understanding of a sphere, seem sturdy and reliable. Others, such as the elusive meanings of the words "pain" and "happiness," are frustratingly elusive. Language, cursed with materiality and temporality, is doomed to fail in its effort to communicate purely. But we must flounder in speech nonetheless, for otherwise we abandon the hope of understanding one another altogether.

LANGUAGE AND PSYCHOLOGY

Classical psychology arose during the heyday of modern philosophy and found itself in routine conversation with modern philosophers. Sigmund Freud, for his part, considered psychology to be first and foremost a branch of science. He stated explicitly: "the contribution of psychoanalysis to science consists precisely in having extended research to the region of the mind" (Freud 2004, 147). The first puzzles of psychology are posed as scientific puzzles, and a new and daunting project of studying, classifying, quantifying, and describing phenomena. In a discussion about the relationship between psychology and the sciences, Freud is said to have declared: "the poets and philosophers before me discovered the unconscious; what I discovered was the scientific method by which the unconscious can be studied."[6]

Freud pointed out that the field of science would be incomplete and impoverished if the scope of scientific investigation failed to extend to such a pivotal and central component of human existence.[7] The discipline of psychology has labored rigorously for more than a century to develop this science of the mind, of the psyche. By creating *correlation* and *correspondence* between episodes, symptoms, patients, and so on, the psychologist is often able to provide accurate predictions of future behavior. Freud's hope was also that such a field could expand the field of medicine to this arena, and he often considered the psychologist to be a hybrid between philosopher and physician.[8] Historically, the study of health and medicine has relied thoroughly on the correspondence theory of truth, searching for correlations between physical events to better determine plans for treatment. Freud felt that psychology was positioned between philosophy and medicine, and *both* of these fields in the late nineteenth and early twentieth century were dominated by the trajectory set by Plato. We should not be surprised to discover an early propensity in the discipline of psychology overall to think with the modernists about language as aiming toward the synchrony of common understanding. The purpose of words, at this level, is primarily aimed toward knowledge and understanding, even if such a goal is always understood to be out of reach.

For some scholars in the field of psychology, the "bond" between the modern and correlational language and psychology is vital. Gregg Henriques (2011), for instance, argues that psychology is in desperate need of a "unified theory" that clarifies "psychology's relationship to the natural sciences, the social sciences, and the humanities" (4). Such a unified theory is desirable, for Henriques, because of the sloppy inconsistency that is generated by the vast disputes in the discipline of psychology over even the foundational issues in the discipline. Henriques, following Robert Sternberg and Elena Grigorenko, sees in the fragmentation of psychological paradigms a grave weakness that undermines the field. In their article "Unified Psychology," Sternberg and Grigorenko (2001) propose "converging operations" in psychology that allow multidisciplinary aspects of psychology to return to a common set of ideas. This convergence requires a reasonable consensus regarding the foundational paradigms of psychology, alongside a willingness to acknowledge that psychology has multiple paradigms and disciplines. The key for this new movement in psychology is the pursuit of "coherent foundations," which Henriques (2011, 5) says are necessary to rectify psychology's current weaknesses. Henriques compares psychology to the disciplines of biology and modern physics, which have disputes that rest on a broad foundation of agreement.[9]

While many psychologists look with skepticism at the efforts of "unified psychology," this movement emblemizes a yearning within the discipline for a holistic perspective on human psychology. And the trajectory that leads to this particular expression begins with Plato and is sustained by the modern optimism that flourished during psychology's nascent period. The yearning of Henriques matches that of Freud, that psychology could take its rightful place alongside other disciplines that attend to the scientifically quantifiable needs of human persons and communities.

My aim is not to undermine the medical coherence of psychology nor contest the need for better synchrony between the psychological disciplines. Instead, I wish to underscore the powerful pressure on psychology to accommodate the theories of truth and linguistics that best accommodate the "convergence" of psychology into common modes of discourse. In its current state, psychology remains torn between competing perspectives, many of which attempt to be inclusive and explanatory for all psychological phenomena. Henriques (2011) wants to "assimilate" these perspectives into a common language (9); other theorists repeatedly propose that their own disciplines should be considered foundational for psychology. This contest masks an almost universal allegiance to the *linguistics of synchrony*.[10]

Can language be considered outside of its necessary role in forging common understanding? Might language have another, more primary "register" before or beneath the form it takes in the sciences? If so, such an inflection on language will be hard to name and more difficult to nourish. And yet, it might be that psychology is impoverished for ignoring a deeper operation of language that precedes the drive to use words to create knowledge and understanding.

HERMENEUTICS AND UNDERSTANDING

A world without the rigorous pursuit of understanding would be quite obviously chaotic, anarchic, and miserable. This is what drives Protagoras to posit the very invention of language as an instrument of social organization and technological advancement (Plato 2009 40.322a). The dynamic of language under this orientation is necessarily driven by the initial disposition of the self. Pre-linguistic human existence, for Protagoras, is beset by perils that language alleviates. Wild beasts are fierce and dangerous when faced alone, but with language and coordination such dangers can be minimized or even overcome. Thomas Hobbes (1904) famously proposed that life without language, community, and contract is "nasty, brutish and short" (84). For both Protagoras and Hobbes an assumption underlies the relation between the self and everything else. They both narrate the tale of how the ego encounters the world. The journey moves from lonely isolation to community. This movement is utterly familiar to Western philosophy; it is so familiar that it almost becomes unnoticeable. It is this caveman-meets-world metanarrative that troubles Levinas and leads him into an intriguing critique of this aspect of Western thought.

As a paradigm of this ego-driven orientation, Levinas points to the concept of the *conatus essendi,* a term he develops from Baruch Spinoza (Levinas and Kearney 1986, 24). The Western *conatus* refers to the persistent self-interest of the ego, driven by the laws of survival to sustain and fortify itself. Spinoza pointed out that "each thing, in so far as it is in itself, endeavours to preserve in its being" (Spinoza 2000, 171). For Levinas, this is a basic account of the natural egological orientation of beings. By attacking the primacy of this basic philosophical orientation, Levinas is leveling a critique that threatens to rattle the foundations of Western thought. Levinas contends that the self is not the protagonist of the story, and that the self-meets-world model of epistemology already overlooks a more primary mode of human existence. Before I encounter the Other as partner for survival, as object for knowledge, or even as interlocutor for speech, I encounter the one I am more primarily *for.* The *for-the-other* is prior, for Levinas, to the establishment of the agendas of understanding and cooperation.[11]

There are certainly branches in both philosophy and psychology that have demonstrated keen awareness to the problem of Western "egology."[12] The hermeneutic tradition attempts a self-aware analysis of this process, and scholars have shown an increasing sensitivity to the perils identified by Levinas. If the process of understanding both begins and ends with the self, the other person plays a necessarily secondary role in epistemology. Though more recent developments in hermeneutics challenge the primacy of the ego, this is blatantly the case in Hegelian hermeneutics.[13] Hegel directs attention to the burgeoning process by which history progresses toward full self-understanding. He analyzes in great detail the dynamics of the encounter of the self with the Other and traces all conflict and progress to a pre-original encounter between the ego and the Other. This encounter begins with the simple primacy of the ego, whose identity is essentially for itself and self-identified. Hegel (2009) writes: "Self-consciousness is primarily simple existence for self, self-identity by exclusion of every Other from itself. It takes its essential nature and absolute object to be Ego; and in this immediacy, in this bare fact of its self-existence, it is individual" (88). Learning, conflict and progress occur when the ego encounters the "antithesis to an individual" (ibid.).

In the twentieth century, Paul Ricoeur offers a more nuanced and advanced articulation of the hermeneutical process, pointing to a series of movements that begin with an outward movement. Ricoeur (1992) calls this initial movement an "attestation" (299–302), which can be as simple as a disposition or as complex as a formed idea or thesis. The attestation undertakes an epistemological journey, moving away from the self, being transformed through the response it receives in the world. The response may be the direct feedback of another person, or even scientific evidence that confirms or contests the attestation. Even as Ricoeur sharpens the hermeneutic "circle" and refines its method to be increasingly humble, there remains in place the sense that the ego is protagonist in a journey that originates with and returns to the self.

To question the egocentricity of the hermeneutic circle is not to challenge its practical and epistemological value. Without such modes of knowing we would lose deeply essential modes of learning and adaptation. In this chapter I follow a suspicion, planted by Levinas, that Western philosophy has presumed that the hermeneutic process attends to the *primary* or even the *only* mode of understanding and communication. The possibility I wish to explore here is that hermeneutics, for all its value, already operates at a secondary linguistic level.

Deep Language

Though Levinas suggests an innovative approach to language, it has been one of the greatest puzzles for his readers. He points toward the evasive Saying that inhabits, interrupts, and persists within the louder and more tangible Said. The Saying, he tells us, lingers in the Said. But this lingering is the trace of the infinite in the finite, which remains as an untraceable trace, that which "cannot be tracked down like game by a hunter" (Levinas 1981, 12). This trace of the Saying that remains in the Said is also a kind of annoying reminder of the slippage of meaning between what one intends to communicate and what is actually conveyed. Leibniz yearned to complete the project that has long been a fantasy of Western philosophy, to craft a language that eliminated the remainders and traces of meaning that forever convolute communication. Levinas uses the term "Saying" to refer to that which resists this enclosure of meaning into the field of "being" or "essence."

Levinas was not the only one to demonstrate this ambiguity of language, nor the only one to focus philosophical attention on the consequences of the slippage. Both Heidegger and Derrida make much of this abyss that opens up in language between interlocutors and, especially, between a text and its readers. What is unique about Levinas's suggestion is that he immediately redirects the ambiguity of language to an anarchic ethical obligation (Levinas 1981, 121). Something more important than clarity is lost when meaning escapes the boundaries of language and semiotics. For Levinas, we not only have to adjust to the fact that language does not attend to a synchronizing eternal truth, we also have to adjust to the fact that the loss of synchrony obliterates the stable metaphysical plane on which we fix universal moral obligation. The destabilization of meaning is also a destabilization of ethics. And on the other side of universal moral certainty, something Kant would guide us toward, there is the frightening specter of anarchy.[14]

The lure of synchrony, in both its linguistic and moral expressions, was partly the lure of *reasonable* responsibility. If the other person is an alternate version of the self, then we should find in both language and ethics a kind of reasonable ground to stand on ethically. On this ground I can forfeit some of my resources to meet the needs of the other person, but I certainly cannot be expected to forfeit them all. There are many models for rational ethics and morality, from Kantianism to utilitarianism to notions of Aristotelian virtue. In each case the self has a road, laced with reason and deduction, to a moral standing that is based in a coherent and communicable logic.

Levinas takes no direct issue with these modes of ethical deliberation and is reluctant to take sides regarding which moral pathway is the right one. His aim is to show that all of them attend to what I am calling the *myth of synchrony*. They all hope for a shared, reasonable, logically coherent ground that makes responsibility reasonable.

Perhaps people turn to the calculus of Jeremy Bentham's utilitarianism because it provides an alternative to anarchy, even as they see the dangers inherent in the logic of consequentialism. And perhaps we gravitate toward Kantian or Aristotelian ethics not because we think they succeed but because the only apparent alternative is chaos and lawlessness. Levinas offers another pathway, but perhaps it is no less frightening.

For Levinas, the destabilization of language and meaning leaves us in a different posture in the world altogether. And it is worth noting here that the turn that Levinas takes here is the leap upon which his whole project is founded. Also lost in the unraveling of synchronous language and meaning is *any moral defense I would have to protect me from being utterly and completely responsible for every other*. In fact, for Levinas, before there is any philosophy there is first a face that calls me to responsibility. And this primordial appearance of the Other in my world is already ancient and abundantly bearing upon me even as I become aware of it. The science of morality is only, then, a fumbling response to a more basic and fundamental reality: I am utterly hostage to the suffering of the other person (Levinas 1981, esp. 6, 11, 15, 59, 112, 114).

Levinas worries about the games of language, hermeneutics, and ethical theory not because such endeavors are unnecessary; they are, in fact, indispensible and unavoidable tools of epistemology and communion between persons. Levinas worries because these enterprises are perilously inclined to forget that they are not primary, that there is something deeper and more fundamental to the encounter with the other person than the exploration of meaning and symbols. There is, before and beneath these moves, raw and scandalous obligation. And philosophy must always exist, for Levinas, in the mode of catch-up, attending to a debt that is older than time.

For my part, I wish to suggest that there is a deeper intonation of language than the one that we find ourselves using in the business of synchronizing meaning. This more original form of discourse can be identified in the disposition of the one who *prays*, though I do not suggest that any form of religion is necessary for us to examine the linguistic aims of prayer. The mode of prayer, or supplication, is a fundamentally different mode of discourse. As one prays (presumable to a deity), one forms words not with the hope of crafting common understanding. In the mode of supplication the accuracy of symbols is secondary to the hope embodied in the discourse.

My three-year-old son awoke from his sleep as I wrote this page, in tears about some dream that haunted his nighttime rest. I listened as he tried to tell me about his experience, but his words, sometimes challenging to follow even when he is lucid, were blurred and indecipherable. I asked him to repeat himself several times, and each time he made the identical but nonsensical series of syllables. For me the words struck me as first of all an intensely difficult puzzle to decipher. I was frustrated that he could not form more articulate complaints. I asked him questions to better understand him, determining whether he needed a drink of water, another blanket, a trip to the bathroom, a hug. His mumbling sent my mind racing through the events of his day; I've been with him without interruption since the moment he awoke this morning. As he cried in my arms, I remembered his frustration when he had to wait his "turn" to go down a playground slide. I don't know if I was right in this assumption, but when I told him "It's your turn now, Luke," his delirious cries immediately ceased and he smiled himself back to a deep sleep.

When Luke awoke and chose to use words instead of mere cries, however mangled by delirium, he was directing language toward *me*. And in the stupor of his state, the words surely sounded perfectly in his mind as he spoke them. To me, the sounds Luke made were more than a linguistic puzzle; they were first of all the realization of responsibility. Somewhere in the confusion of his Said was a Saying that I chased, headstrong. There was nothing *playful* about the exchange, even if our misunderstandings and interactions are often playful. In this case, his effort to communicate was a summoning, an enjoinder, a request for a response. As I discovered that Luke's cries contained attempts to form words, I was immediately aware of the unfairness of his request. The combination of factors that made his speech indecipherable left behind no reasonable route to understanding; the "trace" of Luke's meaning was evasive indeed. Yet the difficulty of my responsibility was no factor whatsoever in the hold his suffering laid on me. As I listened I found myself, in the words of Levinas, "wanting and faulty" (Levinas 1981, 91). Language has a deeper structure than the layers of understanding that provide the framework of the Said. At a deeper register, words are all prayers offered to the other person. The Greek term *deēsis* refers to a form of communication that is first and fundamentally supplication. To speak in this way is to speak with an awareness of the abyss that separates words and undermines communication. *Deēsis* refers to language before (or after) the allure of synchrony lays its hold on the discourse. In "The Transcendence of Words: On Michel Leiris's *Biffures*" (first published in 1949), Levinas writes: "The contact in which I approach the neighbor is not a manifestation or a knowledge, but the ethical event of a communication which is presupposed by every transmission of messages, which establishes universality in which words and propositions will be stated. This contact transcends the I to the neighbor, and is not its thematization; it is the deliverance of a sign prior to every proposition, to the statement of anything whatever" (Levinas 1993, 144–50). Before, beneath, and within the Said is a "contact" with the neighbor that is beyond knowledge and meaning. Language, by this reckoning, is first of all obligation.

Luke's earnest eyes look into mine and he speaks, and in that moment both his words and my responses are characterized by responsibility and by hope. I am responsible for the suffering I hear in the *deēsis* of his prayers. He hopes, perhaps without reason, that his needs will cross the abyss of muddled language. I hope that my racing brain will form the right words and that my hands will form the right response. We cannot say that *deētic* language is an event that happens *instead* of the typical pursuit of a concrete and common Said. Rather, *deēsis* is an event best characterized as "otherwise" than the essence of the dialogue. So the words "my turn" are both expressions of meaning and also traces of meaning's "beyond." Understanding's "otherwise" is responsibility.

PSYCHOLOGY AND DEĒSIS

The stammering with which I address the Other must remain forever connected to the injunction to understand the Other. These layers or modes or manners of speech are irrevocably intertwined. The Said is the very nexus for the Saying, the condition for the trace. Language exceeds verbalization, and my psychologists are trained in looking for nonverbal traces in the Said that is silence, speech, signals, postures, glances, tears, and so on. These traces are, for Levinas, glimpses at *holiness*, at the utterly transcendent person whose world invariably escapes comprehension. In psychoanalysis these traces should be considered far more than clues that could easily be missed or pieces to a complex puzzle. The trace of the Other is a raw and asymmetrical injunction. To see the fleeting ghost of pain on the face of the Other is not first of all to *learn* something but to be *captivated* by someone and called to responsibility. The psychotherapeutic and psychoanalytic relation is predicated upon this nonreciprocity. I speak to the Other who seeks my counsel as one summoned to the impossible task of understanding the incomprehensible and expressing the ineffable. Here the *deēsis* of language interrupts and is also sustained by the formal components of the psychoanalytic encounter. And for the ways in which my utterances will inevitably fail in this venture, I am responsible. I am hostage not just to the suffering of the Other but to the diachrony of language that leaves me forever tardy for the event of understanding.

As such, psychotherapists might think of the vehicle of language in the mode of address common to religious prayer. As such, the words I speak attend to a responsibility that I know I cannot surpass or satisfy. The one who prays never thinks that language is adequate for the prayer. The words of prayer are laden with hope and uncertainty. Perhaps, to further borrow from religious terminology, the speech of the Other can be thought of as a kind of *revelation,* something Levinas occasionally suggests. The speech of the Other, considered in this way, is not first of all a puzzle for the psychologist to unravel, not a collection of symptoms that the client unintentionally or intentionally discloses in the encounter. Even when the Other *does* seem to present symptoms that easily match some theory of human psychology, Levinas raises a word of caution. When the theory fits, we see less and less friction between ideas and persons, often evident as only a flicker on the face of the Other. As revelation, the words of the other person render me doubly responsible. I must read and interpret, for sure, and this is the exercise of hermeneutics. But deeper and more primary, for Levinas, is the discovery that the language of the Other has laid me hostage to the need of the Other. As with revelation, a response is demanded, and shutting the book does not alter the command. Religious revelation is often interpreted and reinterpreted to domesticate the text, rendering it safe and unthreatening. Similarly, in psychology, we can categorize, diagnose, and dismiss the revelation of the Other without attending to the dual responsibility carried by language.

To put it another way, psychology dwells in the tension and legacy of Babel. The fragmentation of language is both blessing and curse. To help others, a goal to which psychoanalysis surely aspires, one must uncover meanings, rearrange the bricks of ideas and themes, and formulate some understanding of the other person. In this project, we may legitimately yearn for a more synchronic form of communication, a more mathematical language that conveys emotions, thoughts, and experiences with directness and clarity. The inability of language to perform this task can be maddening. But at the same time, the psychologist must regard this slippage as the opening of being to its beyond, the opening of interpretation to the radical interruption of the other person. Here we find that language flashes, if only briefly, its deeper reverberation of *deēsis*.

Levinas, using another quasi-religious term, calls this interruption an *election*. To encounter the Other is to be involuntarily elected to stand for, take responsibility for, and even to substitute for the suffering of the Other (Levinas 1981, 15). But to be elected is only just the start; election requires listening, attending to the layers of meaning, altering and repeatedly updating one's understanding of the Other, her need, his hopes, her world.

To return to Michael: the encounter in my office is a weekly struggle over language. He looks, quite specifically, to disrupt me. I lack the expertise to determine which of his complaints and threats are sincere—perhaps all of them. But the words he summons when we sit across from one another are undeniably framed to elicit a reaction. He knows the psychological keywords that make my face twist and my eyebrows rise. I hope that someone with educated expertise in psychotherapy is helping him determine the right course of therapy for his particular suffering and its consequences. What finally dawned on me, thanks to Levinas, is that I have taken the Said of his language into my mind like pieces of a puzzle, attempting to arrange them in a way that make sense of his odd and contradictory claims. Yet it seems that Michael is seeking the disruption that confirms that his *deētic* speech has been heard.

I mention Michael and his struggles with therapy as an example rather than a case study. Michael's language appears to be a scramble for terminology that would trigger a second kind of communication. He uses the trade words well, the language of psychoanalysis that leads to diagnoses, insurance claims, and transactions. But I have not heard him yet, if I have not allowed his words to be *deēsis* and not seen that his plea is for something that precedes and transcends these categories. In his case, the language game ended up being deeply self-destructive, precisely because it helped him avoid any real connection with therapists who could provide him with vital assistance. This spiral led him to an inpatient hospitalization where the steady pressure of earnest mental health professionals finally melted his resolve against therapists. There are no magic words that could have prevented Michael from this destructive movement. I have only begun to guess at what it means to attend to his language in this register. My proposal is not that therapists adopt a new strategy for therapy. Rather, I think Levinas's work attunes us to the language struggle epitomized by Michael, and to similar struggles of various degrees in every client, in every speaker. Levinas reminds me that Michael's problem with psychological jargon is my responsibility. The failure of language is my burden.

Michael and I continue to chat because I hope, and maybe he hopes too, in the irruption of something amid the business of speaking and listening. We hope in the flash of the Saying in the Said, for the trace of the holy in the face of the Other, for a glimpse at the *deēsis* amid the banality of our conversation. In this way, I suppose, I hope in something that is properly deemed impossible. Our conversation shifts and rearranges an ugly assemblage of broken and misused words and labels. But despite this, if I remember to wait for it, sometimes I hear Michael *pray*.

THREE

Asymmetry in Psychotherapy

Kevin C. Krycka

> The relations between me and the Other commences in the inequality of terms.
>
> — Levinas, *Totality and Infinity*

Levinas cautions us to refrain from holding too firmly to the comforts of the known and recognizable, as this tends to obscure the Other. Psychotherapy, in its decided preference for the comforts of symmetry—seen in the countless ways we support positivity, finding balance, harmony, equality, fairness, diversity, or even justice in our practice and the lives of our clients—does damage to our capacity to face the Other in our lived world. Relishing such preferential leanings will bring us eventually to refuse to honor the significance of the asymmetrical nature of dialogue, of relationship, and of our practice.

This chapter could be an intellectual debate. However, we will take a different course here. We will use case examples to ground the proposal that the horizon of asymmetry can assist us in our work as therapists. I define this horizon as our capacity to exceed—overflow—the limitations of our own ways of thinking about and performing our psychotherapeutic work and advancing improvement in our clients' lives. I suggest that asymmetry can be the ground upon which we orient toward a horizon that both unsettles and frees. Symmetry and (not versus) asymmetry are characterized as being at the heart of genuine meeting in psychotherapy. We have a feel for this difference. Personally and culturally we tend to avoid the uncomfortable asymmetrical, yet if we are to be more open and responsible to the otherness of the Other, we would not only not violate him or her but also not cut ourselves off from the deeper meaning we would develop from our openness. A dominant theme in Levinas's works is the meeting of the Other. For Levinas the authentic meeting of persons exists as an ethical relation, described as an "original responsibility" and call of the Other (Beals 2007; Kunz 1998; Levinas 1981, 1985, 1969). At first reading, it might appear as if Levinas's notion of meeting as ethical encounter is more aspirational than realistic. If Levinas gave us more concrete examples of how this would work out in a real life situation, we might save ourselves a lot of time "translating" Levinas to psychotherapy. He does not give us such examples.

As psychotherapists, not philosophers or saints, we must make meeting—or simply the possibility of meeting in genuine encounter—with our clients an everyday occurrence rather than something rare and too special. Meeting, for all its complications and risks, is possible as an everyday part of our work when we consider the unequal nature of this particular kind of relating called psychotherapy. In this chapter we explore what Levinas does little of, in fact had little interest in doing: investigating the psychological environment of the psychotherapy room in which our particular kind of meeting commences.

My assertion is that genuine meeting in psychotherapy occurs within a horizon of asymmetry. In order to verify this claim, I explore Levinas's thematic of meeting (that is, ethical responsibility) and relation in a case example. Through this case we can see how meeting commences as one embedded and imbued with unevenness, inequality, and danger, which is sensed (or can be) by both parties. Of course, both parties can exert forces that may ultimately break the promise and bond of ethical relationality and the therapeutic relationship in particular.

As the chapter title and above quote from *Totality and Infinity* (Levinas 1969) suggest, meeting in psychotherapy begins when two or more human beings, unequal in character and motivation, intentionally commence a relationship. Psychotherapy, then, is a process of navigating together the territories of the therapeutic relationship initially internally bounded by dichotomous notions of sameness and otherness. The therapeutic relationship, never guaranteed as a place of genuine meeting and which never begins on identical ground, can be psychologically understood as *felt datum* and *asymmetrical horizon* together.

As felt datum, genuine meeting involves the sensing therapist and sensing client. It includes the felt sense we have of each other in the moment. One's felt understanding contains the prevailing sociocultural "facts" embedded in this kind of relation. In other words, a therapist's role is formally sanctioned by contemporary society and the profession of psychotherapy that imbue it with a form of distancing from the client, an "as-if above" relationality, while the client or patient is specified as "below." As horizon, genuine meeting is more than one's feel for the meeting in this moment and sense of the inequalities present in it. Genuine meeting has the capacity to reverse the "given" asymmetries fostered by culture and our profession and unsettle them. In genuine meeting, the client and therapist can come to a good enough resolution of the built-in power asymmetry of the therapeutic relationship, leading each to eventually honor the Other for their unique status and power. It is the capacity of the genuine meeting to unsettle that I describe as an implicitly asymmetrical relationality, one that is generative of therapeutic promise.

The brilliance of Levinas, and I believe a key insight for psychotherapy, is to describe how the genuine meeting of persons does not occur by merely adjusting our attitude toward our therapeutic relationships, as if we were moving chess pieces about on a board. The face of the Other cannot be satisfied in a purely cognitive or emotional game on our part, substituting an urge toward sameness with the countermove to embrace otherness. Meeting demands that we *not* perceive the other person in ways that reinforce sameness or distinctiveness: as a purely transcendent other who functions psychologically as isolated specter or sublime vision.

Rather, I believe Levinas calls us to resist falling into sentimentality, which seeks to cover the brute facts that will ultimately deny the dignity of others, much less the possibility of meeting. New therapists and experienced ones may fall into deep feelings of sympathy for their client's situation or experience, leading them to fantasize about a "good resolution" to their plight. It might seem that sentimentality and/or romanticizing the therapeutic outcome would be aligned with the preference for symmetry as I define it. However, glorifying the asymmetrical—the tendency to see mostly crippling power dynamics between therapist and client, for instance—is also a move to reify our therapeutic relations. Casting therapy as either purely symmetrical or purely asymmetrical would be just another kind of totalizing, this time in a superior mode of positivity.

THE UNFORESEEABLE HORIZON

> The Other, in the hands of forces that break him, exposed to powers, remains unforeseeable, that is, transcendent.
> —Levinas, *Totality and Infinity*

The unforeseeable Other is part of therapeutic meeting. It is an integral aspect of the living and lived relation between therapist and client. So as not to despair over this situation, it is good to remind ourselves that we will never comprehend with full certainty the depths of our client as she lives her world. The relation we forge together in meeting will likewise always be somewhat obscured from clear vision and remain unforeseeable, only partially revealed. Even that which is revealed will prove elusive, like a trace that cannot be entirely trusted to deliver us the truth about the other person.

In psychotherapy, the unforeseen and partially revealed other—including the relationship itself—is a doorway for our work. One does not end a session as separated individuals going their own ways. Rather, both client and therapist "emerge" from meeting in a truer standing with each other founded in the courageous intention and ability to meet one another's asymmetrical presence with openness, curiosity, and acceptance. Doing so is no easy task. It will require of the therapist willingness to dispose herself or himself to the Other in all her dis-ease while at the same time encountering the tendencies to reach for the "pill" to ease and comfort.

It should be noted that occasionally psychologically valuable terms are employed, like "curiosity" or "thematize," which are used by Levinas differently than we do in our profession. The common term "thematize" is suspect in Levinas's work as it could be taken to mean a limiting generalization where original life is flattened out, made to be even where in fact it is not anything like this (Beals 2007, 67). The term "curiosity" is also used differently by Levinas. His use specifies something other than wonder and the disposition to hear and listen. For Levinas, curiosity is based in the needs of the ego, a compulsion to grasp, contain, or possess an object in totality. Note, too, that his is a specialized use of "ego," which does not fully coincide with the psychoanalytic use, for instance.

Levinas unsettles our common usage of certain terms like these in order to help us appreciate why one does not seek mere knowledge about another as a curiosity, as if the other person were a thing of interest, an object. However, a valid psychological use of the terms "curiosity" and "thematic" can retain the openness and disposition to the Other, for which Levinas is most known, if we keep in mind his distinct challenges to the use of these terms.

We can never tire of investigating the factors that interfere with or hinder the development of effective relationships with clients. Most likely we all recognize that with a little good fortune and technical skill we can learn how to "be with," to "hold open a space," to invite those who suffer (including our selves) to dwell and reflect — all necessary ingredients for doing good work. Yet, the possibility that there must be more at play here is salient. In the case below, it becomes clear for instance, that something was missing in the relationship; a deep understanding of the client's inner life and of the repetitive cycles of the mutual dis-ease present in the therapy was not initially evident. In the case below, we use the first-person perspective. As disarming as this might be for a formal case presentation, the perspective helps the reader enter into the lived experience of this therapist early in his training.

JAKE

Many years ago I had a client who was very demanding of my time and emotional energy. "Jake" was a young man in his early twenties expressing deep ambivalence, even despair, toward a part of his life, a part he was only now coming to fully understand. He did not need to mention the object of his concern; it was enough for me to know that the territory of disturbance he was experiencing set him off balance in many areas of life. He was a graduate student in fine arts who came in regularly every week and early to our sessions only to complain about how poorly he was being treated (by his family, peers, the faculty, and by me). My best client-centered reflections (Rogers 1959) failed to soften the hostile atmosphere that accompanied him every week. I dreaded these sessions.

Jake grew increasingly distraught at my empathy, which at least in part consisted of well-intended attempts to smooth things over between us, even though I wasn't completely sure how I had so disappointed him. He questioned my motives and expertise. When I pointed out that "we were in this together," perhaps a naive attempt on my part to find some point of mutuality, his rage only increased and he became even more visibly upset.

Jake and I worked together in psychotherapy for just over two years. At the conclusion of our time together, Jake had learned to ride the crests and valleys of his emotional life better but not always successfully. His demands that I change, that his family change, and that in fact the world change to his specifications never dissolved completely. However, we both noticed one sliver of change. To Jake's demandingness was added a newly recognized source of comfort: a kind of resting in the knowledge that he had gone through a powerful period of exploration and was emerging, not whole or healed but as a man who could navigate powerful emotional ambiguities without being wrecked on the shoals of a life organized around negative and positive emotion.

Jake looked to me as someone with the power to help him: his body posture and his eyes pleaded for some assistance, however small. In the moments I perceived his pleading I felt honored, privileged, and intimidated by his demand. This encounter occurred early in my career and the intimidation factor was strong. I did not yet know that a client's trust in me and my profession came at least partly from their need and my willingness to be open to their suffering, if even temporarily. This is a scene many psychotherapists encounter.

Our meetings, and perhaps all meetings with psychotherapists, took place in the space of inequality: the unequal space of client and therapist, of doctor and patient, of seeking other and quiet witness. These are nonetheless generative situations that can open our neighbor and us into what Levinas calls relationship. These meetings are implicitly rich, very frequently tacitly felt as important, and only rarely explicitly allowed to be part of our therapeutic framework in any other but a negative, diagnostic view. If we can sense this basic inequality for ourselves, as felt datum, the feel we have for the relationship can be the ground upon which we orient our work toward a horizon that might unsettle us, but which frees us nonetheless.

THE PROPOSITION

I propose that genuine "meeting" occurs in the interplay between symmetry and asymmetry as we work together in psychotherapy. These dual aspects, if you will, of the therapeutic relationship do not function as binaries that stay in tension but as complementing dynamics. Levinas employs several other sets of terms in couplets to help us explore meeting: "sameness" and "otherness," "synchronic" and "diachronic," "totality" and "infinity" (Levinas 1969).

To help us more fully consider the dynamic roles of symmetry and asymmetry in psychotherapy, I suggest we adopt the attitudes of openness and curiosity, which are placed at the service of being faithful to the phenomenon (Valle, King, and Halling 1989). Adopting openness and curiosity are no easy feat, particularly in contemporary culture, which values certainty and predictability over much else. As Wertz says, to accomplish this stance we need to adopt a "peculiar posture as well as the rigorous enactment of multiple active modes of understanding" (Wertz 1983, 198).

The "peculiar posture" of remaining open, curious, responsible, and fearless, indeed an unusual stance today, requires that we have courage in any case, perhaps more so with clients with whom we feel troubled. Still, even as we are successful at these two things — openness and responsible curiosity, we will remain challenged by finding words for what we find when we look closely at our working with troubling clients.

Gemma Corradi Fiumara (2001), an Italian phenomenologist and psychoanalyst, speaks to this issue as the problem of dealing with the "unfathomable depth" we find as we touch what is essential to life. She advocates that we become tolerant of the uncomfortable feelings that will surely arise as we search into new territories and resist the weight of the "immense terminology for discrete details of observable reality" (94–95). Tolerance of our uncomfortable feelings, courage, fearlessness; these are qualities to which we aspire in our work in general, and which will best assist us in navigating the geography of working with troubling clients.

JAKE AND ASYMMETRY

My encounters with Jake underscore two dramatic manifestations of asymmetry in our work together: (1) the im-balances we both felt. These include Jake's own feelings of hostility, disappointment, and rage as well as my own severely conflicted feelings regarding Jake and my capacities as a therapist; and (2) the confrontation of our preference for *harmony*. This manifests in our desire for "equalization" and even *resolution* in our working relationship, including Jake's own hoped-for resolution of self-ascribed, troubled family dynamics and my hope for some calm sessions.

In a cursory way, we can see a few asymmetries that are probably obvious. First, there is the im-balance of power between therapist and client; I am the therapist, Jake is the client. The origin of the dynamics of power, whether created by our culture or profession, matters little here. As therapists we are supposed to have some answers or at least guidance that our client (Jake in this case) does not himself yet possess. This is a common asymmetry in psychotherapy. There will likely always be the specter of power in this kind of relationship we call psychotherapy. In Jake's case, this built-in asymmetry was at one point a hindrance to his experience of being accepted or respected and a valuable condition that was finally made psychologically available as an explicit subject during the final phases of therapy.

Second, our mutual preference for symmetry became startlingly clear as we got to know each other. At first I noticed that Jake was not able or willing to sense his powerful feelings as anything other than totalizing disturbances. Eventually, he did come close to experiencing his vast emotional range as a horizon of experiences that do not paralyze. I wonder, if we had continued to work together, how sitting with his ambivalence for this uncertainty would have unfolded. Would we have crossed over the unsettling horizon that holds potential for freedom *and* the threat of disillusionment of his ideals or values? I cannot know for certain.

For my part, I noted that I did not enjoy our work as I did with other clients. We seemed better suited to be in a sparring match than in a relationship, which of course was diagnostically helpful but made our meetings full of tension. I came to notice an almost reflexive insistence within me of seeking and hoping for the positive, at all costs (for example, a positive feeling, a calming metaphor or image, a soothing look). With the help of good supervisors, eventually I came to see my own hesitancy to explore Jake's darker moods and ferocious appetite for blame, judgment, and despair with him as an avenue toward genuinely meeting Jake.

I came to suspect that I, along with my profession, might be colluding with our clients to move almost brutally away from any feeling, thought, or sensation that would contest our positive trajectory where our hoped-for good feelings and pleasant metaphors reside. My suspicion continues to be that much of contemporary literature on psychotherapy implicitly advocates for what amounts to a full-scale march toward balance, harmony, and equality as a normative standard in our profession.

Let me conclude this section on working with Jake with this thought: perhaps paradoxically, seeking the most prized realization prevents it from being found. Below I explore what I am calling the horizon of asymmetry along two avenues: (1) the notion of imbalance (asymmetry) as a generative space that may unsettle but is freeing; and (2) a commentary on contemporary urgings toward the leveling of human experience as seen in "evidence-based" practice in psychotherapy.

ASYMMETRY AS GENERATIVE SPACE

There is a dual—or twin—relation between symmetry and asymmetry in psychotherapy. Rather than seeing these as dichotomous or antithetical to each other, recognizing them as implicit and integral can assist us in therapeutic work. In this sense, when Jake touched on his most fearful feelings, there opened the horizon of asymmetry within him, which then assisted in generating new psychological territories to explore. If Jake had inhabited only the obverse, the feared emotional states haunting him, he would have likely spent many sessions focusing on finding the positive alone. However, as Jake grew to honor the asymmetrical along with the symmetrical, I believe he came to a more practical, useful, and encouraging conclusion by the time we finished our work together.

Any notion of the asymmetrical begs inclusion of notions of the symmetrical primarily because our language is weak at holding more than one concept at a time. Ideally, I would find a new, fresh way of expressing this idea without being too burdened by the weight of commonly used terms in psychotherapy. But, instead of creating new terms, I have decided to use unusual ones and chose the terms "asymmetry" and "symmetry." These are terms that do not frequently find themselves in the lexicon of our profession. What do I mean by asymmetry as a basis for generativity in psychotherapy?

The Experience of Symmetry and Asymmetry in Psychotherapy

Let us take symmetry and asymmetry separately at first, and then draw them together.

The Experience of Symmetry

Symmetry is first and foremost an experience: the feeling we have inside during moments such as harmony, tranquility, centeredness, or balance. To put it differently, we have the feeling inside, the felt sense if you will, of opening up rather than constricting or closing. This territory is quite well known to me as a focusing-oriented psychotherapist (Gendlin 1996) trained originally in the person-centered approach (Rogers 1959). These openings and relaxations felt by our clients or us are sometimes prized as indicators of movement forward, and sometimes they are. Also, the experience contains something inexplicable, intangible, what I would say is the wordlessness of it all, something rarely appreciated and even abandoned as useless in many professional discussions.

There is, as well, the pull for its permanence. Symmetries tend to be self-reinforcing in that we both, therapist and client, want more of this. After all, is this not the reason the client comes to us? Isn't permanence a different way of expressing what we mean by success in therapy? Who doesn't want more of this good feeling?

Here is where we get into trouble with the desire for symmetry. The pull for permanence can be found in the desire-and-aversion dynamic. These are psychologically visible dualities. They show up at intra/interpersonal levels as anxiety over conflict, avoidance of exposing one's own ideas to judgment or fearing being judgmental toward others, being vulnerable or intimate, or expressing disapproval and disagreement. For Jake, these dualities presented themselves as unsolvable internal mysteries, genuine moments of despair at not quite being able to feel life. Initially, Jake was unable to sense even one polarity or the other. There was only a "grey feeling, like nothing is...real sometimes."

The Experience of Asymmetry

Asymmetry is noticed as a bodily sense. Like symmetry, it has its own feel, but in this case at least at the beginning, asymmetry is sensed as an un-comfortable feel for the moment (even if it is a feel for a moment in the past); the feelings Jake wanted to deny and avoid. Unlike symmetry, asymmetry is a sense that we move from or at least want to move from, it is a sense not of opening but of something other, an other that we cannot fully understand or speak. It is an experience we also concretize but, in this case, concretize as an incompleteness—a becoming mysterious, a nagging, an over-there, just at the edges of our known horizon.

In Jake's case, the feelings he and I had, though certainly not mirrors of each other, were similar in regards the sense of imbalance, discomfort, and helplessness we both experienced. Additionally, Jake occasionally expressed pain over the realization that I was "above" him, in the sense that I was the doctor and he the patient as well as in his perception of me as whole, stable, and reliable while his inner and external life where anything but these. Part of the fabric of our work was to help him experience his life in the moment rather than merely approaching his concerns as a subject to be studied. This would reinforce psychological distancing, which in his case would serve to keep alive the psychologically safe distance created when *talking about* salient issues. I believe we as therapists exercise the capacity for symmetry and asymmetry through the choices we make in situations like that with Jake. For a certain time in our therapeutic work together, we chose to avoid connecting to the deeper realizations that would come through discussing his sense of our relational imbalance.

As therapists, when we assuage the asymmetrical, not only are we disposed to *not* want to hang out with our uncomfortable feelings, hopes, or desires, but we forestall knowing their deeper character for a simpler reality—essentially giving us an im-balanced, even myopic view of what is going on. For a while, Jake and I worked within a psychological reality that was neat, but thin; instead of living-with-more-than the content presented in-session, of standing with or next to its exceeding overflow, we generally preferred to tacitly agree with this limiting maneuver.

THE HORIZON OF ASYMMETRY AND OVERFLOW — EVIDENCE SEEKING

Turning now to my second avenue, let me say more about the twinning of symmetry and asymmetry as it relates to contemporary practices that these ideas might affect.

I am suggesting that avoidance of the asymmetrical feeds from and into the cultural and scientific fascination with sameness and evenness, resulting in a leveling of human experience and expectancies. Culture and science both need to have similarity over dissimilarity in order to function. They may tolerate variance, but they will always want to spring back to privileging the symmetrical. Variance is seen as confounding the establishment of similarity. Instead, I see a horizon of a different order worth exploring in psychotherapy, a different contour by virtue of the quality of its lived nature.

I define the "horizon of asymmetry" as our capacity to exceed, to overflow, the totalizing desire for the permanence of balance and harmony. Asymmetry is horizontal in the sense that we most often inwardly experience it as in-the-distance, as something that could come into view but isn't quite yet. Still, we do have a feel for just that sense of "not-quite-here" that we can explore.

Exploring the lived quality of any experience—symmetry or asymmetry—can become the ground upon which we reorient our work. I would underscore, though, that orienting toward symmetry is adopting the already known as the basis for the work. Orienting toward a horizon that unsettles but frees, while a lesser-known path, is one at least pregnant with discovery.

Orienting toward the unsettling is a stance that undoubtedly may be personally changing. It may challenge certain paradigmatic ways of thinking about and how we perform our work. I believe that with the notion of a generative asymmetry, we are better positioned to respond in-depth to the many contemporary approaches to human life that reveal the near gravitational attraction to the symmetrical.

As I have suggested above it is the tendency of those theories, persons, or psychotherapies that prefer symmetry to propose methods that level out the nuance and texture of the lived world. This idea, that it is better to have the benefits of symmetry rather than enjoin the efforts of asymmetry, is not new, of course. All you need to do is step outside your reading room and wander into a bookstore (or search online) to find an author who speaks of the benefits of honoring the harmonious, equality, or justice. However, I would like to move our attention to one manifestation of symmetry-production in the health professions that is of particular concern and importance. There are other examples, of course, but this one I know most intimately.

Evidence-based practices (EBP) are those that conform to the ideals of symmetry: equality of terms, maintenance of distinctions, and a belief in neutral universality. They are said to produce stable practices that will uniformly improve our living, will be applicable across the greatest number of circumstances, and will be valueless. Regarding the latter point, by "valueless" I mean practices that have diminished the person to a function, a function that merely responds to the practice, not engaging it where there would be a greater chance of personhood to arise and the practice to adjust. Conformity justified by the high value of symmetry rules in much of today's health practices.

Emerging in the past decade or so is an alternative from the human sciences called "practice-based evidence" (PBE). These new practices help us break out of the singularly linear analyses that have offered limited temporal analytic power in getting at the order of cause and effect, the feedback loops, and the synergistic relations—beyond interaction effects in analysis of variance or multiple regressions . The new generation of PBE crops up in medical practice/training, psychotherapy research/practice, nursing, and a variety of others. With the help of crossing with systems theorists and sociologists, practice-based evidence is gaining ground. Essentially, PBE is inductive rather than deductive, responsive to the local environment, and important for this conversation, is relational in nature—and a bit more messy (Elliott, Greenburg, and Lietaer 2004).

Final Remarks

Neither symmetry nor asymmetry needs to arise within a totalizing scheme. The relation of one to the Other does not nullify either nor produce their separation. We also have no need as of yet to imagine an *integration* of these themes. Doing so would be premature and may simply become a new version of the totalizing efforts inherent in the ideological privilege of symmetry. Likewise, there is no need to suppose universal or existential truths into which the asymmetrical and symmetrical are absorbed. Levinas (1969) would be reluctant to agree that synthesis of these themes would be desirable. The asymmetrical always hangs open, never truly closing into synchrony and symmetry.

Of course, the symmetrical and asymmetrical in psychotherapy, like desire and aversion, are multiply determined states. Yet, when unnoticed, avoided, or myopically privileged, they substitute a genuine feel for life with something less like living. Keeping these two mutually occurring dynamics in tension—without actually recognizing each as a generative opportunity or moving away from the undesirable and moving toward the desired—results in stalling the work. This is not merely a psychological reality. It is a normative duality that shows up in other ways: in the policies and strategies we make as health-care workers, theoreticians, methodologists, and so forth.

Inasmuch as the symmetrical and asymmetrical are structured in our work, as psychotherapists we may be participating in a delusion when we avoid these in the here-and-now of the therapy session. The delusion to which I am referring is not only of psychological origin. I reference a quasi-delusional state that is characterized by compensatory moves to join the hegemonic preference for symmetry and thereby mask its heteromonic experiential neighbor. Problematically, to join the symmetric is to participate in reifying both symmetry and asymmetry as a form that is above. Instead of standing with and next to these as generative dynamics needed together, we embolden distancing ourselves and shielding our clients from their own heteromonic experiences and thereby avoid the actual feel we get as we sense this dynamic intimately.

In a very circumscribed way, the humanistic values we espouse (Bohart et al. 1997, 2001) may lead us to naively be for the Other without understanding that being such will destroy the visages we cherish of being a saintly or at least a helpful person. To inwardly recoil from the starker reality of the destitution of the Other and her lived experience of dis-harmony, dis-unity—to avoid what Levinas calls "the face"—these are at the core of our avoidance. If we knew the costs going in, I wonder, would we be more timid in our claims for harmony, balance, justice, peace, fairness, and the like?

In short (and I will say this brutishly), we have become inured to the nuance of being human such that we rarely recognize in our public and private spaces the place of staying a while with the unfamiliar, the unclear, the very spaces we feel as "anything but" harmonious. We neglect the invitation of the Other to acknowledge and explore the asymmetrical, to see it as potent. We often instead run over the moments where the symmetry is wavering or nearing collapse—those moments of overflow, of experiential fullness beyond the given—to give quick support, to shore up the wound of genuine encounter.

As Levinas states, "To contain more than one's capacity is to shatter at every moment the framework of a content that is thought, to cross the barriers of immanence" (Levinas 1969, 27). The genuine meeting that I have characterized as the heart of psychotherapy brings both the client and the therapist to exceed themselves. I propose that we can have a feel for the asymmetrical as well as the symmetrical. We can learn to invite both: to invite the feel we have of imbalance, harmony, of curious interest in the incomplete, unworded, unknown of connection to the unanswered without perturbing its uncertain, un-centered character. To do less would be to invite being a shadow. Echoing Levinas (1969) once again: "to the extent I reduce my experience to a mere version of it, I remain unrecognized" (252).

There are psychological barriers and not insignificant cultural ones that must be recognized and confronted if we are to have genuine contact and dialogue in psychotherapy. As Fiumara (1995) has said: "We are inhabitants of a culture that knows how to speak but not how to listen. Against a tradition that has endorsed the power of discourse, where warring monologues are mistaken for genuine dialogue" (xx). I have suggested that to move genuinely toward a full hearing of the lives of our clients, we need to adopt a listening stance that is neither naïve nor feeble. This requires a courageous move on our part, a move that Levinas has described variously in his works as resisting the pull to confuse authentic dialogue with its representations—seen in concepts such as infinity and transcendence or through exceeding one's limits simply for the sake of exceeding them.

With Jake and other clients besides him, we confront our own tendency to avert our eyes from the harsh lived reality of our relationships. Beyond this important first move, there was significant work that Jake and I needed to do that confronted the monologues of our given assumptions and positions. Then, and only then, did the generative space of communion emerge between us. In the end, while there was more to be accomplished between us and in our individual lives, we left feeling *real,* a sense that disclosed the *more-than,* however raw and incomplete.

Levinas (1969) states, "the relations between me and the other commences in the inequality of terms" (225). At a certain level, all human relations begin in an inequality of terms. We see this in many ways that often enough emerge during the course of psychotherapy (that is, the power structure of therapist over client, confronting it, and moving toward incorporating this reality into the therapeutic work rather than denying it). Further, it is suggested that we need to acknowledge our own experience of asymmetry, of the basic inequalities that define us and our work. Regarding the latter point, it has been suggested that coming to awareness of this is, in part, an aspect of a psychotherapist's natural process of maturing in the field. However, it has also been suggested that caution be exerted in the therapy relationship regarding how or when inequalities will ever be addressed explicitly. Much depends upon the nature of the mental state of the client and the capacities of the therapist.

Let me conclude by suggesting that as practitioners concerned with the face of the Other, we and our work will be served best to the extent we can:

- leave open the doorway inside and in our systems of thought or theories, for all that we *instinctually* want to avoid in *this particular* experience;
- recognize the inherent imbalance between me and the countless others we know and encounter—we will forever be different from each other;
- speak up when we feel we shouldn't for the asymmetricality embedded in our relations, not to contest them only but to use them as generative spaces.

In short, psychotherapy can midwife the asymmetrical by shrinking avoidance of it.

FOUR

Martin Buber and Emmanuel Levinas

Alexandra L. Adame

Writers in the tradition of existential-phenomenology have long wrestled with the question of what it means to be authentically human and how this knowledge may be applied to society at large. The dialogical tradition within the field of psychology (e.g., Farber 1966; Friedman 1992; Goldberg 2000; Hycner 1991) overlaps significantly with existential-phenomenological thought and focuses specifically on the notion that people always exist *in relation to* others. Stewart and Mickunas (1990) note, "one discovers his [her] own authentic humanity only by recognizing the humanity of others. Authentically existing individuals who recognize each other's humanity constitute a community" (67). When one rejects the notion of self-contained individualism (see Cushman 1990 for a detailed critique of Western individualism), one turns to questions of what types of relational stances we take in relation to others (from dyadic to societal levels) and thereby also consider what our responsibilities are toward other people.

In this chapter I will draw together Martin Buber's philosophical anthropology and the ethics of responsibility posited by Emmanuel Levinas in an exploration of the interrelated concepts of authenticity, community, and responsibility. In order to illustrate the theories in living contexts, I will also ground this discussion with some concrete examples from my clinical work and research with grassroots peer support and advocacy organizations.

Buber's work has been the inspiration for many of the dialogical and inter-subjective approaches in psychology (Binswanger 1963; Boszormenyi-Nagy 1987; Bugental 1987; Ehrenberg 1992; Friedman 1960, 1992; Goldberg 2000; Hycner 1991; Jourard 1971; Laing 1969b), and Levinas has written more specifically on questions of ethics and responsibility in our relationships with others. Feminist writers have also extensively taken up the subject of relational ethics (e.g., Graf-Taylor 1996; Prilleltensky 1997; Walters 2003). I will echo the sentiments of much of their work, although feminist theory will not be the main focus of this particular analysis.

There are some significant and important differences in the philosophies set forth by Buber and Levinas (Atterton, Calarco, and Friedman 2004). One of the main points of departure between Buber's work and Levinas's work is the concept of mutuality in relationships. Buber writes about a symmetrical and reciprocal relational stance between two people as a vital component of the *I-Thou* relation, while Levinas's early writings hold that our relationship to the Other[1] is fundamentally defined by an asymmetrical ethical inequality between us that requires us to bracket our ego-centric interests and acknowledge the ways I am responsible for the Other (Kunz 2006a). It is beyond the scope of the current paper to address these differences in greater depth; instead I will draw from these great thinkers in a way that promotes dialogue about how we go about fulfilling our responsibility to the Other.

I begin by briefly explaining Buber's relational ontology of human existence upon which I base my dialogical approach. Here I distinguish myself from Levinas who bases his existential philosophy on an *ethics* of responsibility for the Other as distinct from Buber's relational ontology. However, I will soon return to a Levinasian ethics of responsibility in my proceeding discussion of authenticity in relationships. Authenticity in relation to the Other is an outgrowth of fulfilling our responsibility to Others and denotes a fundamental respect of their humanity (or, if you will, honoring of their existence). Together, living authentically, we form a genuine bond in community. The notion of community thus ultimately underlies the notion of dialogical responsibility.

THE ROLE OF DIALOGUE

I base the various ideas set forth in this paper on Buber's relational ontology that he explicated most directly in *I and Thou* (1958), *Between Man and Man* (1965), and *The Knowledge of Man* (1988). Buber contends that humans are fundamentally relational beings, and the *I* or the self never exists in isolation. When we speak of an *I* we simultaneously imply a relation to another being, and we are free to choose whether we respond to the Other as an *It* or a *Thou*. In other words, Buber says that our choice is not whether or not to be in relation to Others (we always are) but, rather, the nature of that relationship as either a circumscribed means-to-an-end relation (*I-It*) or an intimate moment of meeting where we stand in reverence of another who also chooses to reveal him- or herself in equal presentness of being.

In an I-Thou encounter, a person turns toward the other person and confirms his or her being and reveres the Other for simultaneously opening him- or herself in such a way. Friedman (1960) explains that the realm of I-Thou "is characterized by mutuality, directness, presentness, intensity, and ineffability" (57). As we turn toward the Other, we are mutually open to the encounter and give the other person the opportunity to confirm us as well. We are most authentically ourselves in the immediacy and mutual confirmation that is felt in the I-Thou encounter.

In contrast to an I-Thou encounter, an I-It relationship is monological and purely subjective rather than dialogical and interhuman. Friedman (1960) explains: "the I-It is the primary word of experiencing and using. It takes place *within* a man and not *between* him and the world. Hence it is entirely subjective and lacking in mutuality" (57, italics added). The other person is not in genuine dialogue with us as we set him or her at a distance and do not attempt to experience the Other's side of the relationship. Instead, we are using the other person as a means to an end rather than a partner in dialogue.

Carl Goldberg (2000) is a psychologist who has been influenced by the work of Buber, and from a clinical perspective he posits, "difficulties with intimate relating are responsible for much of the pervasive sense of alienation and existential exhaustion that characterize postmodern society" (561). Clients may excel in some areas of their lives, such as their careers or financially, yet may still be plagued with feelings of loneliness, inadequacy, and apathy because of the lack of genuine intimacy, connection, and community with others. Goldberg argues that such malaise is a manifestation of the Western notion of the self that dichotomizes self and Other/world, and this Cartesian dualism creates an existential state of isolation and profound disconnect from our relational nature.

Buber's and Levinas's philosophies challenge such false dichotomies and further challenge the notion that we are circumscribed monads rather than relational and dialogical beings. Lest we create another false dichotomy by setting up the I-It stance in opposition to the I-Thou stance, let us now examine the reason Buber believes we need to maintain a flexible dialectic between the two ways of being in the world.

Buber recognizes that much of our day-to-day lives are lived in I-It encounters, and he does not construe the I-It relation as bad or wrong per se, but it is a less meaningful and potentially dehumanized way of experiencing the world. Commenting on the need for I-It relating in day-to-day life, Friedman (1960) says, "it is only the reliability of its ordered and surveyable world which sustains man in life. One cannot meet others in it, but only through it can one make oneself 'understood' with others" (60). Without the realm of I-It, we would not have a sense of continuity and constancy across time and place, and without order and utilitarian knowledge we would be lost in a reality without finitudes. Another way of understanding the need for the I-It relational stance is articulated by Paulo Freire (1998): "Men can fulfill the necessary condition of being *with* the world because they are able to gain objective distance from it. Without this objectification, whereby man also objectifies himself, man would be limited to being *in* the world, lacking both self-knowledge and knowledge of the world" (499; italics in original).

The relational *I* is also a conscious and self-aware being who has the ability to reflect on itself as an object and also as a being-in-the-world. The I-It realm provides the infrastructure for our I-Thou encounters, and thus the two modes of being are interdependent. Buber suggests that our goal ought to be a flexible dialectic between I-It and

I-Thou encounters in a person's life in order to maintain both the stability and the authenticity of one's existence. Remaining in an I-It mode becomes problematic for our clients when this style of interaction becomes an end unto itself rather than laying the groundwork for genuine dialogue. For instance, using standard intake questions about a client's psychosocial history certainly serves an important role in obtaining critical information about a person's life and what brings them to therapy. However, staying in the mode of information gathering without delving deeper into an exploration of the *present, experiential meanings* of those experiences—as they unfold in the context of the therapeutic relationship—keeps this mode of interaction at an I-It rather than potential I-Thou level. Buber explains that all I-It dialogue has the *potential* to become an I-Thou, and alternatively, every I-Thou must eventually become an I-It once we reflect upon the encounter as an event bounded in time and space and fixed meanings. Psychotherapy as such is a relationship where the potential for I-Thou is experienced between client and therapist.[2]

There are clear parallels with the I-It realm and the structure and pacing of psychotherapy, which typically unfolds in thoughtfully structured patterns of interaction—such as a regular appointment times, occurring within the time boundary of 50 minutes, and meeting in the same room for each session where the therapist and client usually sit in the same seats. Many therapists and clients alike will attest that the pacing of therapy reflects the notion that I-Thou encounters are far more rare than our typical I-It modes of interaction. For instance, it is not unusual in long-term therapy to go for several months without having a profound "aha" moment of insight or emotionally cathartic response. Yet, as one former client put it, "I needed the predictability and calmness of our usual conversations to create the safety I needed to really be open with you." In my role as clinical supervisor, I remind anxious therapists-in-training of this necessity of creating reliable and safe conditions for the client in order to create the potential for moments of genuine dialogue to unfold. My supervisees are not atypical of many beginning therapists who are often concerned about "making something happen" or trying to come up with brilliant insights with their clients. In other words, they are striving for the I-Thou rather than focusing on creating the conditions for the I-Thou to occur spontaneously, which, by definition, may or may not occur. Buber reminds us that when we strive for the I-Thou as an end unto itself we have paradoxically turned it into an I-It—an object to attain, achieve, or self-possess. Yet what unfolds in genuine dialogue occurs exclusively in the between, which is neither mine nor yours exclusively, thus creating a unity in dialogue that also does not negate the uniqueness of each partner in dialogue. For both the new clinician and the experienced one, setting the stage—helping form the conditions necessary for genuine dialogue is continuously part of our work.

LEVINAS AND THE ETHICS OF RESPONSIBILITY

Emanuel Levinas also writes about the nature of human relationships in texts such as *Totality and Infinity* (1969), *Otherwise than Being* (1981), and *Ethics and Infinity* (1985). However, unlike Buber, Levinas is concerned primarily with ethical matters and holds that our ethical responsibility to the Other precedes questions of ontology, freedom, and intentionality. Levinas was fond of quoting a line from *The Brothers Karamazov* that captures the essence of his ethical stance: *"We are all guilty of all and for all men before all, and I more than the others"* (Levinas 1985, 98–99; italics in original). He goes on to explain that "this is not owing to such or such a guilt which is really mine, or to offenses that I would have committed; but because I am responsible for a total responsibility" (99). Similar to Buber's notion that we do not choose whether or not to be in relation to the Other, Levinas says that we do not choose whether or not we are responsible to the Other. We are already guilty before the Other, and our freedom lies in how we choose to respond to the call.

One of the key distinctions between Levinas's notion of responsibility and Buber's I-Thou relation is that Levinas posits an unequal relational stance between *I* and *Thou*—the Other calls upon us to responsibility from a position of height and infinite transcendence: "The Other qua Other is situated in a dimension of height and of abasement—glorious abasement; he has the face of the poor, the stranger, the widow, and the orphan, and, at the same time, of the master called to invest and justify my freedom" (Levinas 1969, 251).

The ethical dimension of height implies a notion of transcendence that calls us to infinite responsibility in the face of the Other. We are most authentically ourselves and are fulfilling the purpose of our existence when we fully offer our resources to the needs of Others. We do not respond to the needs of Others with an expectation of getting something in return, nor do we neglect our own needs and practical limitations in terms of time and resource commitments. Clinicians know this all too well, especially those who work with the more severely distressed where self-care is critical and where we would rarely "see" immediate change.

Buber's writings on the I-Thou stance have a similar emphasis on the delicate balance between self and Other in a reverential moment of meeting. Further, Buber appears to agree with Levinas on the point that responsibility to the Other is the foundation of a relational ethics when he states, "responsibility presupposes one who addresses me primarily, that is, from a realm independent of myself and to whom I am answerable" (Buber 1965, 45). In turn, I am focusing on the common theme of responsibility to the Other as a way of drawing out some of the important commonalities between Buber and Levinas.

Finally, Levinas (1985) reminds us that "at no time can one say: I have done all my duty.... It is in this sense that there is an opening beyond what is delimited; and such is the manifestation of the Infinite" (108). In the same sense that Being is an ever-evolving process, our responsibility to Others does not have an endpoint or tangible goal. In fact, Levinas (1969) writes, "duties become greater in the measure that they are accomplished. The better I accomplish my duty the fewer rights I have; the more I am just the more guilty I am" (244). With these ethical principles, along with Buber's relational ontology in mind, I will now turn to the concept of authenticity in our dialogues with other people.

DIALOGICAL RESPONSIBILITY

I have previously written about the concept of responsibility in a broad way that goes beyond the confines of *personal* responsibility (in the individualistic sense of the personal), and reconnects the personal to the political in a practical way (Adame and Leitner 2011).

Following from my previous discussion of a dialogical self that is always in relation to others, I would like to propose the notion of *dialogical responsibility,* which integrates key elements of the work of Buber and Levinas in new ways. Dialogical responsibility harkens back to the familiar feminist slogan "the personal is political," and consequently our so-called personal choices and actions ought to be thought of as having far-reaching implications to the world at large.

Dialogical responsibility follows from the notion that our existence is integrally intertwined with others as well as the natural world. Because our existence is co-constituted in these ever-evolving relationships, we are also responsible for the role we play in other people's lives (as they are in turn responsible for the role they play in ours). For Levinas only here in the political, the relation with "the thirds," can I expect reciprocal responsibility. Implicit in Buber's concept of genuine dialogue is responsibility to the Other, which we fulfill by bringing ourselves fully into relation, holding nothing back as we respond to the needs of the Other.

Buber's notion of the I-Thou relation already expands far beyond the two people engaged in the encounter but is often interpreted as meaningful only in the context of the two-person dyad. By connecting the I-Thou relation to some of the principles of Levinasian ethics, I am attempting to expand the typical notions of the I-Thou dyad to an awareness of the nature of dialogical responsibility. In a related sense, many writers (e.g., Cushman 1990; Hillman and Ventura 1992) have critiqued many forms of psychotherapy as being narrowly individualistic and ultimately self-serving, disconnected from issues of oppression, social injustice, and economic disparity that ultimately underlie so much suffering in the world. Imagine the shift that might occur in our clients' lives and as well in society if we focused even a fraction of the attention we pay to self-image and self-presentation toward the needs of others. Such a reformulation could result in a shift in consciousness — from being primarily ego-centered to a consciousness of social justice, an ethics of care, or feminist ethics, or perhaps, a Levinasian ethics.

Much of my thinking about dialogical responsibility has been shaped by my research on grassroots political activism efforts advocating for human rights in the mental health system. More specifically, much of my research has centered upon the experiences of psychiatric survivors, which is a term embraced by people who have been harmed and/or oppressed by the mental health system and thus have "survived" their treatment rather than a particular diagnosis of mental illness. In one project I asked psychiatric survivors to talk about their journeys of survival, and whether they spoke about surviving traumas experienced in the mental health system or other instances of suffering, many spoke to the strength they drew from their advocacy work in the movement as well as more general efforts to be of service to others. For instance, one participant explained how she understood her process of survival and healing:

> Meaning of recovery—Well at first I thought it was personal, which was about me getting better so I can get on with my life. Now I realize that my life is all about helping others in the same boat.... And now it's even wider than that. It's really as you say, about organizing and activism, and some other of those initial discrepancies that put me into distress to begin with. Like how come most of the world doesn't have access to hot running water everyday like I do? I cry when I'm in the shower about the fact that I still have hot, running, clean water anytime I want. (Adame and Knudson 2007, 171)

For many, living a good life essentially meant assisting other people in need in whatever small or large ways they were able to contribute to the betterment of our shared existence. The findings of this study marked a turning point in my own thinking about the nature of therapy and psychological distress, as I was expecting to hear *personal* stories of healing and growth and came away with a new understanding of a good life defined by an attunement to social justice, collective responsibility, and service to the needs of others.

In his book *The Way of Man*, Buber (1966) recounts a Hasidic parable about God calling to Adam that I believe helps to explicate the notion of responsibility, albeit in religious metaphor. In the story, God asks Adam, "Where art Thou?" This at first glance seems an odd question since God is supposedly all-knowing. So why does God ask this question of Adam? Buber explains that it is the *effect* such a calling produces in us (for we are all Adams) that is significant. The experience of the call stirs our hearts to search for meaning in our existence and thereby encourages us to take account for our lives.

However, Buber also acknowledges that most of us are guilty of hiding from the question "Where art Thou?" and, by avoiding the call of the Other, we fail to take responsibility for our part in the unfolding drama of existence. Furthermore, we become estranged from ourselves when we avoid the call of the Other. Buber (1966) says, "man cannot escape the eye of God, but in trying to hide from him, he is hiding from himself" (12). In Buber's story the Other is God. However, I use this religious analogy to apply also in the secular sense to any dialogue of call and response between two relational beings such as takes place in psychotherapy. In either case, the call of the Other both asks us to respond genuinely (with one's whole being) to him or her and also asks us to attend to our place in the world—thus answering the question, "Where art Thou?"

Dialogical responsibility also takes into account this simultaneous unity of attending to the Other as also attending to the self and vice versa. The Other is never seen as a means to the end of self-realization, self-salvation, or self-fulfillment. Both Buber and Levinas agree that the Other is regarded as an end unto itself, and any personal gain born of that commitment is simply a side benefit of that connection. Buber and Levinas both stress that responsibility to the call of the Other and authenticity in our response form the basis of a relational ethics. In *Between Man and Man,* Buber (1965) criticizes philosophers who focus on self-development and personal (self-bounded) responsibility. He explains: "Where no primary address and claim can touch me, for everything is 'My property,' responsibility has become a phantom. At the same time life's character of mutuality is dissipated. He who ceases to make a response ceases to hear the Word" (45).

Buber explains that the sort of individualism that has emerged from romanticism, scientism, and modern culture misses the point of ethics altogether as we become obsessed with self-salvation and control of other people and things rather than the salvation of the world. In such a circumstance, others exist to support and nourish our own project of self-development, and the relation remains at an I-It level rather than genuine meetings of mutuality and reverence. Such a stance also makes responsibility to the Other a side issue that we may or may not choose to engage, rather than a foundational ethics in which we are beholden to the call (Levinas 1969, 1985, 2003a).

The numerous consequences of such a stance are reflected in the violent, destructive, and thoughtless treatment of other people and the environment—all of which may be significant aspects of our clients' lives in one way or another.

It is also important to keep in mind with all this talk of responsibility to the Other that we do not lose sight of the reciprocal and ultimately self-sustaining nature of this ethics of care. In other words, a common critique of such a system of ethics is that I will be emotionally drained and overwhelmed if I feel the afflictions of the world too acutely. A fair warning to keep in mind. However, both Buber and Levinas are clear that, as we fully respond to the needs of the Other, others turn to us as a Thou as well and we are continuously renewed in our relationships with others.

Commenting on Levinas's work, Diprose (2009) notes, "as for responsibility for the other, I do not get reduced to pure passivity or to a thing because the uniqueness expressed in my corporeal reflexivity emerges through and is supported by the welcome of the other others who are responsible for me" (131). According to Levinas, we are not passively or oppressively beholden to fulfilling the responsibilities of others, and as previously discussed, we must limit our commitments to those we feel we have the time and resources to give without exhausting ourselves completely. As Diprose notes above, as we are fundamentally responsible for the Other, our uniqueness of being is likewise supported and fulfilled when the community takes reciprocal responsibility for us as well.

Authenticity and Community

Living authentically in our relations with others underlies the notion of genuine community where we are guided by localized ethics of care and a strong sense of responsibility for the greater good. However, it is painfully obvious that such community is hard to come by, particularly in Western culture with its heavy emphasis on competition, scientism, radical individualism, and consumerism, to name just a few ways in which we become alienated and isolated units. Rollo May (1967) notes, "when people feel their insignificance as individual persons, they also suffer an undermining of their sense of human responsibility" (31). May warns that the great danger of our time is the increasing sense of apathy, meaninglessness, and loss of purpose in our actions. Instead of simply going through the motions in life, May urges us to act from a place of caring (congruent with Levinas's sense of responsibility) in all of our interactions, recognizing that each of us has a role to play in the unfolding drama of existence. As therapists, we can ask ourselves whether or when we ever would expect our clients to articulate or consider authenticity and community as part of being a human in the world. Perhaps we do not frequently engage this notion for ourselves or in psychotherapy because it is so hard for us to come by it ourselves, and this results in our never bringing up this call at all.

Freire (1998) articulates similar concerns about the dehumanized ways that people interact in mass societies in which genuine community and dialogical responsibility are lacking: "Men begin thinking and acting according to the prescriptions they receive daily from the communications media rather than in response to their dialectical relationships with the world. In mass societies, where everything is prefabricated and behavior is almost automatized, men are lost because they don't have to 'risk themselves'" (516). Freire's sentiments resonate with the work of Buber and Levinas, who also hold that living authentically requires us to risk ourselves in open presence and confirmation of the Other, even if this means possible disconfirmation of ourselves in the process. For our clients—and perhaps for us as well—it is "safer," more predictable, and less anxiety provoking to live our lives in socially prescribed ways of what we come to know as a "good life." However, whose definition of "the good" are we living out when we relinquish personal responsibility to the dictates of mass society in the scenario described by Freire?

Unquestioning conformity to societal definitions of what is "normal" and "good" is what Fromm (1994) calls an "escape from freedom," an escape from the state of anxious ambiguity that arises when we choose to define our values in local dialogues with our fellow human beings rather than blindly embracing universal axioms for living. Taken to extreme conclusions, blind acceptance of society's norms has the potential to lead to a fascist or totalitarian state in which individual voices is silenced within the masses. In contrast to such scenarios, both Buber and Levinas suggest that we ought to recognize our fundamental responsibility to the Other in all of our actions, and in doing so, we recognize the personal impact (for better or worse) that we can have on people's lives.

My previous research with the psychiatric survivor movement provides another poignant example of how it is possible to look beyond personal self-interest and recognize how our existence is ultimately connected to others in local and global contexts. Dehumanizing treatment in a psychiatric hospital further traumatized one participant who had previously survived devastating childhood sexual and emotional abuse. However, after she got out of the hospital she began to seek out connections with others who had similar life experiences to her own: "When I started trying to do these connections to other people, out of a couple of those workshops people decided that they wanted to stay connected to each other. And we were from different parts of the country, so I started this little newsletter to stay connected. Actually trying to feel like I was of service, of use to somebody else with the newsletter" (Adame and Knudson 2008, 153). She acknowledged that at first those efforts at connection were primarily in support of her own healing process, yet soon her workshops and newsletters transformed into something more than "personal" healing:

> I think the definition of healing is: It's not about me. And it's not about how I think things should be. It's just like, what piece can I do? And then just leave it. If it's going to have an impact, it will. And there have been a couple of times in my life when I was selectively mute. I just stopped talking. And now it's like I go in front of a microphone, and I'm actually happy to have the privilege. I think to me, my work now is a privilege. There's so many people who went through things similar to what I did, who would like to have their voices heard in Washington. And then I get behind the microphone and get to say what I think. And that keeps me going. Because I don't wash down what I'm saying because I think of the people that are still in the institutions.... So it's really fun because it's—the fear is gone. For the person who's lived her whole life fear based, it's like oh, give me the microphone. I've got something to say. I represent a group of people that I honor deeply, and it's been a real privilege. (Adame and Knudson 2008, 154)

As can be seen in in the above example, a newfound relational aware-ness can also awaken us to a heightened sense of responsibility to the needs and rights of others. Both Levinas and Buber argue that a central component in living ethically in a community is authenticity in our response to others. Echoing Levinas's a priori ethical stance of readiness to respond fully to others, Buber reflects on authenticity: "I call a great character one who by his actions and attitudes satisfies the claim of situations out of deep readiness to respond with his whole life, and such a way that the sum of his actions and attitudes express at the same time the unity of his being in its willingness to accept responsibility" (quoted in Walters 2003, 34).

Finally, Buber warns against the types of communities that elimi-nate personal responsibility or, worse, give the semblance that people in the crowd have choices and responsibility when in fact this is an illusion. Buber was specifically commenting on the difference between communal socialist communities, such as the kibbutz, where the indi-vidual and collective exist in a fairly balanced mutually self-sustaining relation, and totalitarian communities that have only the illusion of individual influence over the collective. Again, Buber points to the dialectic between a person's responsibility to the collective and the collective's responsibility to its members that underlies the notion of genuine community.

The psychoanalyst D. W. Winnicott also commented on the notion of genuine community in a way that is greatly reminiscent of Buber's description: "When healthy persons come together they each contribute a whole world, because each brings a whole person... they are capable of becoming depressed, rather than automatically joining group manias and seeking domination of others" (quoted in Praglin 2006, 7). In other words, when we relate to others as whole persons or as Thou, this also means we bring our struggles as well as our strengths to the dialogue in a genuine community. Recognizing human shortcomings and struggles as well as strengths and passions aids in not being naively idealistic or positing simplistic utopian solu-tions to complex social problems. Here again we see the balance between the personal and the collective when we speak of participa-tion in genuine community.

CONCLUSION

Buber's and Levinas's writings help to illuminate salient issues for psychotherapy in particular about what it means to practice dialogical responsibility. These thinkers remind us of the process by which "authentically existing individuals who recognize each other's humanity constitute a community" (Stewart and Mickunas 1990, 67). There are numerous contexts in which we might have our consciousness raised about the dialogical nature of our existence and our interdependent web of responsibility to others. In this chapter, I have presented psychotherapy as one place that *could* be seen as an example of a deep recognizing of each other's humanity. Genuine community begins with and is sustained by our commitment (via our actions and attitudes) to responding to the call of the Other. Buber's relational ontology and Levinas's ethical stance challenge us to break out of our Western cultural viewpoint of self-contained individualism and to take up the notion of dialogical responsibility. Buber (1957) once said, "the world is not comprehensible, but it is embraceable: through embracing one of its beings" (27). In other words, it is through the experience of I-Thou relating that we can grow to truly appreciate the greater connectedness of the world and achieve a sense of dialogical responsibility for our fellow human beings.

PART TWO

APPLICATIONS

FIVE

The Aftermath of Murder

Marie McNabb

INTRODUCTION

Several months into therapy with a young man orphaned by murder, I found myself agitated and isolated. Our work was going well, but the content was disturbing and sad. The typical difficulties in PTSD treatment were emerging in our work, and I also recognized signs of my own vicarious trauma. I found relief in passages from Emmanuel Levinas's book *Totality and Infinity*. But something about the relief was unexpected and remains so. Why was Levinas helpful when his words about murder are not practical and he gives no advice—when, in fact, his typical statement is that one cannot murder a face? At that time I wrote an essay for my graduate supervision group, which provides a record of my struggle and to which this chapter returns.

CASE SUMMARY

My client, a young man in his early twenties, had been ordered to undertake therapy due to problems he was having at home and at work, but he came regularly and seemed to enjoy having a private place to talk. My therapeutic approach was client-centered and I allowed him to choose topics, only raising the absence of his parents and the chaos of his childhood when the impact emerged clearly within his current struggle. But I had a growing awareness of murder's potential impact on a person's development. All children sort out their sense of identity using interactions with their family and the norms of society, but for my client the murder had decimated his family and left the norms warped and inadequate. For example, my client told me of a dream where he struggled to write his last name—the name he shares with his siblings and his uncles and aunts but also with the murderer. A last name is not so complicated for most of us.

Meanwhile, another therapist had met with a party to the case and was telling me graphic details about the murders. After two or three such meetings, I wrote:

> As I met with her, I dutifully took notes and tried to participate in her wonderings about what this or that implied and what areas she should discuss next. But I wasn't thinking clearly. A couple of hours later I waited for my client to come to his session and I admit I wished that he wouldn't. It was just a vague feeling. I just didn't care whether he came or not. "Come my lad or go my lad"—words that came to me from a long ago memorized sonnet. He didn't come. A day later, I felt agitated and close to tears. I couldn't get the words and images out of my mind.

But in general my client did come to his sessions. After about six months, our therapy, which had been slow to develop, began to solidify with some intensity and attachment. In spite of his declaration that he would "never trust anyone again," my client began to reveal worries and anger. In the essay, I recounted an exchange with him that left me shaken and confused about my role: "My client was upset about his every move being watched and judged and how everyone is convinced he will fail. I asked him whether this applied to me; did he think my care for him could withstand some of his bad behavior? Having asked, I immediately knew I couldn't answer directly and ours eyes locked. His eyes showed both question and anger. I saw his rage and my heart jumped." Effects were showing up in my own life: too much couch time, too many adrenalin-inducing books, and a hesitance to use supervision. I began to have mild panic attacks, and I reconsidered the security system at my house. Afraid of hurting others, boring them, revealing ignorance, or breaching confidentiality by talking too much about the case, I felt stressed and alone.

Posttraumatic Stress Disorder and Vicarious Trauma

Posttraumatic Stress Disorder (PTSD) and its treatment are a complex topic. Some background may be helpful. One understanding of its symptoms and treatment is that the client, having witnessed and survived deadly violence, responds to the horror with a variety of defenses, including avoidance, emotional numbness, and assuming responsibility for some element of the event (Steiner and Matthews 1996). "What keeps PTSD alive, in part, is some aspect of the trauma that is unavowed but crucial to the event, involving some imagined or real responsibility or failure" (377). The treatment seeks to carefully relieve this responsibility, freeing the client for rage and mourning. Steiner and Matthews (1996), describe the treatment of a young man who witnessed the murder of his beloved stepfather and who added several minutes of time into his memory of the event. He believed he could have stopped the murder—but did not. Through treatment, careful and supportive, he remembered more accurately that the murderer had burst into the room and fired almost instantly. Realizing he had no responsibility, no power, he was able to let himself off the hook but then had to experience the awfulness, anger, and loss (376–80).

Vicarious trauma describes the reactions found in therapists working with victims of violence. Symptoms resemble those of PTSD, including some I noticed in myself such as withdrawal, heightened emotions, and anxiety. Lisa McCann and Laurie Pearlman (1990) propose that therapists are affected by client stories of trauma in line with their own active schemas, including questions of safety, power, intimacy, and a meaningful world. Therapists must confront—in their own lives—the questions raised by their clients' trauma.

Protection and isolation are aspects both of PTSD and of vicarious trauma; avoiding reminders of the event is one of the diagnostic criteria (APA 1994). Most of the time my client dismissed the significance of the event, as did his remaining family. This implicit warning to avoid the topic serves a protective function but leaves the client isolated and complicates therapy. Therapists can also isolate themselves in order to protect colleagues and even supervisors. In the essay written at the time, I began to describe some of the details and then stopped myself: "I hesitate to continue. Why would I spread these images to other people? The other day, I lectured my daughter about not going to work with the flu. I said, "The virus can die with you or it can move to three or four new hosts...think of the impact you can have by simply keeping it to yourself." I am searching for some way to process this knowledge that doesn't impact anyone else around me."

But is it knowledge that we attempt to avoid? The word "vicarious" implies that those who support others through the aftermath of violence can come to react as if they too had witnessed it. The fact that the therapist envisions the murder may be an aspect of vicarious trauma that is so obvious as to be overlooked. Images have power whether carried in memory or created by imagination, especially images of senseless, intentional, and personal violence. I have specific and detailed images of murder scenes from my work with traumatized clients including rooms, furniture, clothing, and bodies although these elements were never described to me. The idea of murder raises paradoxical anxieties about death and about continuing to live surrounded by inhuman humans. But the image of murder, of victim facing perpetrator, isn't an idea. It is an image, flexible and lifelike, and I cannot help but place myself there and attempt an alternate resolution, as perhaps our clients do when they continue to assume responsibility.

Levinas's Words

In the midst of this back and forth—for both my client and me—between processing and protection, I wrote an essay, which I have referred to above. In the essay, I reviewed and applied Vicarious Trauma literature, but I found true relief in the words of Levinas, and specifically in two passages from *Totality and Infinity* (1969).

First, in reflecting on the experience of asking my client if he trusted me, facing his rage, and finding myself silent, a quote from Levinas helped me stay in the intensity of the moment—to experience and to respect the enormity of what it means to be fully present to an Other, even in a small moment. (In the essay, I wrote my reactions to Levinas's words in the brackets.)

The face resists possession, resists my powers. In its epiphany, in expression, the sensible, still graspable, [I wouldn't have asked the question if I didn't think I "had" him.] turns into total resistance to the grasp. [What Pandora's box have I opened?] This mutation can occur only by the opening of new dimension. [We are together, but where are we?] For the resistance to the grasp is not produced as an insurmountable resistance, like the hardness of a rock against which the effort of the hand comes to naught, like the remoteness of a star in the immensity of space. [There was a plea as well as a challenge.] The expression the face introduces into the world does not defy the feebleness of my powers, but my ability for power. [I couldn't speak—or I didn't speak?]. (Levinas 1969, 197)

Second, I stumbled upon more than sought-out words about the moment that caused all of this, the moment of murder. Following the passage quoted above, Levinas writes of murder and I wrote at the time, "his words slowed down and nuanced the video of the murder playing in my head." I looked unsuccessfully in these Levinas passages for something specific that would explain or resolve my reaction to the scenes of murder; but instead I was drawn to words and phrases scattered over the pages:

> To kill is not to dominate but to annihilate...to renounce comprehension absolutely. Murder exercises a power over what escapes power....
> I can wish to kill only an existent absolutely independent...pointless to insist on the banality of murder...negation of being...exposed to the point of the sword or the revolver's bullet...that intransigent no...the very unforeseeableness of this reaction...defenceless eyes, nudity of the absolute openness of the Transcendent.... Infinity presents itself as a face in the ethical resistance that paralyses my powers and from the depths of defenceless eyes rises firm and absolute in its nudity and destitution. (Levinas 1969, 198–200)

In retrospect, I wonder if I was trying to idealize the situation of the murder, to redeem it in some way. I willed the victims in this case to have faced the murderer with an "intransigent no," to have gone to their death in dignity. I think now this was wishful thinking. They may well have gone to their deaths in rage, oblivion, or begging for mercy. I wonder if Levinas's words helped because of exactly what I wrote at the time, "his words slowed down and nuanced the video of the murder playing in my head." Of course, we all know what a murder is. We hear about them almost daily. We "get" it and we move on. Levinas's words held me in the moment of the murder—not the grisly details but the time and space between two people. Levinas holds me there through his phenomenology of one human facing an Other, through his words of ethical awareness and responsibility. In this holding still, I give the interaction some of the respect it deserves. Murder happens and is not ethical, and it is our clients' reality. No obvious answers exist for the questions around murder, but I want to stay with the questions.

The Question of Murder

Heidegger (1996) writes specifically about questions and answers and points out the luxury of finding the right question, one that asks exactly what is needed and always already carries the glimmer of fulfillment. The only way that we come to know anything is by finding the ground common to the question and the answer. But this notion does not apply to another person, Levinas adds as a significant distinction. In the face of an Other, we are not the same knowledgeable and understanding being who smoothly handles so many questions about the world.

I ask myself, "Why were Levinas's words helpful when I was so distressed by this case?" but there is no answer. I do not have a question as much as I have a dissonance. His words about murder sit across from the growing connection with my client, which in turn sits across from my agitation and self-doubt. Levinas's words continue to calm me, but they do not give me any resolution. Nothing feels completed by his words.

This lack of completeness may be more present in the therapeutic process than is generally thought. The human face is always a little disturbing, because dealing with it by reaching for the tools of logic is often disappointing; much trial and error is demanded. Therapists know this well and find other less tangible resources, seemingly "out of nowhere," to negotiate hours with distressed people, such as Levinas's words were for me. When I am working with a survivor of interpersonal violence, the dichotomy between rational explanations and irrational dissonance is heightened and my fear is unsurprising.

The ground for my client and me was murder, the most devastating and in a way the most intimate of human facings.

Another question has been with me all along. A big question that comes because I read Levinas alongside a murder made real for me by my client. Gadamer (1998) writes, "Thus questioning too is more a passion than an action. A question presses itself on us; we can no longer avoid it and persist in our accustomed opinion" (366). This second question presses itself on me: "Does a murderer meet their victim? Is there a face-to-face, a Levinas face-to-face, a genuine recognition of the Other as Other—when one person kills another?" I ask this question with shame; it sounds macabre. Discussing it with colleagues has proved uncomfortable and ends up feeling like an argument. This question may be a way out of intense experience and into something black and white, seeking the luxury of a question. Furthermore, it is likely unanswerable; the victim cannot tell us and a murderer will probably not.

Whatever is faced and rejected in murder faces us as therapists in its wake. We face our clients week after week increasingly aware of the damage and dissonance they live with as well as our responsibility to them. Perhaps vicarious trauma is evidence that our clients raise for us the primary question they both resist and cannot ignore: What is the face-to-face at the moment of murder? Since the words of Levinas raised the question, I look to him for further help in examining my experience, attempting to understand the level at which damage was done and the nature of that damage.

KNOWING AND FACING

Partly as a respite from the intensity of murder, I want to return to how we know and understand the world and how well these ideas apply to relationship with an Other. Within ontology, the study of the ultimately real or of Being, we find understanding as foundational to human existence. In "Is Ontology Fundamental?," Levinas acknowledges Heidegger's contribution to understanding how we exist in the world, how our understanding unfolds and builds only through interaction with the world, and how it is through an examination of our human existence that we get a sense of what Being is. "The essential contribution to the new ontology can be seen in its opposition to classical intellectualism. To comprehend the tool is not to look at it but to know how to handle it. To comprehend our situation in reality is not to define it but to find ourselves in an affective disposition. To comprehend being is to exist" (Levinas 1996, 4).

Ontological understanding, therefore, involves a sort of construction, a drawing on past or language or culture or embodiment, making a scaffold from which we might grasp something new or put words to an idea glimmering on the horizon. This explains much of our Being but is not what happens in the approach of one human to another ("approach" being Levinas's shorthand for two people coming face-to-face). Levinas sets the human encounter outside of comprehension or knowledge, that is, that which can be grasped or delineated. My own experience of facing an Other leads me to this same limit to ontology, this separate thing that is the face-to-face.

I am aware of the "sizing up" of another person upon an introduction. There is comfort in the familiar back-and-forth that works out whose role is going to be what. But prior to the sizing up, the sorting out, and the assigning of social roles, there is an instant of simply the presence of that other person. This presence is just a flash but it happens. This instant is unsteady, nothing is clear and anything could happen. To use Levinas's expressions, anything could be asked of me, demanded of me. And I am bound to answer.

I am unsettled facing another person in a way unlike facing any other being or thing. From reading Levinas, I find within the unsettledness of facing an Other the presence of the infinite—to the simple wonder that I exist at all, on this earth, at this time. This awareness finds me, briefly but surely, each time I face another person. It is what I want and what I have, all at the same time. It is what I value and what I can so easily lose. I can call it infinity, call it existence, call it life; it is present each time I actually look at another person.

We rush past the unsteadiness to the comfort of knowledge. In "Transcendence and Height," Levinas wrote, "Intentionality is a movement of the mind adjusted to being. It takes aim and moves toward a theme. In the theme, being comfortably accommodates itself" (Levinas 1996, 19). So we size each other up, we figure out whether there is relationship or if we need conversation. We try to move to what we already know and away from that flash of awareness.

We make this move out of expedience. We make it out of fear or in an assertion of power. But at some level we make it out of awe.

Therapists work in the face-to-face and are in the unsteadiness of relationship almost all the time. Anything could be asked, demanded of me. I am bound to answer. When working with clients after violence, we are with people for whom the unsteadiness is magnified by the horror witnessed and by the simultaneous wish to tell one's reality and not inflict it on anyone else.

Therapists are in a bind. We naturally wish to flee awfulness into the refuge of knowledge. We are of our culture, as are our clients, and we first and foremost look to objective knowledge for answers. Having witnessed the senseless, our clients ask us to "make sense"—to pull an ontological rabbit out of our hat. Levinas tells us this is a futile movement. Facing, even that of murder, lies outside of knowledge. But if interpersonal violence is not a knowledge problem, what kind of problem is it? Levinas uses the word "ethical" to describe the sphere of not-knowing. We could certainly use an ethical solution to accomplish healing of this damage.

What Levinas May Say about Murder

When writing this chapter, I had two moments, two facings. Facing my client—close at hand, very angry and scared, was unnerving. I also faced the murder, using details from the other therapist, embellished by imagination, scary and bloody as a man with a gun faced a woman in bedclothes. The juxtaposition of these two moments draws each other out. So I ask the second question: Did they truly face each other? Even for an instant? Perhaps it is macabre, but to ask in the presence of my client is to ask it on his behalf and to demand an answer that arises from experience.

Reading Levinas's essay "Is Ontology Fundamental?," I watch for his opinion on this question. He addresses it, however not clearly. He writes: "A human being is the sole being which I am unable to encounter without expressing this very encounter to him. It is precisely in this that the encounter distinguishes itself from knowledge. In every attitude in regard to the human there is a greeting—if only the refusal of greeting" (Levinas 1996, 7). Meeting a person is unavoidability in the ethical realm, outside of ontology. There is always an encounter. Even in murder, there is an instant in the face-to-face. But then Levinas seems to contradict himself in the following passage:

> At the very moment when my power to kill realizes itself, the other (*autrui*) has escaped me. I can, for sure, in killing attain a goal: I can kill as I hunt or slaughter animals, or as I fell trees. But when I have grasped the other (*autrui*) in the opening of being in general, as an element of the world where I stand, where I have seen him on the horizon, I have not looked at him in the face, I have not encountered his face. The temptation of total negation, measuring the infinity of this attempt and its impossibility—this is the presence of the face. To be in relation with the other (*autrui*) face to face is to be unable to kill. (9)

Here he suggests a space in which either relationship is achieved or is not. A person intent on murder can keep their victim "on the horizon" and not yet as a face. Once relation is achieved, murder is impossible. The creation of a space where an Other is seen as a human but not approached seems to contradict the heart of Levinas's teaching. Is there first a body and later a face? How would anyone achieve such an exception to approach?

The common psychological thinking about murder offers some possible ways: A killer keeps enough distance that the face is out of view. A killer "sees" characters in a video game. Murder is a reenactment of a psychological death of self, experienced long ago. The damage to the psyche through pain or abuse or organic injury has changed people into things. Levinas refutes these common ideas that people are ever seen as things. I agree with him. From my experience and the richness of Levinas I hold that a face cannot be made into just a thing. One cannot *decide* ahead of time not to see a fellow human. One cannot intentionally keep an Other out of focus. Even in murder there is an approach, one to an Other. But it goes wrong.

Levinas in "Transcendence and Height" describes movements between people that are founded on knowledge as unethical, referring to the "the indiscretion of intentionality" (1996, 16). He means those times when we intend toward a person the way we intend toward objects in the world. It is always a violent action and at its maximum it is war and murder. This attempt to intellectualize an Other is one way that an approach goes wrong. Murder involves two distinct actions. One can face an Other and *then* choose an assertion of power. One can face an Other and *then* "pull the Other into knowledge," where outcomes can be weighed and lead to a decision to murder for advantage. Is this, however, as easy as a murderer might think?

Finally, murder could be a reaction to the infinite, revealed in the face of the Other. The killer faces his victim, and is—as we all are—unsettled. Anything could be asked, anything demanded, most specifically: Do not murder me. The unsettledness of the killer may be worse when the intent was to see the Other as a thing, and instead a face appears, a human face declaring the impossibility of murder. A murderer sees that something that evades naming; and seeing the Infinite, seeing life and feeling its transient nature, flashes upon it and ends it. Murder attempts to be bigger than infinite. As I wrote in my essay: "In every honest exchange we realize the Other's right to say *no* is always maintained—to say no even to the point of death. The very possibility of that intransigent no stirs in each of us vulnerability and rage and the killer could not stand that moment. My client and I need more moments where we do stand it, and someday we may talk about it."

Perhaps to tolerate these experiences is what we offer our clients. They ask of us to not abandon them but to stay to the extent we can in the dissonance of how a human facing went so wrong, *that* a human facing went so wrong. They ask us to step outside the safety of knowledge, where one foot is always in the already-known and familiar world, and join them in the chaos. The symptoms of vicarious trauma may prove that we join them, intentionally or not. This relational space needs to be slowed down and nuanced. I have one final reflection where Levinas helps with this point.

In "Essence and Disinterestedness," Levinas examines the subtleties of approach. When we are proximate to an Other, approach an Other, there is potential in the air. Finally we commit in some way. As humans, we are always committing—and thereby defining who we are—by our choices. Each moment in life can be seen as an opportunity to choose. Levinas's expression for this choice and commitment, particularly with respect to other people, is the *Saying* and the *Said*. And it seems accurate to think about language, volatile and vague, when thinking about how hard it is to be in relationship to other people. In unsteadiness I face an Other with 200,000 words of the English language at my disposal. Ultimately, I speak and in choosing my words, I am committed. The Said I commit to comes at the expense of the others I did not choose: "The correlation of the saying and the said, that is the subordination of the saying to the said, to the linguistic system and to ontology, is the price that manifestation demands. In language qua said, everything is translated before us, be it at the price of a betrayal" (Levinas 1996, 112). This certainly describes therapy as we and our clients attempt to speak within the woundedness of the human situation, the dissonance of facing each other. We subordinate all that *could* be said to the linguistic system as we choose what we *do* say. An essence will fill that commitment, once made. Furthermore, time maintains a constant, separate, and structural presence over both the infinite and the waiting essence:

> But if time is to show the ambiguity of being and the otherwise than being, its temporalization is to be conceived not as essence but as Saying. Essence fills the said, or the epos [word] of the Saying; but the Saying, in its power of equivocation, that is, in the enigma whose secret it keeps, escapes the epos [word] of essence that includes it and signifies beyond in a signification that hesitates between this beyond and the return to the epos of essence. This equivocation or enigma is the inalienable power in Saying and a modality of transcendence. (1996, 116)

This is a hard quote to follow, but I think Levinas points to the crux of human existence, which we live in always, as surely as we live in time. As we choose a word to say to another person, *as we Say,* we commit and fill the word (and world) with our meaning. But he wants us to note two key aspects of Saying. First, we always hold something back—this is the enigma. We hold back because no word is quite perfect but we also hesitate because of the unsettledness, that volatile hint of infinity, that facing an Other always brings with it. Second, what we say always returns to us, but amplified. The actuality of what we said is not within our control; rather, it joins the world and we may be struck by a larger significance. (As a murderer is struck by what death really looks like.) And we cannot escape—time presses us forward, into choice, into *saying.*

Through this quote Levinas gave me the image of a split in time/ being where an infinite number of *saying*s become a single, chosen *said*. That split in time is transcendence, or it provides the opportunity for transcendence. Because I have made choices, because I chose words at times when the right words felt like a matter of life and death, I understand experientially that the potential for transcendence is there.

Murder is a *saying* without a *said*. Saying is equivocation, enigma, secret. Murder suspends us in *saying*. It is not just the wasted potential of the life that is ended, but the breach of the fundamental human contract to face each other with a willingness to commit. A murder cuts this willingness off midstream, in the mid-stream-of-time. We remain not just traumatized but dissatisfied, frustrated. In a moment that would most demand an explanation, we are suspended.

Suspended there with our clients and this seems like a curse. But it can be an honor as we face them, particularly as they ask the impossible of us. "The putting into question of the I by the other is ipso facto an election, the promotion to a privileged place on which all that is not-I depends" (Levinas 1996, 18). Working with my client, I believe I felt the weight of this promotion, the impossibility of escape, and the severe damage done to this young man: relationship as such had been contaminated, I feared beyond repair. Murder is the inability to *stand* the awe revealed in an Other's face. The challenge of therapy is to *stand* it, to show our clients over and over that there is another outcome.

CONCLUSION

> At stake is a movement oriented in a way that is wholly otherwise than the grasp of consciousness and at every instant unravels, like Penelope at night, everything that was so gloriously woven during the day.
>
> — Levinas, *Basic Philosophical Writings*

So often every attempt at understanding in therapy unravels. With my young client, I was often surprised when he did come to his session, bringing the large purple monster that "hunkered down in the toy corner." With this chapter, I fear I have written disturbing words and possibly only muddied the water. Yet I am left with the incredible implication of Levinas's thought—we do not have rationality to anywhere near the extent we think we do. Even our questions are often illusions. As therapist in the territory of murder, I cannot have one foot in the already known and familiar (ontology), hopefully eyeing the horizon, moving safely ahead one step at a time. I value this message that Levinas sent through his words and that reached me in a particular way at such a difficult time: I felt so clearly my fear, my election, and my responsibility.

Six

The Tragedy of Domestic Violence

Jackie Grimesey-Szarka

The demise of a nation begins in the homes of its people.
— Angolan proverb

Introduction

The home is our sanctuary, the place where we can feel at ease and enjoy the pleasures of living and where we long to return after a difficult day. Home is that which we carry in our hearts as we journey through life, the security from which we explore the world beyond, and that to which we relate and compare experiences. These things are true for most of us, but for others the home holds a very different meaning. Just as it can be welcoming, it can be imprisoning; just as it can be security, it can be danger; just as it can hold the greatest joy of our lives, it can contain our deepest sorrow. These alternatives are often only too true for persons victimized by domestic violence. Suffering control and abuse at the hands of another who should love and care for you best is one of life's greatest tragedies.

Emmanuel Levinas founds ethics in the immediate world of our interrelationship with the Other. His philosophy illuminates key dynamics that can help us understand the interrelationship between victim and abuser and further examine solutions such as shelter programs, batterers' treatment, and governmental systems designed to combat domestic violence. I would like to acknowledge my choice of examples and my use of the terms *he, she, abuser,* and *victim.* I recognize that other alternatives exist and do not pretend to account for or encompass the enormous depth or breadth of all relationships or all people suffering from these dynamics. Rather, I am drawing from my own experience of over ten years spent working with domestic violence survivors, victims, and service agencies.

"A man's home is his castle," so the saying goes. Levinas describes the home as the place where we can exist in egoism, where we enjoy the fruits of our labors and deposit possessions. At home we sit back, kick off our shoes, reflect and recollect the events of the day. "Concretely speaking the dwelling is not situated in the objective world, but the objective world is situated by relation to my dwelling" (Levinas 1969, 153). Home is the place where we welcome the Other and serve them through generosity. For those with whom we live, however, Levinas describes a different sort of relationship, one that is more familiar, more taken for granted. We are able to relax around them and forget ourselves in egoist enjoyment. Levinas states, "The Other who welcomes in intimacy is not the *you* of the face that reveals itself in a dimension of height, but precisely the *thou* of familiarity: a language without teaching, a silent language, an understanding without words, an expression in secret" (155). This relationship with familiar others is beyond the ethical. However, we must not reduce the familiar other to an object of our need or enjoyment. The attempt to reduce and totalize the Other is at the core of the ensuing cycle of domestic violence. According to Levinas (1969), "Violence bears upon only a being both graspable and escaping every hold" (223).

A troubling aspect of domestic violence is the lack of discernible warning signs during the initial relationship period, where violence may come only later. Rather than exhibiting violence or danger, the initial period is one of excitement and doting attention. One is romanced and *swept off one's feet*. What warning signs do exist, such as jealousy, intensity, or attachment are easily written off as *just being in love*. Levinas characterizes love as a *need* that can be satisfied. Loving is therefore dissimilar from *desire,* in which we recognize the Other as infinitely outside of our egoist needs or categories. "This Desire is a desire in a being already happy: desire is the misfortune of the happy, a luxurious need" (Levinas 1969, 62). He goes on, "Need indicates void and lack in the needy one, its dependence on the exterior, the insufficiency of the needy being precisely in that it does not entirely possess its being and consequently is not strictly speaking *separate*"

(102). He thus shows how separation and happiness is necessary in order to inhibit the totalizing of the Other.

In domestic violence, however, the relationship is characterized by enmeshment and trauma. The lover, coming from a place of uncomfortable deficiency, seeks a companion for an *other half*, manifesting a desperate need. The needed qualities are projected onto or magnified in the loved one by the lover. The lover does not really desire the loved one but wants the enjoyment gained from the relationship (Burggraeve 1985, 33). To need the Other and search for the Other as a need-fulfilling *object*, rather than desiring the Other as a transcendent person independent of ourselves, is a recipe for domestic violence.

Slowly and insidiously affirmations such as "I love you so much I want to be with you all the time" become "You are to be there for me, for only me, at all times"; "I get lonely when you want to go with your friends" becomes "You will not see those bad influences any more"; and "I really love that red dress" becomes "You are to wear and do exactly what I tell you to, when I tell you to." Eventually power and control are gained, even supremely, and emotional abuse becomes the rule. If the emotional abuse becomes no longer effective, then physical violence may become the method used to keep the victim within the confines of the abuser's totalization. The degree of violence used is often the degree necessary to maintain control. Similarly, the abuser may give only the degree of deference necessary to prevent the violence, from the victim or society, from impinging upon them.

A victim caught in this situation finds herself surprised and bewildered. She often has no understanding of the abuser's totalization and seeks desperately to identify the reasons for his behavior. The easiest place to look for the cause is within herself. This self-blame is facilitated by the accusations constantly heaped upon her by the abuser and by society. Levinas points out that when we focus on the inward self, attention to an outward focus is prevented. As time passes and the abuse becomes more intense, the more desperately the victim may try to analyze and change her own behavior, often supporting the abuser's totalization. However, as Levinas states, we cannot totalize the face of the Other. Even if the Other allows totalization, she remains infinitely Other. We can never truly know the Other and he or she can never truly conform or become an object for our needs. It is not a *fault* that we cannot totalize the Other, it is the transcendence of the face continually overflowing any adequate idea we may have of it. Levinas (1969) explains that "It is not the insufficiency of the I that prevents totalization, but the Infinity of the Other" (80); "Over him I have no *power*. He escapes my grasp by an essential dimension, even if I have him at my disposal" (39).

Communication between the victim and other people is very threatening to the control being established by the abuser. For this reason, the first major mechanism of control often unleashed by the abuser is the isolation of the victim. The abuser cuts off the victim's contact with friends, family, and the world. This may be accomplished through threats, through shaming the victim to the point of her not wanting outside contact, or through being so nasty to others that they avoid the couple due to fear or disgust. Levinas (1969) discusses isolation in stating: "the separated being can close itself up in its egoism, that is, in the very accomplishment of its isolation. And this possibility of forgetting the transcendence of the Other—of banishing with impunity all hospitality (that is, all language) from one's home, banishing the transcendental relation that alone permits the I to shut itself up in itself—evinces the absolute truth, the radicalism, of separation" (172).

In imposing this isolation, the abuser stops real communication with the victim, and conversations are sometimes kept to orders and insults, to rhetoric, which resists true discourse and solicits the Other's compliance. Halling (1975) illuminates Levinas's ideas on rhetoric: "in speaking rhetorically to the Other, the Other is for me the one who is going to be persuaded, not the one who is allowed to speak to me, or even to listen to me on his own terms. The relationship is then defined from my point of view in terms of this specific intention that I have with respect to the Other. It is a relationship of exercise of power" (214).

Discourse with the outside world could uncover the abuser's ugly secret. Discourse within the home could amplify the face, which calls the abuser into question. Levinas says that the person needs the world. Responsible communication is the means by which the Other discloses the truth of their world. The abuser must strictly monitor communication. The outside world is therefore often oblivious to what happens within the home. The home, as Levinas (1969) points out, "has a *street front,* but also its secrecy" (156).

Isolation also involves the question of freedom. The abuser seems to calculate that, if the victim is free, then the abuser's freedom is limited. The victim's freedom is thereby perceived as threatening. Levinas states the contrary; rather than limiting freedom, the Other invests freedom and calls us to use it responsibly. For a totalizing abuser, acknowledging the face of the victim or the responsible use of their own freedom is avoided. The abuser lives in what Levinas calls *the illusion of independence,* believing and behaving as if he was independently free. In reality, he is extremely dependent upon others, including the victim from whom he lives and who provides him his very freedom. His dogged attachment to his freedom becomes a concealment for the pain of the shame he feels deep inside. Levinas (1969) describes shame as "where freedom discovers itself murderous in its very exercise" (84). Once this shame becomes unbearable, it is released upon the victim through further abuse.

Levinas tells us the face of the Other is infinitely out of my grasp and beyond comprehension. The Other comes from a position of height, having rights above my own, and calls me, my freedom, and my egoist enjoyment into question. The face of the Other is the first truth; it speaks and says "you may not do violence toward me." For a couple embroiled in domestic violence this is equally true, but for the abuser any independence of the victim is perceived as a threat.

The abuser uses violence to totalize the victim and maintain his facade. Totalization, however, is impossibility because the Other is infinite, always more than his controlled victim. Since the presence of the face of the victim calls the abuser into question, it is perceived as a threat. Levinas (1969) states that "The face is a living presence; it is expression. The life of expression consists in undoing the form in which the existent, exposed as a theme, is thereby dissimulated. The face speaks. The manifestation of the face is already discourse" (66). Victims often desperately search for behavior they can change in order to prevent further violence or to regain the glory of their early days together, however their search is in vain. The violence is not about any specific behavior, not about what they did or did not do; the violence is not within their control. Simply their presence, the existence of their face, is all it often takes to provoke the abuser.

This is especially true when the victim tries to do something new or different, even if the intent is to please the abuser. Breaking the pattern structured for them by the abuser, exposing the victim's infinite nature even in beneficial acts, calls the abuser into question. The abuser senses danger when the victim shows herself to be the person she is, which he cannot allow. Even if initially he is pleasantly surprised by the change, it can become a provocation for violence. Victims are often put down or humiliated when they attempt something new. Any break in totalization calls the abuser into question. Because the abuser is not open to her as other, he is threatened. Any attempt to change may be thwarted. The victim often lives in what Levinas (1969) describes *patience,* the experience when "the imminence of defeat, but also a distance in its regard, coincide" (165). The victim learns to live with violence, to accept it, but still holds onto hope for the day that it will end. This dynamic is reinforced by society through victim-blaming beliefs like "you made your bed, you must lie in it." If we accept the premise that the victim did not provoke the violence, then we must also accept the premise that none of us is immune from becoming embroiled in such a situation. In fact, the latter premise is true. Levinas reminds us that we are capable of good, of indifference, or of evil. We are all capable of falling toward the ends of this continuum given the proper circumstances.

Once the cycle of domestic violence is established, few efforts to intervene can stop it. The most common factor capable of facilitating change is the involvement of the couple's children. Women will often accept all means of abusive treatment, but when the violence becomes directed toward their child, or when the child suffers through fear or aggression, this is unacceptable. The child presents their face as other and calls both parents into question. The child questions the parents' freedom to stay and be victimized, and the child's gaze may provoke the realization that the parents' views are arbitrary; they may begin to recognize their responsibility. The child's face comes from a place of great need, destitution, and dependence, calling the parents to be responsible. Levinas (1969) further points out that both suffering and responsibility are passed down through the generations. This helps us to understand the intergenerational nature often involved in domestic violence. Parents who recognize the face of their child can return to themselves when the child calls them into question. They can find the center of themselves, existing in the Other, in their child and begin to accept the responsibility of their power and freedom to protect and serve the child who comes from on high and has rights over them.

If the relationship remains violent and the victim does choose to leave, many things can further complicate this picture. The most overwhelming factor is the fear of what Levinas (1969) calls the *there is*. The unknown looms menacingly out there in the world. "The silence of infinite spaces is terrifying" (190). Even if their life is filled with unhappiness and suffering, this may be less terrifying than the prospect of an uncertain future. Second, what sticks most power-fully in the minds of victims are the good times. The bad times are also remembered, but the good times are remembered with even greater intensity, and the memories leave the victim wanting those good times to return. Suffering is truly the absence of enjoyment, the absence of the good times they remember and believe can return. Victims believe the abuser is, in Levinasian terms, *fundamentally good* and that his abusive behavior is a violation of his own goodness. They believe that, if they themselves are just good enough, if they do every-thing right, if they help the abuser, then his fundamental goodness will break through and become the norm. A third factor that strongly resists change is the incredibly strong sense of hope the victims hold to through it all, returning an average of seven times before making any permanent change in an abusive relationship.

Dr. Lenore Walker (1979) has developed a *cycle of domestic violence* (55–70) utilized by many agencies in their work with victims. The cycle begins with escalating tension, leading to violent explosions, culminating in a *honeymoon* state where conciliations are made and hopes are rekindled. This cycle creates resistance to change at every stage. Tension enlists self-blame and guilt, violence induces fear, and the honeymoon encourages hope. The cycle of violence theory pow-erfully illustrates the concepts discussed above and is relevant to the lives of many, but not all, victims. For some, the honeymoon never arrives or exists only as a short period of calm. Both abuser and victim get caught within the grasp of this vertiginous cycle of totalization.

Fortunately, hope can create an incredible resiliency in survivors of domestic violence. Forging through the terror of the *there is,* victims who reclaim their lives and survive their ordeal are able to build a new world. As Levinas (1969) states, "To be free is to build a world in which one could be free" (165). Many women who have traveled this road return to help others along the way. In "Useless Suffering," Levinas wrote that suffering is useless unless it is in the service of another (1998a, 91–101). Similarly, we can learn from our suffering and use this knowledge to help others. Levinas describes that in suffering: "a radical difference develops between suffering in the Other, which for me is unpardonable and solicits me and calls me, and suffering in me, my own adventure of suffering, whose constitutional or congenital uselessness can take on a meaning, the only meaning to which suffering is susceptible, in becoming a suffering for the suffering—be it inexorable—of someone else" (1998a, 93).

The first modern battered-women's shelters began during the 1960s and have spread throughout the country, largely through grassroots efforts of survivors reaching out to serve others. These agencies have become a surrogate home for many victims and survivors. The philosophy of grassroots domestic violence advocates is largely in sync with that of Emmanuel Levinas. Advocates welcome the Other and give generously of themselves. Shelters give victims the space to recollect their experiences and to represent themselves. "Recollection, in the current sense of the term, designates a suspension of the immediate reactions the world solicits in view of a greater attention to oneself, one's possibilities, and the situation" (Levinas 1969, 154). Victims are better able to reflect in a supportive shelter environment when no longer submerged in their violent situation. Many realizations are reached and critical decisions are made during this time. Levinas questions whether "the *view of oneself* characteristic of care can be brought about without a disengagement from the situation, without a recollection and without extraterritoriality—without being at home with oneself" (170).

Advocates recognize the face in its infinity and the position of height from which it comes. They realize that victims have the right to freely feel, think, and make their own choices. Ideas are offered by advocates and contemplated, taken in, or cast off, but the most important thing is that victims have advocates *with them*. Advocates recognize that each survivor is the expert in their own situation, and even if similar histories are shared they are not *alter egos*. Advocates must always be careful to not totalize the *victim experience* model or to impose on their decision making some idea of the *good life* to which they should aspire. A domestic violence agency may be the first place a victim is able to experience a true *face-to-face* relationship where they are safe and free to be the person they are. "It is only when I respond to the other as an integral person that I am face-to-face with him" (Halling 1975, 210).

This can be tricky and difficult when an advocate witnesses the trauma that someone suffered and that person then chooses to return to the situation only to be abused again. Also tricky is advocating for the wishes of the victim under tremendous pressure from the courts or others to "get her to do x, y, or z." The shelter must remain a safe and welcoming place, regardless of the choices the victim makes. Burnout and vicarious traumatization are ever-present dangers for advocates working with victims of abuse, and this is another critical pitfall to avoid. Nevertheless, sharing experiences is priceless for both survivor and advocate. This illustrates the paradox of power and weakness, stated eloquently by Jean Vanier (1992): "You know people in pain; we can never be neutral to people in pain. It is the power of the powerless...those who are powerless have a gift to give, to transform our hearts" (38).

I share many of these experiences from working in grassroots agencies for many years. Organizations like these have come to be near and dear to my heart. I know the importance they can have for a victim of violence. As a movement grows and becomes more mainstream, however, it can become more conservative. I worry about current trends in this work. Levinas warns us that goodness can become bogged down in bookkeeping, policy, and procedure. As agencies become more professional, this danger becomes greater. Also, with the growing numbers of victims seeking services, creating a true face-to-face relationship between victim and advocate can become a luxury rather than the norm. Moments of familiarity, of silence or discourse over cups of coffee are sadly now few and far between.

As shelter programs proliferated and the public became more educated about the problem and dynamics of domestic violence, the questions asked began to shift from "What did she do to deserve it?" or "Why does she stay?" to more appropriately "Why is he abusive?"

or "How does society create or condone this violence?" Services have similarly begun to address the problem of abuser violence. Initially, the treatment of choice was *anger management.* This approach missed the fact that power and control—not anger and impulsivity— are the primary and central themes in these relationships. Anger can, of course, be a response to the Other. For those with whom we are familiar, however, the dynamics are very different and much more complex. Halling (1975) explains: "a response such as anger may be the attempt of the Same to dominate the Other. Anger can be used in the service of rhetoric, in the service of need and possession...anger may also take place within the context of the recognition of the Other as Other, and as exterior to myself" (215). More recently, the thera- peutic approach toward *batterers' treatment* addresses the patterns and core issues in the abuser's use of emotional, sexual, and physical abuse to maintain power and control over the targeted victim. This approach has shown greater promise than anger management, but the picture is still uncertain. Even with less than optimal success factors, some components of what the batterers' treatment model attempts to accomplish can be understood through the philosophy of Levinas.

Abusers think they are like Gyges—the mythical *unseen seer*— thinking they see and know everything and they are hidden and secure from the outside world. Levinas (1969) describes the Gyges myth as "the very condition of man, the possibility of injustice and radical egoism, the possibility of accepting the rules of the game, but cheating" (173). Batterer's treatment can effectively shatter this Gyges image by introducing Others not so easily susceptible to the abuser's totalization, Others who have employed these very methods themselves. Treatment involves the use of group therapy where the indiscrete faces of Others serve to powerfully call each person into question. Gyges could not survive in such a situation and the poten- tial for abusers to finally acknowledge their behavior is therefore pos- sible. Levinas (1969) states, "In this commerce with the infinity of exteriority or of height the naivete of the direct impulse, the naivete of the being exercising itself as a force on the move, is ashamed of its naivete. It discovers itself as a violence, but thereby enters into a new dimension" (171).

In order for batterers' treatment to be effective, the abuser has to recognize that his or her behavior is problematic and has to want to change—not just to regain the victim or just to appease the court but to change in recognition of their responsibility and in desire for something more. Levinas (1969) states: "Morality begins when freedom, instead of being justified by itself, feels itself to be arbitrary and violent" (84). The attitude must be one of openness, of approaching truth in the face of the Other, and thereby allowing teaching to take place. The group therapist must also approach treatment in this manner and remember the infinity and fundamental goodness of each individual. The therapist must strive toward Levinas's (1969) description of teaching: "alterity is manifested in a mastery that does not conquer, but teaches" (171). These are not easy tasks for either abuser or therapist and can become complicated, perhaps even made impossible, through court orders that commonly require the abuser to seek treatment. Nevertheless, court actions have been instrumental in driving home Levinas's point that "My freedom does not have the last word; I am not alone" (101).

Court and state involvement throws another level of complexity into this picture, which is well beyond the scope of this chapter. However, several brief points can be explored here through the philosophy of Levinas. The court and state represent what Levinas terms *other Others* who are also violated by domestic violence. Recognizing that domestic violence is now against the law, unlike years ago when the sanctity of the home was nobody else's business, crimes of domestic violence are prosecuted by the state, sometimes even without the victim's testimony, and mandatory arrest can be enacted when the police arrive upon the scene of a domestic assault.

The power asserted by the state is paradoxical, however. As systems seek to protect society and the victim from further abuse, they can also take away the freedom and responsibility of the victim to make decisions. As Levinas (1969) points out, "The State awakens the person to a freedom it immediately violates" (176). Levinas would likely see such a system as necessary for social order, as a kind of enforced peace. Nevertheless, these systems constitute a totalization and a continuation of the power and control that has oppressed the victim in the first place. As Levinas warns us: "The inter-human can subsist, but can also be lost, in the political order of the City where the Law establishes mutual obligations between citizens" (qtd. in Burggraeve 1985, 165). As he explains, justice does not equal reciprocity, and as freedom is upheld oppression inevitably follows: "Truth is thus bound up with the social relation, which is justice. Justice consists in recognizing in the Other my master. Equality among persons means nothing of itself;...it already rests on justice—which, when well-ordered, begins with the Other...and in this sense justice coincides with the overcoming of rhetoric" (Levinas 1969, 72).

CONCLUSION

Domestic violence is a microcosm of other forms of violence that plague our world. Sadly, our homes are often a training ground for future generations of victims and abusers. Domestic violence is akin to war, the ultimate evil in which the identity of the Other is destroyed and fixed in totality, where hunger and fear prevail. War, whether between countries or within our homes, involves "the attempt to deny the radical otherness of the Other by imposing our will on him" and, conversely, "peace, which would come from the primordial reality of the face-to-face relationship" (Halling 1975, 206). I believe that a genuine application of the philosophy of Emmanuel Levinas could end the historical, social, and interpersonal tragedy of domestic violence. At the very least, a careful study of his ideas would help us understand and address this tragedy. We may not yet be ready to widely embrace such a philosophy, but if we could make this leap toward recognizing the priority of the Other, toward valuing and desiring the infinity of each person, and toward acting on our own responsibility, then a higher, peaceful, more joyous world would surely await us all. How could we not desire such a future?

SEVEN

Levinas in the Hood

Heather Macdonald

INTRODUCTION: MISSION IMPOSSIBLE?

As a psychologist who performs psychological evaluations, I am often under the spell of knowledge. In other words, it is my job to report on the knowledge and understanding I have of another person and to believe that this knowledge has the power to serve the Other. I seek to understand the relation between the assessor and the client in terms of comprehension: understanding him or her through rational knowledge and by some abstract theory of analysis. While under this spell of knowing, I am allowed to view myself outside the intersubjective relation with the Other, as a single solitary hermetically sealed package that gives primacy to cognition from an omniscient viewpoint. But according to Levinas (1969), when I assume that objectivity in relationship is the ultimate form of self-transcendence, I have totalized that person, reduced them to a knowable thing that cancels out the opportunity for real ethical love and social justice.

Therefore, as soon as I read the referral questions for the assessment of a 17-year-old African American female who is pregnant, I am in a serious dilemma: How do I conduct this mission of knowing without totalizing the Other? How do I conduct myself in the spirit of ethics and social justice? This seems like an impossible task especially when the assessment process typically begins as an informational disclosure. Initially, I am lost in the rhetoric of totality, or what Levinas (1969) would call obsolete knowledge, where the psychologist may readily categorize the client's experience according to the previously set standards of the *Diagnostic and Statistical Manual of Mental Disorders* (American Psychiatric Association 2000).

For many years, scholars have argued that psychologists who conduct testing and assessment with clients in a multicultural setting must understand the complex role that cultural diversity plays in their professional activities (Sue and Sue 1990). The challenges of understanding clients in multicultural assessment as described by Richard Henry Dana (1998) have highlighted test fairness and the impact of the testing instruments themselves, with clients from diverse groups. This has raised the possibility that psychology has failed to meet the unique mental health needs of ethnic minorities and that mental health providers have lacked sensitivity in their treatment and assessment models.

Stephen Finn (2007) and Constance Fischer (1994) have argued for a collaborative model of assessment. Through the model of collaborative assessment they have emphasized that nothing is more fundamental than experiences and events in the lived world of the client, and that everything in the assessment must refer back to this world, including test results and diagnosis. The individualized assessment gives a portrait of the person and characterizes his or her point of view and approach to situations.

However, there appears to be very little mention, in previous literature, of the issues of political power and social justice within the context of working with ethnic minority populations while conducting psychological evaluations. The term "political power" can be defined from many different perspectives, but for the sake of this discussion, "political power" is defined in the sense of relationship where one person may appear to have more "power and control" and may inadvertently reproduce and extend the larger political structures at play within the society (Collins 2004, 13). This is exactly where Levinas (1969) locates his ethics and social justice: in relationship to the Other. His philosophy is helpful in understanding what it might look like to be in a relationship founded in social justice. I had been struggling with these ideas as I began the case with Dedra and had been acutely aware of my growing discomfort in my mission of knowing as an assessor.

The county worker who had made the referral explained to me that Dedra was due to deliver within the week and was unsure if she would be wiling to complete the assessment process. The case manager felt the assessment would be important to determine what kind of mental health support my client would need as a new mother. The worker had concerns about the presence of a possible mood disorder, such as bipolar disorder, since Dedra had exhibited symptoms of extreme irritability, depression, and impulsive behaviors that had started prior to pregnancy. Dedra had retuned home to her mother after more than a year in foster care, and since that time Dedra had become "obsessed with death." However, the worker could not explain to me over the phone exactly what she meant by Dedra's "obsession."

It was fortunate that I worked at an agency that often encouraged clinicians to have initial meetings in the home of the client in order to gather background and experience in the context of the client's world. It was good that I was able to visit Dedra in her home and to see her world, even though nothing could have prepared me for the events that followed.

This chapter is a means to explore those events and to depart from the tradition of psychology that teaches that the foundation of the self is in the self. Within this chapter, I am concerned with two fundamental questions: Can Levinas (1969) help transform this mission of knowing in such a way that I am able to recognize that the Other "is more primordial than everything that takes place in me" (67)? And does the philosophy of Levinas work in a cross-cultural context, when the assessor is Caucasian and the client African American?

Using examples from three assessment sessions, where the ethical response to the Other is called into question, I will propose that Levinas (1969) is portable and cross-culturally applicable. The first session will describe my initial meeting with Dedra in her home where the "face of the other" (78) is revealed. The second session will explore Dedra's "obsession with death," its relationship to the African American context, and the importance of music as a way to reduce the I and avoid totality. The final session will describe some of the feedback letter I read to Dedra, which is an attempt to be a placeholder for the infinity of the Other.

The First Session: Ethics Ruptures Being (Dasein)

There was no way to predict the outcome of meeting with my client for the first time. I think of that moment as a collision, a massive disruption of language and narrative. Theory and metaphor got tossed about on the surface like useless items after a shipwreck. If Levinas (1969) heard the story he would probably shrug his shoulders and say, "The face speaks" (66). Maybe it is just that simple.

As I drove to my client's home that morning, the streets were quiet. The air smelled like doughnuts, and the usual group of men huddled together out in front of the corner market. It was easy to find the apartment where my client lived and I parked just outside her building. I pulled multiple bags out of the trunk of my car. The bags were heavy, full of assessment test materials, and I could feel my hand scrape along the edge of the trunk as I pulled them out. I quickly shut the trunk and looked around to see if anyone else was present. I wanted to be sure I had a safe route to her doorway.

A screen door with rows of thick black rebar stood at the entrance of their home. There was no doorbell so I pounded on the screen. Eventually, Dedra's older brother answered and let me inside. The walls of the apartment were bare and a large screen TV blasted at full volume in the middle of the living room. Shoes and clothes spilled forth from plastic hefty sacks scattered around the apartment. Everything smelled like marijuana.

We moved into the kitchen and stood around the table. I introduced myself to Dedra, her mother, and older brother. Everyone looked stunned and stared at me in a grave silence. My first thought was, "Something is really wrong." I began immediately to interpret their facial expressions as shock at having a "white lady" with many bags intruding into their home.

Dedra's mother spoke first and said in a thick southern accent, "Do you realize that you have blood all over your face?" My second thought was: "This family is psychotic." As my heart began to pound inside my chest I asked, "What do you mean?" Dedra spoke up, "She is right, it is blood."

All four of us crammed into their bathroom and looked in the mirror. Sure enough I had blood smeared on both cheeks. At the same time I noticed I had large cut on my hand from a loose metal fragment on my trunk lock. I must have wiped my hand across my face multiple times before entering the apartment. Everyone started talking at once and flew into action. Hot towels appeared out of nowhere, as did alcohol, bandages, and band-aids. As I stood in the bathroom I had enough awareness to realize that our roles, the traditional categories and the typical frameworks we might have used for perceiving the white female psychologist visiting an African American family for mental health "treatment" had been nicely shattered.

One could go wild with analytic interpretations of these initial events with Dedra and her family. A clinician I consulted with on the case suggested that the client's psyche might be responding to this event as a foreshadowing of the birth of the baby or that the blood was a reflection of the violence in the community. But is there any possibility of going beyond representation and beyond metaphor to suggest that something far more important occurred in that first meeting?

In that moment we were all liberated from our self-belonging by a tear, an interruption in the signifiers and the signified, and so totality broke into pieces. According to Levinas (1969) the undoing of totality is the moment when the common face turns into the uncommon, into the unfamiliar and into the uncanny. In other words, it is the moment when totality shatters, the face of the Other appears, and one is led into that asymmetrical and nonreciprocal responsibility to and for the Other (Critchley and Bernasconi 2002). My bloody face put me in connection with Dedra outside the anticipated meaning for our meeting, and this allowed for the face of the Other to emerge. In essence the face says, "Here I am, I have a right to be and I summon you to recognize that right."

Perhaps this why Levinas (1969) used such volcanic language when describing the Other? Words such as *evasion, rupture, invasion* indicate real contact with the Other's otherness. I would also argue that the bewilderment that follows the rupture is the incubator for an ethical consciousness.

When the subjective self becomes unseated, an opportunity arises to abandon the familiar, the visible, and the known. Peter August (2010) described this opportunity as "a threshold, an in-between so slim and slippery that it exists only in its own disappearance but which I am trying to welcome in such a way that I am not too held by my own categories" (4). For the rest of the time I spent with Dedra, I tried to follow the initial rupture and bewilderment to wherever it took us. I tried to let the face of the Other introduce into me what was not in me.

THE SECOND SESSION: THE DETAILS

Dedra sat down on a kitchen stool and looked at me from across the table. I noticed for the first time the features of her face. Her eyes were a deep brown color with eyelashes that curled perfectly above them. She had full lips and high rounded cheeks. Her skin was an earthy brown color that shone in the light. While I looked at her, she inspected my face at the same time. No blood. She looked serious, and I refrained from commenting further about the previous session. Her belly was enormous beneath a bright yellow cotton t-shirt. She said, "I am having a boy." She picked up her phone and sent a text while appearing to ignore me. A knot formed in the middle of my chest as I pulled out the *Minnesota Multiphasic Personality Inventory* (*MMPI-A*) questionnaire and a cognitive test battery (Butcher et al. 1992). Something felt wrong. A text came back to her with a ring tone I recognized and I said, "Hey, that is Lil' Wayne." She gave me a brief upward glance, and with several keystrokes on her phone, the whole song played.

We talked for some time about her love of music and various rap and hip hop legends. She articulated which songs she liked and why, but then her mood seemed to shift, and she said, "You can't really explain music. You just listen to it." We ran through a few more songs on her phone, each of us commenting on the rapper's flow and alternating tempos.

Although we shared some ideas about music I still felt like an intruder. I felt like she knew something I did not, that I could give her those tests and it did not matter since I would still be the one who did not know or could not know. The blood, in essence, was still on my face.

She had mentioned to me before that she wanted "white people" out of her business and that this assessment would finally get the white people "off my back." This was something I had heard before with other clients and had to try to navigate. The topic of culture and unequal privilege will often tear the fabric of the known and unseat the "usual arrangement between events and ideas" (August 2010, 2). But in Dedra's case we had already worked backward, we had already forgotten ourselves in the initial authentic exchange. I was confused about what to do next.

Dedra paused before asking the next question, "Do you know about the death of Oscar Grant?" It appeared that Dedra continued to rely on interruption to create our relationship rather than sticking to the known categories—reaching further out to the unknowable Other upon which social justice is based.

I replied, "Yup. He was shot a week ago by a police officer just outside our office where I work."

Dedra nodded and then looked away in a manner that told me I had missed the point. The fact of the matter was that I did not know Oscar Grant, did not know her experience at all, nor could I ever really understand it. I could only notice things and notice the details as they revealed themselves in our interactions. As Levinas (1969) asserts, over and over again, "The face is present in its refusal to be contained," there is no "adequate idea" (194) or logos endiathetos by which to grasp the face. Levinas reminds us that the face cannot be seen, touched, or known. So, what does one see?

In Dedra's case it was a mirror. Dedra took me into her room because she wanted me to see her mirror, which somehow related to the original referral question regarding her "obsession with death." In her room there was a bed, a maroon carpet, and a wooden dresser with a mirror on top. On the left side of the mirror was a column of five newspaper obituaries she had cut out and shoved into the edge of the wood. I leaned in close to read each one. All five people who died were African American and male. Oscar Grant was the last in line; a policeman had murdered Oscar while he lay handcuffed, facedown on the ground.

When I looked up I observed Dedra's reflection in the mirror, with her swollen belly and her baby boy about to come into the world; I felt my whole body flush with emotion. She wanted me to know the odds. This was not about pity, sentimentality, helplessness, or liberalism. Dedra existed in the quickly disappearing space right between birth and death and she knew it.

Dedra wanted me to get the message: there is an inequitable distribution of power in our culture, a loaded dice game wagered with human lives. Levinas (1969) wrote in *Totality and Infinity* that "The unforeseeable character of death is due to the fact that it does not lie on any horizon. It is not open to grasp" (233). For Levinas, death and the face of Other come from "beyond," and Dedra instinctively understood this idea. She could die as a result of someone and for someone; that death was always in context of the Other.

I said, "Dedra—this is so cold."

She nodded, "You better be cold. Because that's how it is."

Dedra and Levinas (1969) have taught me a similar lesson: that there is nothing noble about social justice. Social justice does not involve having "good intentions" as a white person. In fact, Levinas warns us repeatedly that this is the most dangerous kind of morality or ethics. There was no moral "high ground" to walk in my relationship with Dedra. She endured my presence in her life. She did not ask for it nor did she welcome it.

The best justice, Levinas (1969) reminds us, does not come from the laws of government or a moral code, it comes from that great hidden god-place in relationship, where we lean in and are "listened into the world" (August 2010, 1). Where we are in relationship with one another in the direction of forgetting ourselves, where the map becomes murky and runs off in stained ink. But there are no losses if we submit to the Other; we already have blood on our faces and hands.

Levinas (1969) stated in *Totality and Infinity:* "But the manifestation of the invisible cannot mean the passage of the invisible to the status of the visible; it does not lead back to evidence. It is produced in the goodness reserved to subjectivity, which thus is subject not simply to the truth of judgment, but to the source of this truth" (243). Social justice is to stand with Dedra in a state of awe and complete attention, to die psychologically to the social structures in the mind and to stave off any hidden wanting; to be present to unjustifiable suffering and to be blasted by it.

Social justice means that two people endure the initial shock of otherness, of not understanding one another, and then are willing to be transformed by that very lack of understanding. Social justice is not discovered in an abstract manner, rather, it is made in the relation between two people.

THE THIRD SESSION: THE MUSIC

When I sat down to write the report for Dedra, I was once again in the same dilemma: How could I write about knowing Dedra and show that "what takes place in the Other is more primordial than anything that takes place in me" (Levinas 1969, 87)? In other words, how could I write a report founded in social justice?

My supervisor at the time was upset when she learned that in much of my formal assessment report I wrote about music. But I felt it was the only way I could make sense of my experience with Dedra. In the report I often used lyrics to support my ideas around the data. I felt that music could speak to the subconscious pool beneath language; music has a wisdom that the data points lacked. In short, music was a way to avoid totalizing the Other. Lil' Wayne, Jay-Z, Soulja Boy, B. B. King, Coltrane, had so much to say on the experiences of grief and survival; the music could fill in the gaps left by my testing measures. Eventually, through much editing, I wrote a report that I felt was fair, and in a language that minimized the violence of words and of the *Said*. I also wrote a long a feedback letter to Dedra. She wanted me to read it out loud to her in our final meeting. In the final paragraphs I read,

> In the opening statement of his autobiography *Blues All Around Me* B. B. King (1996) states, "When it comes to my own, others may know the facts better than me.... Truth is, cold facts don't tell the whole story.... I'm not writing a cold-blooded history. I'm writing a memory of my own heart. That's the truth I'm after—following my feelings no matter where they lead. I want to try to understand myself, hoping that you will understand me as well." (2)
>
> Your baby boy will be learning about his heart through yours. He will want to know how to live in this world, not just to survive, but how to really share himself and his dreams with others. He will want to know how to become his full potential by following his own truth and you can teach him.

As soon as we finished the feedback session, I gathered up my things and prepared to leave. She walked me to the door and waited for me to exit with her hands on her hips. It was an awkward farewell, an intimate moment across an abyss of the unknowable. Once out toward the car I looked back at her through the closed rebar screen door. She smiled and waved goodbye.

EIGHT

Levinas and Psychoanalysis

Richard N. Williams

The current landscape of psychology reveals neither broad nor deep concern with what can fairly be characterized as the "big picture" issues. It is at the level of the big picture issues that the work of the Lithuanian-French phenomenologist Emmanuel Levinas makes contact with psychotherapeutic theory and practice. This essay concentrates on two interconnected aspects of the big picture as a framework for discussing what Levinas's thought might bring to a discussion of human nature, psychopathology, and psychotherapy: the ethical dimension of human life and the problem of an individual's relationship to others.

In his work Levinas brings to the forefront of discourse about human beings the inevitably ethical nature of our being. This essentially ethical character of our existence is bound up with the irreducible otherness of any and all other human beings with whom we come into real or conceptual contact. For Levinas the ethical dimension of human being runs so deep that it must be understood at the level of the most elemental reality—the level of metaphysics. In order for this ethical reality to find its way to the surface and influence our lives, we must assume that we possess certain abilities that are necessary to make us able to be thus influenced. As I have expressed it elsewhere (Williams 2005, 10): "unless one already supposes human beings to be innately capable of understanding, interpretation, meaning creation, and symbolic expression, immediately given to something akin to 'care,'...in addition to being innately sensitive to a feeling of obligation and rightness, then no real metaphysic of the ethical is possible."

What Levinas adds to the understanding of us as active, rational, caring, and willing beings is a distinctly ethical dimension. I hasten to point out, however, that Levinas intends by the "ethical" something much more profound than what usually comes to mind in treatments of the topic in contemporary psychology and philosophy. Levinas speaks of the ethical as the essential, primary, and fundamental structure of subjectivity (Levinas 1985, 95).

Levinas means to say here that I am an I only because I have encountered another, in contrast to whom I can be an I. The encounter itself is inherently ethical as is the subjective identity it produces. This ethical nature of subjectivity is manifest in responsibility for the Other. For Levinas, responsibility is not something I feel toward the Other based on a rational assessment that for some reason I ought to feel responsible, and a subjective decision to accept feeling so. It is much more elemental than that. The Other approaches me, and in the very act of acknowledging, I both have, and feel that I have, ethical responsibility.

To many who encounter Levinas's work, his notion of the fundamental, ubiquitous, and inescapable nature of ethical obligation and responsibility for the Other seems extreme. It accomplishes nothing less than placing ethics at the heart of Western thought, placing it at the level of metaphysics—the starting point of all analysis and understanding. In some sense it is an extreme position but, for that, all the more compelling. It calls us to consider it. It is not easily dismissed out of hand because of the momentous implications that follow if Levinas happens to be right.

LEVINAS'S PLACE IN CONTEMPORARY THOUGHT AND IN PSYCHOLOGY

It should be noted here that the work of Emmanuel Levinas occupies a unique (or at least, sparsely populated) position in modern thought. On the one hand, he is not confident of the ultimate success of the quest for apodictic knowledge. He is disenamored by the ontological project of the hermeneutic, existential movement, which must surely have seemed to him to be self-focused and egocentric. However, in spite of his skepticism he is decidedly and explicitly not a relativist. He thus escapes the relativism of the various contemporary social constructionist movements. He is bold enough to trust the insight his phenomenological analysis gave him—that at the heart of being lies an overwhelming confrontation with otherness.

The most immediate confrontation is with a particular other—with a face—who quite literally calls us into existence as individual subjectivity. The result of this confrontation is an inescapable reverence for and obligation to that other, and all others, which we cannot successfully deny nor evade, for the very reason that we cannot destroy the Other, because once confronted, it is too late. It must be kept in mind also that this obligation is prior to any reasoned construction of a principle of obligation. It is pre-logical. It is also important to understand that this obligation to the Other is not symmetrical. That is, it does not arise from a social compact nor with any expectation of a quid pro quo. In other words, I can never regard myself as an other's Other. My obligation is infinite and unmediated by principle or expectation of reward. The result of all of this is a new perspective on—or better perhaps, confrontation with—ethics and a new root metaphor for human being and for personality. Rather than being a subset of the contemporary epistemological and the ontological projects, ethics is moved to the center of all considerations of being and thus all psychological understanding. This ethical perspective lies at the heart of psychology and psychotherapy insofar as they deal with questions of who we are, who we ought to be, and how we ought to be with each other. To the extent psychology does not deal with just these questions it is irrelevant to the human condition (Williams 2003).

LEVINAS AND PSYCHOPATHOLOGY

Levinas's potential contributions to the understanding of psychopathology come primarily from three constellations of ideas. The first is that human life is deeply and fundamentally moral. The ethical is at the core of the profoundest understanding of our human existence. In fact, morality—as the real-life unfolding of the primordial ethical obligation to and for the Other—can, in large measure, fill the existential insecurity produced by the failure of contemporary philosophy and psychology to provide certainty about our knowledge, our nature, and what is of value (Williams and Gantt 2002). Levinas (1969, 150) describes the life prior to the confrontation with the Other and the moral obligation it brings as having "a margin of nothingness about the interior life, confirming its insularity,...lived...as the concern for the morrow." To the extent that pathologies and problems in living have roots in a dearth of meaning and purpose in life, Levinas's perspective can shed light on them at their foundation. If, as Levinas suggests, the ethical call of the Other is integral to the formation of the subjectivity that constitutes the person, it is reasonable to infer that this ethical call will be experienced in some discernable way, although perhaps only vaguely. To have such a potentially profound experience as the ethical call or to sense the moral obligation incumbent in it and then refuse to act upon the call has potentially significant effects on the emotional and psychological functioning of the person. An example of just such effects will be given below.

The second potential contribution of Levinas's work for the understanding of what might be referred to as the radical turn outward and upward. If Levinas's analysis is correct, what was ultimately insufficient for philosophy—the radical turn inward toward the question of *Dasein* or being—will likely be insufficient for individuals as well. If meaning and certainty are not to be found within the resources and activities of the ego, concentration on the ego as interiority will likely tend toward egoism, isolation, and a lack of meaning—a sort of existential angst.

The third potential contribution of Levinas's work for the understanding of pathology comes also from the radical move outward and upward, but it centers on the inherently ethical relationship with the Other. Many pathologies and other problems in living stem from bad relationships. They are, in many cases, not fulfilling; they may be harmful. If relationships with others are not founded on a deep sense of ethical obligation to the well-being of the Other, they will presumably be less profound, less stable, and often less moral than if they do reflect such deep ethical obligation. Such relationships, if not inherently pathological, may tend to be at least transitory. They may be based entirely on fulfillment of what are experienced as personal needs, which, according to Levinas (1969, 114–17), are by nature insatiable. Levinas contrasts personal neediness with desire for the Other as may be manifest in spiritual stirrings, the yearning for God, or the desire for wholeness and transcendence. The former pulls us inward as we attend to the feeling of need, the latter pulls us outward and upward toward the Other. Personal needs are insatiable; the desire for the Other is inexhaustible. In short, in understanding pathology Levinas's work quietly reminds us that relationships built on neediness and the quest for satisfaction will have no power either to satisfy or to transcend the mundane neediness and superficiality of what Levinas refers to as a "living from" the world (1969, 111).

There is little in Levinas that speaks directly to the etiology of psychopathology. Nothing in Levinas's work rules out any particular causal factors. However, in bringing his perspective to the level of the analysis of lived experience, the following lines of analysis suggest themselves. The Spanish existentialist Miguel de Unamuno (1985) in his short story "San Manuel Bueno, Martir" describes the tortured life of a young Catholic priest, loved by all his parishioners and renowned for being able to comfort and strengthen his flock in their adversities. He is able to build the faith of many, but he is haunted by his own inability to believe in the reality of God and the things of eternity. Manuel's life is haunted about the edges by a sense of nothingness. It affects his relationships. He feels himself to be living a lie. He doubts his ability to love and serve others. He has no peace. In Levinas's terms, there is in his life no meaningful contact with or appreciation of absolute otherness, with that which is higher than and beyond oneself. Interestingly, Manuel, the priest, is able to have an authentic relationship with the concrete other, but he cannot find, even in the face of the other, the absolutely Other—totality, infinity, perfection, or God. He is not drawn upward by the Other.

The French existentialist Jean-Paul Sartre (1977) described the human condition as our being "condemned to be free." By this is meant we find ourselves faced with the absolute necessity of defining and creating ourselves with no help or justification from a self-existent reality beyond ourselves. This description captures the predicament we often experience in the twenty-first century as a great burden—a sort of infinite obligation to and for ourselves. Other people are a threat to the absolute autonomy of our subjectivity. Their existence is a threat to us—to our very existence—insofar as it constrains our self-creation. This threat is summarized by Sartre in a line from the protagonist in his play *No Exit* (Sartre 1947). Trapped in a drawing room without doors, windows, or mirrors, Garcin is faced with the dissolution of his identity through the medium of conversation with the two women who also inhabit the room. He concludes, "Hell is other people." In contrast, for Levinas, the Other and otherness are not threats to our subjectivity but are the occasion for its coming to be. The heavy obligation of life is not the obligation to make meaning for the self while confined to a world of strict facticity in which others can only be threats. Rather, the fundamental obligation is to the Other. This obligation does not result in the loss of freedom; taking on the obligation in acts of "substitution for the other" is the essence of freedom (Williams 2002). For those who seek therapy because of the heavy burden of self-creation and a poignant sense of nothingness, or for those who are lonely even in the midst of unbridled autonomy, a Levinasian account of life, relationship, and infinity whispers of hope and wholeness. These are to be found not by concentrating ourselves inward—but, rather, outward.

LEVINAS AND PSYCHOTHERAPY

The work of Levinas can serve as a "still small voice" of sorts, calling us to remember in our therapeutic endeavors the importance and power of the primacy of ethical obligation to and for the Other, the wonder of otherness, and the desire for transcendence. However, I believe that if a Levinasian perspective is to find traction in psychoanalysis and psychology or have beneficial influence on psychotherapeutic practice it must demonstrate its usefulness in making sense of a clinically relevant phenomenon that has proved to be elusive in the past. I have suggested elsewhere (Williams 2005) that self-betraying emotions may be such a phenomenon. Identification of and interest in self-betraying emotions grows out of the literature on self-deception—a literature heavily influenced, in turn, by one of the central issues of psychoanalytic theory. Is it possible to both know and not know something at the same time? That is, how is it possible to know the truth about some action, such as its moral content, and yet seem not to know? This question goes to the heart of Levinasian thinking brought to psychology and psychotherapy. The ethical obligation to the Other is as universal and as central to human being as individual subjectivity itself. Yet we find scant evidence that acknowledges the reality or recognition of such obligation; as often, or perhaps more often, we act otherwise.

Self-betraying emotions are essentially emotions created in acts of self-justification precipitated by the failure to respond to an immediate moral prompting (Warner 2001). The following example, told in the words of the man involved in it ("Philip"), illustrates an act of self-betrayal, the emotions generated from it, and the effect it can have on relationships (Warner 2001, 113–14).

> I planned, after an orderly dinner with no squabbling and no stern looks from me, to gather our two little children around the fireplace, read them a story, tuck them into bed, and tell them I loved them.
>
> My train was an hour late. When I finally got home, I went through the door determined to be cheerful and kind. But dinner wasn't on the table. Marsha wasn't even getting it ready. It was her turn to fix it, too. Was she waiting for *me* to do it?
>
> For a moment I felt I ought to help her out. But then I just got bitter. How could I be the kind of father I'm supposed to be in this kind of mess?
>
> I felt like letting out a bellow, but I didn't. I never do. I did what I always do. I hung up my coat (so there would be at least one thing put away in the house) and went to work cleaning up the mess. First I put the children in the tub and got them properly bathed. Then I did the dishes and put away clothes and vacuumed everywhere.
>
> Marsha said, "Please, stop, will you?" I'm sure she felt humiliated to have me pitch in when she had obviously been wasting time. People who don't act responsibly are going to feel humiliated by people who do.
>
> But I didn't say anything back. Maybe I should have given her "what for" or not helped her at all. But I wasn't going to stoop to her level. And I tried not to have an angry expression, even though it was hard. I'm above pouting and tantrums and that sort of thing.
>
> It took till ten o'clock. When we went to bed, Marsha was still upset. After all these years I know her well enough to know that no matter how hard I had worked, she still wouldn't have appreciated it.

For a brief moment, Philip felt the pure ethical prompting to help the other. He immediately turned from that call, however, and in an act of totalizing seized control of the situation and captured Marsha and her feelings. He became convinced of and content with his own reading of her and her situation. Her situation existed for him only as an inconvenience to him and a justification for his own emotions. Rather than being concerned about and responsible for Marsha and those for whom she was also responsible, he held her responsible for his situation and his emotions. She ceased to exist as an other with a face. He concocted his own emotions to justify turning away from the ethical call. He felt victimized by Marsha and by the situation into which he felt himself thrown. He felt angry and justified the anger by invoking her faults and failures.

We find in this account a manifestation of influence without awareness. Note that after the incident, and at some time removed, Philip acknowledges the straightforward ethical call to help his wife. He quickly dismisses it. The evidence that the call continued to influence his behavior, however, is found in the "style" in which Philip went about his domestic duties. He proudly refrained from "bellowing," because he is morally above such displays. He gave the children a "proper" bath and vacuumed "everywhere." Marsha's plea for him to stop was rejected, because in his mind, she deserved the humiliation she felt. He probably felt he was teaching her an important moral lesson. His silence in response to her request that he stop was deafening and sent the clear message of moral superiority. He also displayed his moral superiority by not "stooping to her level" and displaying his anger toward her.

Yet, in truth, his display of anger and condemnation was plainly manifest. Rather than straightforwardly helping Marsha and the children, he helped in a manner that did not reflect the taking on of a simple and pure moral obligation. Rather, his manner of helping was self-conscious, reflecting self-justifying emotions of anger and frustration, and a refusal to recognize the other and her call on him. Such anger and frustration—especially in the stylized and dramatic form in which Philip displayed them—arise from the fact that Philip did, in fact, feel the pure and gentle ethical call but chose to dismiss it, betraying himself by not being true to that primal sense of obligation. He then needed his emotion to justify the self-betrayal—to Marsha and to himself.

In this account of emotional distress and strained relationship, Philip created, described, and responded to his problem by looking inward to his own feelings, both producing and finding a justification, and by looking "downward" by concentrating on and allowing himself to be absorbed and victimized by the oppressiveness and the immediacy of his situation as he concocted it. Philip also looked downward at Marsha from a position of moral superiority. He saw in his totalized view of Marsha only an unworthy victimizer. In contrast to this, Levinas invites us all, whatever the facts of our situation, to look outward and upward, to take up the obligation to the Other. This is the portal leading to freedom (Williams 2002) and to that which is higher and nobler than self.

LEVINAS AND THE MEANINGFUL LIFE

Levinas is explicitly religious—although much hangs on what is meant by the term "religion" (see Williams 2005). Levinas (1998a, 7) used the term "religion" to describe a "bond with the other which is not reducible to the representation of the other, but his invocation." The "other" in this description is not the concrete other person but the absolutely Other, the total of alterity itself—that which is "above" us, what Levinas describes as infinity, that which escapes our categorization and capture. This absolutely Other describes God. Levinas speaks of the desire for the Other as compelling and fulfilling. The particular others by whom we are called into obligation show us the absolutely Other. A Levinasian analysis of the human condition and psychotherapy should not supplant nor be inimical to religion understood as the invocation of the self by the Other. It should, rather, facilitate religious involvement that draws one outward toward the particular others and toward moral obligation and draws us upward toward the infinitely Other as the object of desire (Levinas 1969).

Richard A. Cohen (Levinas 1985, 3) proposes an expression of the central question of Levinas's notion of ethics as metaphysics: "Do I have the *right* to be?" Doubt about the significance, the meaning, the purpose, or even the justification of one's existence are by no means uncommon in the twenty-first century. For anyone feeling disengaged, unsure of his or her worth or purpose, the vision of a fundamental moral purpose to every life can be a healing balm—an answer to a critical life concern. To questions of self-worth, self-affirming therapies such as those originating in the work of Carl Rogers or Heinz Kohut, among others, provide relatively superficial answers—looking inward—bent on convincing an individual of his or her intrinsic worth and finding mainly self-serving, instrumental relationships.

In contrast, anchoring worth in purpose, seeking its source outside rather than within the struggling soul, and helping one articulate a fundamental moral purpose to life, all seem to offer a surer foundation for meaning and a sense of mission than is available in other, self-affirming, strategies. The strength and dignity of moral purpose as an anchor to meaning and health has not been fully explored nor exploited. Some therapists will no doubt recoil at the thought of healing effects coming from a client's taking on a keen sense of asymmetrical infinite responsibility for the other. On the other hand, on a pragmatic level it seems to be simply true that people will do things for others they could never manage to do for themselves on the basis of private commitment and internally produced motivations. It must also be remembered that the Other's call to ethical obligation is, for Levinas, not a harsh demand, but a softer call—more like a plea, characterized by "gentleness" (Levinas 1969, 150). In addition, we should understand that the sort of obligation articulated by Levinas is not one that derives from rational principles, adopted by reasoned assent. Rather, it is a primordial call present at the genesis of our private subjectivity itself. Recognizing, articulating, and affirming this primordial call to care for the other can be healing and life affirming. The therapeutic deployment of moral responsibility and purpose is a key element of the radical turning outward and upward of therapy as informed by Levinas's work.

NINE

Trauma as Violent Awakening

David M. Goodman and Brian W. Becker

INTRODUCTION: HELL IS TINY

C. S. Lewis paints a compelling picture of hell in his book *The Great Divorce* (2001). The allegorical story begins with the nameless main character standing in line at a bus stop in the civic center of a "grey town" that is "always in the rain and always in evening twilight" (1). Surrounding the bus stop are residences spread out in concentric circles littering the dull landscape as far as the eye can see.[1] Without a clear understanding as to why he is doing so, the main character boards the bus that takes flight above the seemingly enormous expanses of hell and takes the passengers on a day trip to the outer recesses of heaven. Upon arriving, the passengers are met by figures whom they had known in their earthly lives. During the main character's conversation with his "Teacher" whose intention it is to invite him into heaven, the main character describes to the Teacher where he had just come from. The conversation plays out as follows:

> "The big gulf, beyond the edge of the cliff. Over there. You can't see it from here, but you must know the place I mean."
>
> My Teacher gave a curious smile. "Look," he said, and with the word he went down on his hands and knees. I did the same...and presently saw that he had plucked a blade of grass. Using its thin end as a pointer, he made me see, after I looked very closely, a crack in the soil so small that I could not have identified it without this aid.
>
> "I cannot be certain," he said, "that this *is* the crack ye came up through. But through a crack no bigger than that ye certainly came."

"But—but," I gasped with a feeling of bewilderment not unlike terror. "I saw an infinite abyss. And cliffs towering up and up. And then *this* country on top of the cliffs."

"Aye. But the voyage was not mere locomotion. That bus, and all you inside it, were increasing *in size*."

"Do you mean then that Hell—all that infinite empty town—is down in some little crack like this?"

"Yes. All Hell is smaller than one pebble of your earthly world: but it is smaller than one atom of this world, the Real World. Look at yon butterfly. If it swallowed all Hell, Hell would not be big enough to do it any harm or to have any taste."

"It seems big enough when you're in it, Sir."

"And yet all loneliness, angers, hatreds, envies and itchings that it contains, if rolled into one single experience and put into the scale against the least moment of the joy that is felt by the least in Heaven, would have no weight that could be registered at all." (Lewis 2001, 137–38)

The enormity of hell is an illusion. Hell fits into a crack in the soil of heaven. It is so small that a butterfly could swallow it. However, one's state of consciousness when in this hell does not *feel* constricting. Rather, as the main character states, "It seems big enough when you're in it." Perceptually, it appears to expand for eternity. Experientially, hell is all consuming.

Oddly enough, even with these insights, many of the passengers on the bus—the visitors to heaven—choose to get back onto the bus and shrink into the prison of a miniscule narrative. For a variety of reasons, they were not able to tolerate, recognize, or desire the transcendence of heaven. The Teacher states that "Their fists are clenched, their teeth are clenched, their eyes fast shut. First they will not, in the end they cannot, open their hands for gifts, or their mouth for food, or their eyes to see" (Lewis 2001, 139). The sameness of a somnambulant existence is preferred; a life of being awake to surprise, variety, and otherness is defended against. They remain asleep.

Emmanuel Levinas wrote extensively about a consciousness caught up in hellacious clenching, grasping, constricting, and egoist slumber. He recognized a human tendency to remain intoxicated by the security of sleep and the safety of totalizing narratives.[2] For Levinas (1985), the complacency of being is the homeostasis point for the ego. The ego's resting point is in a protected state of equilibrium and suspended animation. That is, we prefer our stories to maintain a particular course, a predictable frame of reference — sameness. Consumable and bite-sizable experience is sought in the place of saturated encounter with Otherness. We live out of constricted narratives and remain asleep to alterity, or, as George Kunz (2006b) put it, in a state of "tranquilized undisturbance" (7).

Levinas's ethical philosophy calls the self to awaken through an inexhaustible responsibility to the Other. Jonathan Haidt (2003) argues that "Morality dignifies and elevates" (852). Levinas would likely agree, but he would eschew any glorification of morality as utilitarian or even pleasant. Rather, morality, from a Levinasian frame, involves violence and trauma to one's ego. Encountering the Other brings about a violent awakening to the self. Exposure to the Other creates a violent denucleation and dethroning of the self's sovereignty and dismembers its sense of security and comfort. The self is wakened from the slumber of being and becomes awake to the point of insomnia. In this process, the trauma of the Other's alterity and the subsequent inexhaustible demand placed upon the self frees the self to exit the "complacency of being" and enter the freedom of responsibility (Levinas 1990b). The clinical implications of this slumber-to-insomnia movement are profound.

In this chapter, we hope to constructively problematize Levinas's understanding of trauma and selfhood. The first part will use Levinas's ethical phenomenology to detail the process whereby the self is *violently* awakened in proximity to the Other. Levinas's radical definition of freedom and its relation to the awakening of the self is explored, with specific reference to the traumatic effect of the Other upon the self. The second part explores the relationship between Levinas's thought and its implications for trauma and abuse survivors, detailing how the encounter with the Other (qua therapist) may involve *play* and *nonviolence* in the developmental process of psychological healing.

The Assault of the Other: A Trauma That Heals

> Since the egoism of the self is so entrenched, the shattering of the individual's natural attitude must be radical....In order to achieve authentic subjectivity the individual must become hollowed out, inverted, extroverted, denucleated, even persecuted.
>
> — Michael Oppenheim, *Jewish Philosophy and Psychoanalysis*

The late relational psychoanalyst Stephen Mitchell (2003) wrote about the dysregulating quality of love and the human preference for contrivances rather than the vulnerability inherent in desire for the Other. This orientation toward life ensures that we live out of stories for which we already know the end. We may seek the excitement of new experience or the unfamiliar, but typically we modulate this with defensive fall-backs and "hide outs" (Marcus 2008, 59). Mitchell describes our willingness to take controlled risks as pornographic in nature. That is, we experience the thrill of desire (pseudo-risk) without compromising our safety. We engage in "risk free desire" (Mitchell 2003, 137) and never place ourselves in the "risky business" of love.[3]

During a recent lecture at Harvard, Ronald Siegel (2009) indicated that current debates involved in the formation of the *DSM-V* have revolved around the question of whether there are overarching etiological dynamics taking place in most psychological disorders. Among the contenders for such overarching causes is emotion and experience avoidance. Nearly every psychological disorder can be understood to be a form of emotion/experience avoidance.

We suggest that avoidance of the Other or Otherness might be another way of understanding this. The inherent trauma present in face-to-face relation to the Other is defended against and papered over by alternative perceptual, experiential, and egoistic sources (Fryer 2007). Fryer suggests that, "Everyday life is, from a Levinasian perspective, a constant covering over of our original responsibility for the other person, a continual and deliberate forgetting of our fundamental guilt" (584). Phillip Bromberg in his book *Awakening the Dreamer* (2006) observes that "The need to preserve affective safety organizes the mind's responsiveness to novelty" (4) and that "When self-continuity seems threatened, the mind adaptationally extends its reach beyond the moment by turning the future into a version of past danger" (5). The Other is reduced to the sameness of one's past—the butterfly swallowable narrative—that mutes the terror and trauma of alterity (Goodman and Grover 2008). The Divine is intolerable.[4] In Hebrew Scriptures, the consequences of seeing God are fatal. We find means of hiding behind more palatable idols. We lull ourselves to sleep with counterfeit versions or totalizations.

Levinas argues that this Gygean way of being—maintaining a self that is "buffered" (Taylor 2007), distanced, "masterfully bounded" (Cushman 1995), immune, and grasping at security—is a form of existential "cheating" (Levinas 1969). It is a self asleep in the "normative allure" (Levinas 1998b, 4) of contemporary modes of subjectivity and naturalistic egoism. It is a self lived in the closed circuitry of being without alterity. It is living with "windows closed and doors shut" (Levinas 1969, 173).

Levinas is a philosopher seeking exit from this static and ataractic existence (Kunz 2006b). For Levinas, exit is not found in choice or agency. It is not derived from a rational approach or an inherent drive toward freedom. It is not a throwing off of the shackles of the social order and its conditions of worth. The self, in and of itself, cannot achieve exit from its *for-itself* orientation and the automaticity of its small and repeating stories. Rather, according to Levinas, the self is commanded outside of itself only by the Other.[5] We are asleep until the Other wakes us.

This waking process—the transformation of the ego from self-protective to ethically responsive—is described by Levinas in violent, fierce, and tempestuous terms (Levinas 1969, 1981; see also Huskinson 2002; Ricoeur 1992; Visker 2000); the self is taken hostage, persecuted, accused, and guilty.[6] Visker (2000) illustrates this well: "The Other divides me, 'denucleates' and beleaguers me, does not leave me alone but instead obsesses me and persecutes me, takes me hostage and traumatizes me, brings me to hate myself, to abdicate my place at the center of my own concerns, to give everything up, to give nothing more to myself, and thus to hemorrhage ceaselessly; the Other burns him- or herself into my skins, and penetrates me—in short: the Other does virtually everything to me, except 'let me be'" (248).

The demand from the Other is wounding, disrupting, decentering, and wakes the self from its complacent slumber. In proximity to the Other, the self is not allowed to sleep. The self is jolted awake. It is in encountering the transcendent Otherness—the irreducibility and infinity—resident in the *visage* of the Other that the ego's primacy is called into question (Levinas 1990a). The ego, in the process, is violently wrest from itself—called outside of its complacency, safety, and at-homeness. It is no longer comfortable in its own skin. It is "hunted" and called beyond its inherent smallness and overdetermined narratives. In this encounter the ego is denucleated, dethroned, and interrupted (Levinas 1981). The self's protections are neutralized, and the self awakens to an exposed *otherwise than being* that is less buffered, less defended, and less contained.

Was Levinas a masochist?[7] No, he did not wish violence upon the self. However, he recognized that the ego's current configurations and its corollary definitions of freedom in Western thought lead to a possessiveness of identity and a self-protecting egoism that leaves persons alienated, relationally impoverished, and morally anemic. Is it possible that these conventional depictions of selfhood and freedom actually close us off from others and put us into the sleep of being and out of the wakefulness of a life lived for the Other?

Freedom is redefined and reconditioned by Levinas's thought (Alford 2002). It does not come from unencumbered sovereignty of the ego, self-creation, or autonomous rationality. It is not in living congruently with nature and with one's needs. Rather, it is a life of perpetual sacrifice, of laying down oneself to the needs of the Other; *kenosis* (Levinas 1998a, 1981; Levinas and Kearney 2004; Baird 2007). It emerges in the trauma of exposure to the Other and is a freedom born from responsibility to this Other (Levinas 1990b). Levinas describes the "ethical subject" (Critchley 2007) or the self as a "peculiar dephasing, a loosening up or unclamping of identity: the same prevented from coinciding with itself, at odds, torn up from its rest, between sleep and insomnia, panting, shivering…a malady of identity" (Levinas 1981, 68–69).[8] Freedom, when it needs to be protected, conserved, and in its self-referential form, must be given away and relinquished. It must be let go and given over to the Other

(Levinas 1990b; Robbins 1991). In so doing (in giving away a lesser freedom, that is, unencumbered being), a greater freedom is given by the Other to the self.[9] Formulating Levinas's critique of the agentic and autonomous ego of Western philosophy, Marcus (2008) writes, "Levinas asserts that freedom is conferred, as an investiture, through the encounter with and entrance of the Other. Without the Other, freedom is without meaning or foundation" (43).

Thus, for Levinas, the violence rendered in proximity to the Other is necessary in order that our nature be turned "inside out," to put "our ontological will-to-be into question" (Levinas and Kearney 2004, 76). Levinas is rejecting the complacency of Western identity here. The homeostasis of the natural ego is denied.[10] The violence emergent from face-to-face relation allows us to be welcomed outside of ourselves, beyond nature, and into a freedom born from responsibility (Levinas 1990b). Critchley (1999) reminds us that, for Levinas, "ethics is a traumatology" (185). Critchley continues by observing that "The Levinasian subject is a traumatized self" (195) and, for Levinas, "this is a good thing" (195).

The denucleating violence of the Other provides a calling to goodness, an elevation of the person beyond the "murderousness of my natural will" (Levinas and Kearney 2004, 75–76; see also Cohen 1994; Visker 2000) and out of the false expanses of a constricting hell. Levinas and the Jewish tradition that lies behind his emphases call for an awakening from idolatrous slumber, a subject wide awake—to the point of insomnia. As Ira Stone (1998) suggests, this represents an "insomnia of consciousness" wherein "demands, principally justice, cause us to renounce . . . the sleep of ontology" (29). When describing Levinas's concept of substitution, Alford (2002) states, "The other is my saving grace, an alien presence that allows me to open myself to the world, a foreign body that wedges itself between me and my ego, and so allows me to escape my narcissistic soul by devoting myself to the other in me" (29; see Levinas 1981). Marcus (2008) points us to Levinas's words, "The Other 'devastates and awakens', 'compels me to Goodness'" (27).

Visker (2000) portrays this lucidly in a statement we will come back to at multiple points:

The Other does not enslave but liberates, awakens, disillusions, purifies, and elevates. One cannot but conclude: the Other brings me a
trauma which heals. Even if the Other "paralyzes" me ... he or she gives
the precise movement that I needed — paralyzing my paralysis and so
pulling down the walls which had hindered my movement.... The
Other's face taps a source in me henceforth not to be closed; it inflicts
a wound in me which purifies with its continual flow of blood: the
Other does not permit me to be alone, but leaves me no choice than
to come out of my shell (for he or she smokes me out of every hiding place, every *refugium*), to step outside, to bare myself and stand
in a nakedness which, as Levinas likes to say, is still more naked than
that of my bare skin, for it inverts my skin, turns it inside out, so that
I become an outside without an inside (*envers sans endroit*) that no
longer has any secrets, no longer any interiority, leaving me completely
open, empty, without possibility of holding anything within myself
and thus without possibility of holding anything *for* myself. One must
not forget that it is precisely these extraordinarily violent expressions
that Levinas will take up in order to explain what he means by "proximity," the nearness of the neighbor.[11]   (248)

Seldom in the literature have we seen a more poignant and evoca-
tive description of the violent and freeing effect that the Other has
upon the self. There is something both disturbing and inspiring in
this description.

We will use Visker's depiction as a springboard to enter into conversation with Levinas's account of trauma in order to gain a clearer
and more nuanced understanding of how Levinas and psychological
literature on trauma might condition one another to greater nuance.
We recognize that Levinas is referring to an "original traumatism"
(1996),[12] representing a different level of analysis than we are addressing when we speak about a "trauma" victim; but working to engage
these meanings with particular clients is a part of what is necessary in
the process of translating Levinas's work into clinical relevance. It is
messy and there are incommensurables that we are pretending to be
commensurate. In terms of clinical work, much work still needs to be
done to understand, nuance, challenge, and deepen the meaning of
Levinas's account of trauma.

TRAUMATIZING THE TRAUMATIZED: A NUCLEUS FORTIFIED

> You claim you love me but you keep suffering. You say you love me in the present but you're still living in the past. You tell me you love me but you refuse to forget.... The truth is that I am nothing to you. I don't count. What counts is the past. Not ours: yours. I try to make you happy: an image strikes your memory and it is all over. You are no longer there. The image is stronger than I. You think I don't know? You think your silence is capable of hiding the hell you carry within you?
>
> — Elie Wiesel, *The Night Trilogy*

Using a clinical lens, we will examine Visker's words on Levinas and trauma. First, we start with our more disturbed and perturbed response to his quote. When Visker (2000) writes that the trauma created in proximity to the Other "paralyz[es] my paralysis and so pull[s] down the walls which had hindered my movement" (248) and "the Other brings me a trauma which heals" (248), we cannot but think about some of our clients who are adult survivors of severe childhood abuse. Visker's statement and Levinas's deeper point assumes a narcissism that is upheld by an egoism that wants the world for itself. It notes the phenomenology behind the ego's fantasy and preference for the equilibrium and knowable rhythms of sleep. In other words, Levinas assumes a grandiosity of the ego.

However, there are also ways in which trauma has *contributed* to our being trapped in slumber.[13] Sometimes the ego has been fragmented in such a way that sleepfulness (in whatever form it takes) remains the only recourse of the psyche. When surveying nearly any trauma-related literature in psychology, the clamping down of the psyche into self-protecting and limbic-oriented states is a salient feature. Sleep—in the form of being closed off to alterity, difference, threat, otherness—is the only means of preserving basic function and preventing a dismantling of the ego into fragmented shards of insanity and torment. Dissociative states protect the ego.[14] The psyche has trapped the ego in this sleep to ward off these devastating results. Sleep is the alternative to terror. And, this is not the terror of Levinas's *there is*. Rather, it is terror of the Other as hell (Sartre 1947). For many trauma survivors, the Other *was* hell and *remains* hell.

The Other is utterly defended against, and suffering becomes a suffering by oneself—a "useless suffering" (Levinas 1998a). It is exclusionary. Experience is closed down into solipsistic trauma responses. Exteriority becomes, too frequently, a source of re-traumatization or reactivation, rather than conversation, exposure, or a calling outside of oneself. Disequilibrium certainly takes place, but it is a being off balance that does not denucleate. Rather, it sends persons more fully into the inner chambers of their nucleus. It is a clamoring for nucleation in the experience of fragmentation. And, when this nucleus is constructed, the windows and doors are shut *and* bolted. Traumatized persons are not smoked out of their places of refuge, but rather, the smoke is reminiscent of their burns and scares them into a deeper entrenchment into their hiding places. The Other is transmuted into sameness, typically taking the shape of the underlying emotional scar tissue. As opposed to a "trauma that heals," the trauma victim often finds that his or her trauma continues to wound with a pain that separates, isolates, and exhausts one's resources to remain awake to the Other. Such persons remain within a "narcissistic web of being" or "enclosure" that Marcus (2008) defines as tomb-like (87).

Contrary to Visker's description, this is not a "trauma that heals" but, rather, a trauma that clots the blood and lodges itself into dangerous arteries. It is a trauma that creates an automaticity that paralyzes and re-paralyzes, constricting one further and further into a repetitive and rote series of functions. Movement restricts into an increasing rigidity. Walls become fortified and shells thickened. Already feeling as though one's skin is inside out, the trauma victim experiences the Other as a reversing of this disposition. He or she desperately, and often effectively, becomes an inside without an outside.

In other words, the traumatizing call of the Other can sync up with the lived traumas of one's past in such a way as to bolster and magnify immanence rather than rupture it. Levinas teaches us that Otherness is traumatic, intolerable, unmanageable, and dysregulating. However, what he is really saying is that it is these things to our "sovereign egos." He does not address an allergy to the Other that is born from being mutilated and crushed by an-other. This brings up a series of new questions, ones that any clinician working from a Levinasian frame will undoubtedly encounter with trauma cases.

How can I, as the therapist, *be* a "trauma that heals" rather than one that triggers, activates, and dysregulates? How do I help a client move from a *trauma that anesthetizes* to a *trauma that awakens*? How do I help a client from a *trauma that clots* to a *trauma that increases blood flow*? How do I help a client from a *trauma that causes a burrowing into oneself* to a *trauma that invites one toward the outside*? Let's consider a case to put flesh to this.

Case Study: Jill

Jill was a force of nature. When she walked into the room, whether it was the waiting space or my (David's) office, a hurricane of energy and intensity came with her. At 34 years old, she lived in a perpetual frenzy, bouncing from job to job, apartment to apartment, and doctor to doctor.

It was not uncommon for Jill to spend large portions of our sessions talking rapidly, tangentially, and aggressively. "Life has no purpose." "Everyone is stupid." "God conspires against me in all that I do." And "Nothing will ever change." There was such momentum in her narration that it almost seemed out of her control. She appeared to have little agency as words poured out of her mouth. Her embarrassment was evident at times when she would apologize for "being like this." She could not calm herself down and was disturbed about her snowballing self-presentation.

Jill was tormented by severe anxiety that translated into perpetual worry, intrusive thoughts, constant tension, and panic attacks. She never slept throughout the night, and multiple times nightly she would jolt awake and fling her body out of bed into a ready state, chest heaving and heart pounding. She would then spend considerable time rifling through her drawers trying to organize or find something. There was never a clear goal but, rather, some sense that she was working at something. In sessions as well, she would be pilfering through her purse, tying and untying her shoes, or working at "something." There was never rest for Jill, never even a halting state.

In addition to this anxiety, Jill was plagued by dissociative experiences that were particularly disturbing to her. Jill was sent to physical therapy to have her knee worked on. When touched by the physical therapist, she would immediately experience significant chronological confusion. She wasn't sure if she was about to be touched, was still being touched, or was touched long ago. Furthermore, she would begin experiencing some cognitive slippage as she began having tactile hallucinations concerning the knee in question. Sometimes when Jill returned home, she felt as though the knee had disappeared and was left behind at the physical therapy office. Or, the knee was rotting in the joint and infecting the surrounding area. These were horrifying experiences for her. Touch was dysregulating. She lost herself—or parts of herself—in these episodes. Her daily life over the past 20 years consisted of these dissociative experiences and a chronic terror and anxiety.

She frequently spoke about a desire for all of it to end. But when asked about suicide, she stated that it wasn't even a temptation. Walking through a list of gruesome methods, Jill enumerated with great detail the ways that God would ensure their failure and use her suicide attempt as a means to create greater hardship and exact further cruelty upon her pathetic life.

Jill had grown up in a chaotic home where siblings, cousins, grandparents, aunts, and uncles marched through as though it was a train station. Most family members severely abused alcohol and drugs. Sexual, verbal, and physical abuse was basic to the fabric of her everyday existence. She recalls no warmth or responsiveness from her parents, only volatility, violence, confusion, and debasement. Her body was used for others' gratifications, her emotions used as others' sadistic playgrounds, and her mind was used to contain the insanity of her context. By the age of 11, she was an alcoholic. She kept Jack Daniels in her locker and took swigs between classes. She spent the next decade "walking wounded" (her words). She frequently found herself in other geographical states and in bad situations. By the time she came to me, she had been sober for nearly 10 years. She had yet to find an alternative means of calming her limbic flames.

Particularly in the first months of therapy, many of my words, my questions, and even my presence was experienced as an assault or what she described as a "penetration" that did not call her out but, rather, drove her into greater frenzy and anxious countermeasures. She paced faster on the well-worn path, more aggravated, and less attuned to anything outside. Jill's hell was a small region of persecution, helplessness, and the expectation of being psychically dismembered.

One day, as I was walking down the front steps of my office building about an hour after a session with Jill, I looked up and saw her seated in her car at the curb. Looking embarrassed, she waved, and I waved back. During our next session, I inquired about her still being there. She admitted that she frequently sat in the car for a half hour to nearly two hours after sessions. In a rare moment of lucidity, she explained that she often vomited after sessions, was highly disoriented, and would get terribly lost, even when driving through neighborhoods that she grew up in. Without me knowing, throughout the entire first year of treatment, this had become a normal chain of events.

I inquired further about why she would come back each week considering the long-term pairing of nausea and therapy with me! With some sheepishness in her voice, she expressed that over the course of the year, she had begun feeling some pockets of "calm." There were moments wherein she felt that things "might be okay." These moments were rare—but brand new for her. Additionally, she said that she did not feel daily as though she wanted to die.

She had sat with me, mortified and transformed, over the course of the year. She would generate whirlwinds of information and affective stimuli in the therapy room as a means of generating a protective smokescreen and as a way of communicating the deep chaos she experienced within. However, each time she came, she sat with an other who worked toward attunement without impingement, care without need for gratification, and safety and consistency rather than violence and mayhem. Slight movement in her perception of the Other, her tolerance of Otherness, and her way of relating to herself in the presence of the Other was apparent. Her ability to unclamp without disintegration in the presence of the Other was growing.

Is it possible that one step toward ethical traumatism of the Other might be an experience of the Other as safe and calming? Might the ability to open and close the doors of one's psyche be a basic prerequisite for a trauma that heals? Jill's windows and doors were splintered and ultimately rendered useless by violent family members. Exposed and perpetually raw, her life oriented toward trying to put these doors and windows back on their hinges and install a security system to protect herself from the invading Other. Therapy was a movement toward helping Jill experience less limbic noise so that she did not feel as though she had to be in a perpetual state of protection against the Other.

INSOMNIA: SELF LIVED WITH WINDOWS AND DOORS OPEN

Ultimately, we agree with the sensibility put forward by Alford that, "From the perspective of Levinas, the therapeutic goal is not to refound or reground or integrate the self. The goal is to find productive—that is, involved with other humans—ways to give oneself away" (2002, 73–74). However, too much is assumed here about the self's preparedness for such an orientation in relationship to the Other. We want to nuance this discussion of trauma with a recognition of the developmental process that may require the self to find a form of foundation, grounding, and integration that is capable of hearing the brutalizing and welcoming call of the Other. This founding, grounding, and integration surely need to look different than their present, conventional definitions. This is where Levinas's thought can profoundly condition and enrich contemporary clinical theories and practices. His recalibration of Western notions of freedom, as described earlier, lays the groundwork for a redefining of the self and its development.

We posit that psychotherapy has as its goal an awakening of the self to the Other. In the vicissitudes of the inter-subjective journey between the client and therapist, the client is invited to a fuller encounter with the Otherness of the therapist. A slow and steady dismantling of the broken symbols and idols that mediate and protect takes place. The movement in therapy is from solipsistic slumber to an unending vigil to the needs of the Other. It is the stirring from sleep to wakefulness and, further, to an insomnia of inexhaustible responsibility. The therapist offers such a welcome to the client.

It is important to be aware that different steps, stages, and/or rhythms are necessary in the clinical progression from slumber to insomnia. On the one hand, Levinas captures something of the violence experienced in exposure to the Other. Being called into question, being affected, held hostage, and persecuted by alterity and the fragility of the Other is excruciating. Becoming aware and attuned to the gravity of the Other necessarily disrupts and unsettles. Waking up is painful. In the original *Matrix* movie, Neo, after choosing the red pill and being exhumed from the mucous chamber of the machines, states, "My eyes hurt." In awakening to experience unmediated by the protective sheaths of consciousness, there is pain, confusion, disorientation, and terror; so also, when the psyche shifts from its normative discourses to the phenomenological trauma of the face of the Other. The return to this pre-original and anarchic dyad is radical and catastrophic to one's referential system and anchor points for meaning.

For example, my gentle and assuring presence was accosting to Jill. It could not be adequately thematized in the neat categories of her history. In psychoanalytic terms, it remained unformulated and inaccessible to her psyche—a threat to the equilibrium of knowable experience (Stern 2003). However, her patterns of overdetermined relationality—creating sandstorms of energy and verbiage in the therapy room to keep encounter at a distance—became stale for her as time progressed. She could not maintain them, they began breaking down, and she found herself venturing into the nether territories of something different: small amounts of trust, a sense of comfort, hope, and connection. This created horror, vomiting, disorientation, in a psyche awakening to something otherwise than her previous being. Her experience of the Other (me) was a violent experience.

On the other hand, the rhythms involved in awakening are sometimes peaceful and not violent. Caress to the side of one's cheek, a kiss on the forehead, or a gentle nudge are also ways of being awakened. The assumption of "entrenched" egoism that requires a "shattering of the individual's nature attitude" leads to the necessity of violent denucleation in Levinas's thought (Oppenheim 2006, 39). There may be other parts of the self that are awakened in playfulness, safety, and familiarity. The need to sleep as a means of dissociation and emotional avoidance may become less necessary in the context of laughter and comfort. In this way, Levinas's (1969; 1990) understanding of the Other as providing a welcome, an invitation, and a conversation may be preferred.

Jill and I learned to become playful with one another. I frequently made fun of her purses (they were enormous!) and she made fun of the front office staff (making fun of me would come along further into therapy, when it was safer). We were doing serious work but were working hard to take things less seriously. Over time, Jill described the therapy room as the place where she felt safest in the world. She could be herself, without (as much) fear of reprisal. Defenses, hideouts, and idols diminished in power as their protective purpose became increasingly unnecessary. Over time, subtly, the knob on her limbic volume was turned to a decibel that allowed for other sounds besides the inner noise that plagued her perpetually. Each week, there was a predictable tempo and rhythm to our encounters—she came to trust it and even depend on it. It was as close as she had come to being with an other peacefully.

For some, particularly those who carry a significant trauma history, learning to experience the Other as safe, secure, and loving may be the first developmental prerequisite for experiencing the Other as a "trauma that heals." Much is assumed about psychic development, tolerances, and self-regulating capacities in Levinas's thought. Levinas's lack of developmental theory contributes to some of the difficulty with applicability around this topic. And, to his credit, this was not the place that he was directing his philosophical energies (he had bigger fish to fry). We are carrying his work forward into these new realms because of the value we see in his ethical phenomenology.

This is not the first time this challenge is being posed to Levinas. He has been critiqued many times before by Irigaray (1991) and Alford (2002) for not allowing space in his thought for connection, dialogue, rhythm, participation, attachment, and relationship. Using Winnicott, Alford argues that Levinas overemphasizes the Otherness of the Other, the subject's responsibility to the Other, and the infinite qualities of the Other without properly balancing this with mutuality/reciprocity, sharing, and the play and needs of finite human-to-human relationship. Mitchell (2003) suggests that the dynamic presence of both ends of a continuum between safety/familiarity/predictability and adventure/otherness/novelty is needed for love to remain alive (see also Bromberg 2006). This may capture something of the sensibility we are putting forth here.

The Other necessarily unsettles (which can be tremendously violent to one's narcissistic egoism) and can also invite and comfort. The totality of the "I" does not consist of selfish egoism. There may be parts ready to be awakened through caress. And, for some trauma clients (like Jill), comfort and familiarity are already violent.

Conclusion

The nameless main character in C. S. Lewis's allegorical tale noted that to walk on the grass of heaven was quite painful. It felt so solid, and he felt much like a phantom, having almost no substance. Accustomed to being asleep in the numbness of hell, the vibrancy of experience (even grass beneath one's feet) was too much. It over-activated the senses to the point of registering pain. The Other is much the same in Levinas's thought. The excess of experience resident in the face-to-face encounter overloads and breaks the ego apart. However, it is a "trauma that heals" as it tears us free from the confines of small stories, sleepfulness, and ego imprisonment. This prison break has psychic casualties. In Levinas's words, "The other haunts our ontological existence and keeps the psyche awake, in a state of vigilant insomnia" (Cohen 1986, 28).

Levinas's words are shocking, radical, even unsettling. They stand in diametrical opposition to the fortified and well-boundaried versions of selfhood and freedom propagated in many Western philosophies, societies, and psychologies. His emphasis on violence done to the ego by the Other is a necessary corrective to the complacency and safety-seeking of egoism. However, we have asked about its particular relevance working with trauma victims in a clinical setting. These clients' identities, already traumatized and hemorrhaging, will respond differently to the alterity resident in face-to-face relation. With these persons in mind, we ask of Levinas's work some difficult questions about his emphasis on the violence of Otherness, alterity, and infinite separateness.

Sharing Levinas's sensibilities, our wish is that our clients will find themselves called forth from the narrow confines of the "sleep of ontology" (Stone 1998, 29) and the dissociative slumber of abuse and become increasingly open to the infinite and Other. An insomnia made up of deep and unmodulated awareness, attunedness, and responsiveness to the Other is understood as the greatest of freedoms;

a freedom born from responsibility as Levinas is fond of saying. Alford (2002) reminds us that Levinas "also writes about insomnia as a type of 'ecstasy' that is utterly open to otherness because it neither knows nor categorizes, but just is, waiting for nothing. . . . In fact, insomnia is both, on the border between heaven and hell" (68).

TEN

Toward a Therapy for the Other

George G. Sayre

INTRODUCTION

There is a growing body of literature exploring the implications of Emmanuel Levinas's radical understanding of ethics for the practice of therapy (Gannt 2002; Halling 1975; Hand 1996; Heaton 1988). This makes tremendous sense because both ethics and therapy are, fundamentally, realities of human relationship. Although this scholarship has contributed a great deal to our understanding of therapy, it has limited its focus to the psychotherapist's relationship with the client and has not yet addressed the ethical reality of therapy for the client. While the insights and observations of Levinas have important implications for our understanding of the psychotherapist's relationship with clients, they pose an even more radical challenge to the client's experience of therapy.

Levinas observed that the ethical good is one's lived response to the primacy of the Other over and above one's own self. He does not explicitly address the notion of "health" or "healing" in his work; however, as psychologists and psychotherapists interested in the relevance of Levinas's ethic to the therapeutic process, we make an implicit assumption that there is an inherent connection between that which is ethically good and that which is psychologically healthy. In other words, we are assuming that it is psychologically healthy to be ethically good.

The Traditional Ethic of Therapy: Client-Centered

Although there are nearly as many approaches to the practice of therapy as there are therapists, a basic ethical assumption shared by all is that the client's good is the fundamental good with which therapy concerns itself. The well-being of the client is the fundamental concern—in fact, the purpose—of the relationship. This ethical assumption transcends "schools" of therapy. Although various theoretical orientations differ as to the nature of the "good" that therapy endeavors to bring about, there is no disagreement as to the question of "whose" good therapy is to serve. The ethical codes of the various professional associations that represent and oversee the practitioners of therapy, all place the well-being of the client at the center of concern. In ethical terms, all schools of therapy, from behaviorism to psychoanalysis, can be said to be "client-centered."

Yet this "client centered" ethic is not simply a professional code of conduct; rather, it reveals our understanding of the healing process. We assume that healing comes from being seen, being understood, being cared for. The language of therapy concerns itself with creating a space in which the needs of the client are met, whether emotional, cognitive, psychodynamic, and so on.

In order to facilitate healing, the psychotherapeutic relationship is intentionally constructed to "protect" the client from responding to the needs of the Other, the therapist. As therapists, our own needs are bracketed from the therapeutic relationship. We construct a relationship in which the client is able to experience the hovering attention—perhaps even the unconditional positive regard—of another, free from the ethical responsibility of caring.

If, for the therapist, this is a relationship that is "Other centered," then, for the client, the experience of a client-centered relationship is "self-centered." In the lived ethical reality of the therapeutic relationship, "client-centered" defines the experience for both the therapist and the client. In this sense, therapy as traditionally understood has been an extension of psychology's ego-ology (Kunz 1998) and thus lies in sharp contrast to ethics as Levinas perceives it.

Some might respond that the client is, in fact, confronted with the face of an other, the therapist. After all, as therapists we express feelings and thoughts and perhaps even disclose information about our own personal lives. We experience genuine empathy for our clients as people, and our clients respond to us. However, this is not the face of the Other as Levinas describes it. Levinas emphasizes the witness to suffering, the response to need, in all of its alterity.

Therapy not only does not require the client to respond to the needs of an other, it is carefully constructed to preclude the needs of the therapist from impinging on the client. The face of the therapist that the client sees is a face responding to the client, a face of empathy. We may cry for, be moved by, rejoice with our clients, but we do not bring in our own distinct pain in its profound alterity. We do not say, "I want to talk about me today," or "I'm hurting because my wife and I are having some trouble," or "I'm not sure I want to be a therapist any more, I'm getting a bit burned out," or "My timing belt broke on my car and I'm not sure how I will pay for it." To do so would be to impose our needs upon the client, a violation of the therapeutic relationship.

To the degree that we, as therapists, do show our faces, the ethics of individual therapy demands that we act, in some manner, for the good of the client. For therapy we use terms such as "safe," "holding," and "empathetic." These terms point us toward a pleasant, warm, safe face in which clients find, in the therapist's similarity, themselves. These terms do not point us to the face of the Other as Levinas observed it. The mirroring of the therapist is not the face of an other in all of its alterity that imposes itself upon us, with its own needs, distinct from and potentially at odds with our own. In alterity Levinas describes not "safety," but the horror of the "there is" (Levinas 1996, 56). In the face of the infinite Other, we experience not only caring, empathy, and joy but also responsibility and the terror of their claim upon us.

By limiting ourselves, constraining ourselves within the role of "therapist," we overtly and covertly totalize ourselves. This is true for both the psychoanalysts and the "unconditional positive regarding" Rogerian. Indeed, in different terminology, Martin Buber addressed this same issue with Carl Rogers (Friedman 1996). Whereas Rogers proposed that the therapeutic relationship is one of *I-Thou*, Buber described the limited manner in which we, as therapists, can be present while in the role of "healer."

It is not only the therapist who tends to be totalized by the therapy relationship. As clinicians we are trained to relate to the others in our client's lives as issues. Other than our duty to warn regarding child abuse or the threat of violence, we are not taught to be concerned with the well-being of those in the client's life. As clinicians we have been trained to speak of these others, real people, as objects and issues.

Recall Levinas's basic observation, that to be ethical is to respond to the primacy of the Other. If, as psychotherapists interested in the implications of Levinas's insight for therapy, we return to our assumption that it is psychologically healthy to be ethically good, and the traditional ethic of therapy is an ego-logical one in which the client is primarily self-centered, then we are confronted with the conclusion that therapy as traditionally conceptualized may well be psychologically unhealthy for clients.

One way to counter the traditional client-centered ethic of therapy is therapy with Others: family, group, couples, and so on, where one is, at least potentially, confronted with the face of the Other in their suffering. But even family and couples therapy is often understood by clients and therapists, as "for" the individuals. The primary measure used in couples counseling assessment is not "caring" but, rather, "satisfaction." Thus, clients, even couples, come to therapy not to *love* better, but to *be loved* better. As clients, we tend to seek out couples counseling to ease our own suffering rather than the suffering of our partner, and our traditional therapeutic ethic does not train us to challenge this perspective.

The following experience illustrates the manner in which we, as clinicians, have been trained to hold an ego-logical "client-centered" ethic even in settings in which Others are present. Several years ago, I was working with a fellow, Don, who suffered from terrible post-traumatic stress, much of it with origins in his experience as a soldier in Vietnam. Concurrently with his therapy with me, he was being treated at the VA hospital with medication. Not only did Don suffer severe anxiety, he suffered alone. He was self-employed, providing nighttime cleaning for office buildings, a job that required minimal contact with others; he had no friends, had only a few acquaintances that he saw periodically, and had little contact with his family.

At one point Don brought up the possibility of participating in a therapy group offered at the VA for veterans who suffered from post-traumatic stress. The group included both older vets from Vietnam and younger ones from the Gulf War. He was interested, which surprised me, but voiced doubt that it would do him any good. At one point I suggested that he might go anyway; even if it did him no good, he might be of some help to others. We discussed the possibility that he might be of support to other veterans, especially the younger ones. He seemed to brighten at this prospect. It was interesting to see the change in his face, the lightening of affect, when he talked about what he might be able to say, what he might be able to give, to a younger man who had experienced horrors as he had. He decided to go.

At the session following his first group meeting, Don appeared very glum. He reported that at the beginning of the group, the therapists (there were two) asked each member why they were there, and what they hoped to get out of the process. Don had proceeded to share that he was not sure that it would help him, but he hoped to be of use to some other veterans, maybe just offer some support. He shared that he thought this might help him as he tried to get better, but that, even if it did not, that was fine. In response, the lead therapist let Don know that he needed to be here for himself, not for anyone else. The other therapist suggested that focusing on others was perhaps a way for Don to avoid his own issues, that he should not hide behind the caring role, that this, after all, was their "job." Don felt rebuked: in his words "they acted like I was trying to take over, I just wanted to help." He did not go back.

Now, the therapists' reactions could be understood in terms of power, or role, but I think that the therapists were simply operating from the individualistic, ego-logical ethic of psychology and psychotherapy: namely, that therapy is for the client, and that "healing" comes from having a relationship that is entirely "for you," from being understood rather than understanding, being seen rather than seeing.

An Alternative Ethic for Therapy: "De-Centered"

At this point, I want to emphasize the word "toward" in this chapter's title. I am not claiming to present a "system" or "theory" of therapy. Whether such a therapeutic modality can be developed is beyond the task here. I also want to emphasize the word "toward," because, like other psychotherapists, I am steeped in the ego-ology of our profession. As I sit with clients, even while I am acutely aware of the issue I am articulating here, I frequently find myself at a loss as to how to direct their gaze toward the Other, how to make this a moment of "de-centering."

When considering therapy as informed by the radical ethical observations of Levinas, we are confronted with the question: "For whom is therapy?" This question precedes the issue of "how" one does therapy. For Levinas, the ethical answer is: "For the Other." For Levinas, relational knowledge is "not governed by the concern to rediscover oneself" (Levinas 1996, 92). In this way, a therapy informed by Levinas's ethical vision rejects the traditional "self-centering" process of therapy and calls us to an understanding, and practice, of therapy as a process of "de-centering," for both therapist and client.

Therapy as a process of "de-centering" is not merely an ethical ideal, it is a psychologically coherent perspective. Developmental psychologists ranging from psychodynamic (Erikson, Bowlby, etc.) to cognitive (Piaget) have observed in widely various terms the fundamental quality of human development to be a move from ego-centrism to the capacity to experience the world as greater than ourselves. To become human is a process of de-centering. De-centering is both the means and the ends of therapy.

The notion of therapy as a de-centering also resonates with my experience as a therapist, and my own life. So much of our suffering, at least that which is avoidable, seems to be grounded not in the failure to get our needs met but in our obsession with having them met. I am by no means dismissing the damage done by trauma and depravation, but I am considering the much more frequent, everyday injuries we cause to ourselves and those around us, in our attempt to preserve ourselves.

As I have begun to see therapy as a de-centering process, I am confronted (in individual therapy) with my limitations in facilitating another person's ability to have a true lived response to the face of an other without an other present. This is not merely a theoretical conundrum but a lived experience as I struggle to be a therapist. On the one hand, I strive (with varying degrees of success) to make the good of those I work with primary. I work to place their need, their struggles, suffering, and joys at the center of the therapeutic experience for me. At the same time I hope for them to be free from the tyranny of the self in which they find themselves trapped. Thus, I endeavor for therapy to be not about their needs but about the needs of another—but not myself. Fortunately, despite my training, the ego-logical ethic of my profession, and my own tendency toward self-centeredness, moments of de-centering do happen in the therapeutic relationship. The following narrative describes one of these moments.

Shelly and Mary

Shelly had been mildly "blah" during the summer and fall, then after the Christmas holidays experienced rather profound anhedonia and lack of energy. She had gained weight. She no longer enjoyed her work, her daughter, her husband, or the beautiful house they lived in. When it got to the point that she started staying in bed "whenever she could get away with it," she came for therapy.

It confused and troubled Shelly that she should be depressed, Why her? She made a point of letting me know that she had a wonderful marriage, that she loved her husband, he loved her, that they were best friends. She also had a wonderful daughter, six years old. The previous summer Shelly, her husband, and her daughter had moved into a house they had been building for the last eight years. It had been their dream. It was a wonderful home. But she was unable to enjoy it. By being unhappy Shelly felt that she was being unfaithful, somehow disloyal to her husband. As she shared her suffering, she apologized, minimized it, tried to suck it back in, lest she sound ungrateful and unhappy.

Because she "should" be happy, Shelly hated herself for being depressed. Her Christian faith was important; she felt she was missing God somehow. She experienced her depression, her suffering, as a moral failing. At times she seemed more disturbed by the fact she was depressed than by the depression itself. She was ashamed of it, offended by it. Fed by this shame, her depression snowballed and took on a life of its own. She expressed a desperate desire to be free of this depression.

At the time of therapy Shelly was 35 years old. Her father was a strict Episcopal minister, and her mother was from a once-wealthy social registry family. Shelly's mother was very concerned with class and propriety. Shelly was raised to be concerned with what the neighbors might think. She came from Boston, something she referenced frequently, "where I came from" and "having gotten away from." Her father died when she was 27.

In the first session Shelly reported that she had no history of depression, perhaps some moodiness in adolescence, but nothing unusual. She was on the whole happy and social. She wanted her "old self" back. She talked about a secret feeling, an experience she kept to herself. She told of walking down the stairs in the wonderful house and feeling like she didn't belong there, like it wasn't hers. She wanted to run away.

In the third session, while talking about being an adolescent, she mentioned "acting out." She described this in a vague way, and when I asked her to say more she casually mentioned having been in the hospital, having taken a whole lot of pills and trying to kill herself at 16. She was, quite honestly, unable to recall why or how she felt. The experience carried very little weight with her. It was as if it had happened to someone else, the person she had moved away from.

As we talked about this time, she described the "acting out" in high school in more detail and feeling. She recalled drinking and sleeping around, somewhat indiscriminately—not like a minister's daughter should. As we began to talk, she was able to express the stress, the weight, of living two lives: one on the Friday night and one on the Sunday. She also recalled how, when she was hospitalized, her father did not come to visit during her week's stay. Her mother came once and then to pick her up. After she was picked up and came home, it was never mentioned again.

Shelly became angry. It flooded out. Shelly was angry that "nothing was good enough" for her mother. She expressed her deep fear of her mother's disapproval, of wanting to be validated. She felt haunted by a sense of never being good enough, never being lovable, of always "proving" she was good. Shelly talked about how she hated to go back to Boston because, in her mother's presence, she would become so insecure, she felt fat, unattractive, coarse, and so on. She became increasingly angry toward her mother and experienced many years' worth of unexpressed frustrations and hurt. As she began to express anger toward her mother, she spoke a great deal about her daughter,

Emma, how much she loved her. Shelly explained how hard she tried to have unconditional love for Emma. She was proud that her daughter confided in her, told her difficult things, and could come to her with problems. It was so very important to her that she have a different relationship with her daughter than she had with her mother.

Seven weeks after beginning therapy, Shelly's mother fell and went into the hospital. Shelly was going to fly back to Boston. At this point she had not let any of her friends or family (other than her husband) know that she was in therapy. The conversation turned to how she was going to approach her mother. This was infused with fear and need—fear of rejection and loss; need for approval, for validation and love. In all of this was the belief, the faith, that her mother could grant her a gift, the gift of being okay. As we spoke, I recalled the wizard of Oz. How Dorothy sought out the great and powerful Oz—to save her, to take her home.

Shelly had hidden her depression from her family, especially her mother. With this visit looming, Shelly felt a crisis regarding what to say to her mother. She wanted to say "I love you," but she did not know if she wanted to say it as Shelly with the wonderful life or Shelly who is in therapy and feels unworthy and took a whole lot of pills when she was a kid. For Shelly, the most pressing concern was how her mother would respond to her. Would she be critical or would she be supportive? The more she tried to anticipate her mother's reaction, the more anxious she became.

I said to Shelly: "I don't know what your mother would do if she saw you, but I know she doesn't have much of a chance seeing you because you don't show yourself. How can she love her depressed adult daughter when she doesn't know she has one?"

In response to her anxiety I said to Shelly; "When you talk about what your mother will do, you can't be too certain, because you have a very limited idea of who your mother is." She looked taken aback, shocked by that thought.

Shelly had never mentioned her mother's name. I asked her and she told me "Marion, but everyone calls her Mary." We talked some about what it might be like for Mary to be in the hospital. I asked Shelly if she loved Mary; she looked a bit offended, then said: "I don't really know."

She looked sad. She said that her mother probably wasn't sure if she loved her. I shared with Shelly that I thought that it might be good that, if she does love her mother, she could use this visit to let her mother know that. Shelly said she never knew what to do for her mother, how to help her. I suggested she ask her. During this conversation, Shelly's anxiety faded. She left the session much lighter.

In the session after her trip to Boston, Shelly seemed to feel much less anxious and less weighted down. It had been a good trip. She described how, for the first time, she was able to see her mother without worrying about how much weight she had gained or being proud of how much she had lost. She said she had prayed and felt closer to God. As Shelly put it, "God seems more interested in talking about how I can love my mother than about how judgmental she is."

She also shared two experiences that I think are revealing. One of her maternal aunts was there during the trip, and Shelly ended up talking to her quite a bit about what Mary was like when she was young. One of the stories involved Mary not being accepted into music conservatory. Shelly said she had never been able to imagine her mother as an adolescent before. She had heard the story but had always understood it as an admonition to work harder. This time she felt empathy for the young Mary's disappointment.

The second experience Shelly shared involved her daughter, Emma. The day after returning, she called her mother to see how she was doing. Her mother was not feeling well and was being very negative about the care she was receiving. This was the type of situation that Shelly had the hardest time dealing with. Shelly explained how she would usually become terribly tense and guilty when her mother was critical. This particular time, however, she imagined how hard it must be to be dependent on others. She also found herself sad that this woman did not know how to express herself in any other way. She saw her mother as frightened. She told her she loved her and hoped that she felt taken care of.

After Shelly hung up the phone her daughter, Emma, bounded into the room with a new stuffed animal. She wanted Shelly to help her make a tea party for her bears. What surprised Shelly was that she could turn from sadness to join in with her daughter's joy so quickly. She put it very well: "before I would have been so upset about what my mother thought of me that I wouldn't be able to enjoy my daughter."

SOME THOUGHTS REGARDING THE NARRATIVE

I want to touch briefly on three aspects of Shelly's experience that the ethical insight of Levinas helps us to understand more than we can see with traditional therapeutic language: infinity, responsibility, and truth.

From an ego-logical perspective, Shelly could be understood as dealing with an internalized critical mother, negative self-talk, or some other aspect of herself. An analyst would understand Shelly's experience to exist entirely within her. However, Mary was not an introject, she was a real woman that Shelly was failing to see, a living person condemned to seeing her daughter only on her knees.

One important part of this therapy experience was that we, both Shelly and I, attempted to see her mother as a real, and thus infinite, person. Shelly had a profoundly totalized perception of her mother, as a negative withholding power. The realization that there might be more to Mary than Shelly knew was freeing. Yet this process took courage, because Mary's needs were not about Shelly. Mary was not the mother that Shelly so desired.

I am not suggesting that we simply add ethical prescriptions to our therapeutic repertoire. As Gannt (2002) articulately points out, the ethical perception of Levinas should not be understood to entail an alternative utopian vision to replace all other utopian visions of therapy. Rather, I am suggesting a perceptual shift: that we see our clients as people who are ethically responsible to the others in their lives. From an ego-logical perspective, our only thought regarding her visit to her mother could have been "How will this be for Shelly?" Yet this question, instead of being healing for Shelly, would only have served to thrust her back into her own anxiety, insecurity, guilt, and shame. By considering herself as responsible to her mother, Shelly found some freedom. The question of her worth was not so much resolved as it was transcended.

Lastly, in the beautiful description of her phone call with Mary and the tea party with Emma, Shelly described a profound psychological truth. Levinas observed that ethical truth is the lived response to the infinite Other. In responding to her mother in truth, Shelly was also able to respond to her daughter in truth. That one response was to a face of loneliness and the Other to a face of joy does not matter. In that brief span of time, she was responding to the needs of those around her whatever they might be, caring, sympathy, or tea parties. The truth that Shelly was articulating was that the capacity to respond to the faces that bring us joy, the "come play with me" face is the same capacity that allows us to behold the face of suffering. If we refuse to see one, we cannot see the Other. This capacity to respond in truth to whatever face we see is the outcome of therapy as de-centering.

In Summary

One of the great appeals of Levinas's writing on ethics is that he did not propose a systematic normative ethical theory. Rather, as a phenomenologist he described the reality of the lived ethical experience. For this reason, as psychologists and therapists we find his insights to be illuminating and profoundly useful in understanding the lived experience of those with whom we work. But this very strength presents a profound challenge. In that Levinas has not provided a systematic ethical theory, we do not have the luxury of developing a systematic therapeutic model we can appeal to. Rather, in light of the phenomenological nature of Levinas's insights, we must continually look to our client's—and our own—lived experience in order to learn what it means to practice therapy, to do good, and to become human.

As psychologists and therapists we were taught that people want to be happy, healthy, content, and satisfied. We might have even been taught that they hope to be fulfilled, find meaning, find belonging, and be loved. The people I have worked with in therapy have shown me an additional truth, their desire to be ethical. We are all ethical persons living in response, for good and ill, to those around us. The ego-logical tradition in therapy is to ignore this aspect of our client's humanity. We are trained to see those we work with out of the context of the world of others in which we all live, as if they each existed in the center of their own world. Although this client-centered ethic is sometimes presented as humanistic, it seems to me to be profoundly dehumanizing to deny one of the most profound aspirations of those we work with, namely, to be good.

In rejecting the ego-logical ethic of therapy and moving toward a de-centered understanding, we are better able to understand people within the reality of their lives. By seeing Shelly (and others that I have had the privilege of working with) as an ethical person responsible to others, I have learned a great deal about what it means to become more human. It is my hope that this chapter serves as an encouragement for others to look to their clients to learn how to do therapy in a profoundly ethical manner.

ELEVEN

Therapeutic Impasse and the Call to Keep Looking

Claire Steele LeBeau

I do my thing, and you do your thing.
I am not in this world to live up to your expectations.
And you are not in this world to live up to mine.
You are you and I am I.
And if by chance we find each other, it's beautiful.
If not, it can't be helped.

— Fritz Perls, "Gestalt Therapy Prayer"

I am I in the sole measure that I am responsible, a non-interchangeable I.

— Emmanuel Levinas, *Ethics and Infinity*

"I'll take your word for it," Sam said. He said this virtually every time he left our weekly psychotherapy sessions for three years. Sometimes we would smile because of the familiarity and inevitability of this statement and I would say "OK, let's talk more next week," or occasionally, "Let's take your word for it." Except that they weren't his words. They were mine and he didn't believe in them. The message I gave him every week for three years was one of hope and strength and discovery. My words were about what he could find beyond and through his pain and despair. They offered glimpses into worlds that could offer promise and possibility. But this was not his world. They were not his now. He did not see any future except more of the same.

BACKGROUND AND HISTORY

Sam was a 23-year-old man who lived in the basement of a house that he shared with two other renters. He had been living in this house on his own since graduating from high school. He worked as a laborer but was often laid off during the winter months when the work was scarce. He had a few friends with whom he was greatly attached but felt an imbalance between his affection for them and theirs for him. He experienced himself as radically different and estranged from the worlds of others, and above all else, he felt needy and alone.

Sam's parents divorced when he was nine years old, and they shared custody of him and his sister, who was three years younger. Mostly, he lived with his mother and saw his father on weekends or for the occasional holiday. Sam had worked with his father as a construction worker since he was 14 years old. A year before entering therapy, Sam had completely broken off his relationship with his father because he felt constantly abused verbally by him. Ironically, Sam did not trust his mother or give her perspective much weight, in part because she never had anything but good things to say to him, meaning that she never criticized him or corrected him about anything. Sam felt that his sister was manipulative, and he said that she was really his father's favorite while he was his mother's. Sam seemed to be developmentally quite young, and his life was ruled by a constant fear of failure and rejection, frequent eruptions of anger and frustration, and an overall depression that left him feeling exhausted and unmotivated to do anything.

Sam seemed to have cultivated a remarkable ability to disengage and disassociate himself from his surroundings, his feelings, and his memories. He typically did not remember anything of what we talked about in the prior week's therapy session. He reported having no childhood memories before the age of eight, and only cursory memories of his life before the age of 12. He would often stay up and watch movies, television, or surf the Internet until the early morning when exhaustion would finally work through him and allow him to sleep. When he did get to sleep, he would sleep for 12 or more hours at a time, waking when the day was almost over. He never listened to music of any kind and never read any books. His life was one of a watcher, a spectator, and an observer. He did not remember ever feeling anything but sad and lonely and that everyone around him held a secret understanding of vitality and life in which he could never participate.

After my first session with Sam, I remember sitting in the office of my supervisor, Dr. Jan Rowe, and telling her that I could not remember ever meeting a more depressed person. For the first year of our therapy, I attempted to align myself with any aspect of Sam that seemed rousing and differentiated, his pain, his anger, or even his passion for certain movies. During one session, after several months of simply listening and trying to stay with him in the depth of his pain and despair, I found my own tears rising in my eyes, as he expressed his desire to die and end the pain of his life. I went to sit next to him on the couch, and I put my arm across his shoulder and tried to assure him that he would make it through this. When I told Jan this story, she laughed and said, quite lovingly but with all sincerity, "Claire, you need to just stay in your chair." She meant that I needed to, quite literally, stay put and ride the storm and not try to *do* anything but be there with him. That was one of the hardest things I have ever had to do.

THERAPEUTIC IMPASSE AND COUNTER-RESISTANCE

Most mainstream contemporary psychological literature does not directly address the question of the therapist's experience of not knowing the answers. Understandably, most research focuses on what we can scientifically observe, predict, and control in the application of the therapeutic tools or techniques for specific diagnostic areas. Yet, psychotherapy remains one of the most ambiguous and mysterious of human relationships. So what is happening when it is *not working*, so to speak? There are many possibilities with regard to this question. One possibility, inevitably, is to question who is the one really *getting it wrong?* Is it the client or the therapist? Conventional psychoanalytical theories take up this question and cast the "getting it wrong" as client resistance to perhaps the therapist's interpretation and authority as well as a type of projective defense mechanism. Freud (1989) casts one of the primary goals of psychoanalysis as the project of "removing the resistances which the ego displays against concerning itself with the repressed" (630). The process through which the patient's ego displays these resistances is usually unconscious; and therefore the uncovering and breaking through resistance is a central project for the analyst and a primary goal of psychoanalysis. In this light, it is easy to imagine any and all patient protest of the analyst's interpretations as ego resistance.

While the predominant body of psychotherapy literature seems to focus on the position of the therapist as expert, there are some authors who allow for the possibility of therapist fallibility. One of these positions might be that the therapy has reached some sort of impasse or stasis because neither therapist nor client is able to move beyond a given set of interpretations. These impasses are often claimed to be the result of "prolonged, unrecognized transference-countertransference disjunctions and the chronic misunderstandings that result" (Atwood and Stolorow 1984, 52). In this perspective, the therapist serves as a kind of mirror for the client's pathological self-object transferences (Kohut 1971, 1977). Atwood and Stolorow place the misunderstanding on the shoulders of the therapist—but within a complex of breakdowns in empathy and prolonged misinterpretations by the therapist of client resistance. In recent years, the term "counter-resistance" (Strean 1993) has been used to describe the therapist's portion of impasse. The term has been used to link Freud's four types of resistance from the therapist's perspective and to broadly describe lack of therapist self-reflection or any of the therapist's "attitudes or behavior that impede therapeutic process" (2).

This language changes the focus of who misunderstands, but it still does not specifically address the experiential aspects of the process for the therapist. There are, however, a few authors who offer more descriptive accounts of the therapist's experience of clients' communicating that they have been misunderstood. Some Humanist authors suggest that the therapist is the sojourner in the strange, unique, and ultimately unknowable (in the totalizing sense of this word) world of the client. Others attempt to address the efficacy and value of learning from the client, when the therapist does not understand and, in fact, experiences the unknown or the mystery of the client. Carl Rogers maintained a theoretical position of not knowing and not adopting preconceived theoretical assumptions about the client. In an article published in 1970, he wrote, "What I really dislike in myself is when I cannot hear the other person because I am so sure in advance of what he is about to say that I don't listen...when I catch myself trying to twist his message....It is only when I realize through his protest or through my own gradual recognition that I am subtly manipulating him that I become disgusted with myself" (1970, 11–19). In this confession, we can witness his struggle as a therapist to interrupt his process of trying to understand the client in his own way rather than the client's.

Our perceptions are incomplete. Our comfort in feeling that we have "got it" lulls us into a false sense of security and, more detrimentally, often into hubris. In therapy, the totalization of the client frequently leads to places of impasse and protest. Human beings cannot be concretized, and understanding is never static. My clients will always surpass my attempts to "figure out" or enclose them with my meanings. Only when I am able to make room for *not* knowing, for ambiguity and for surrender, am I open to being surprised and find them in always evolving newness. In this way, clients may also come to know themselves in this light, often doing so by acts of their own courage and agency.

Levinas's Pedagogy in the Therapeutic Journey

For three years, my work with Sam was characterized by a constant ebb and flow between my counter-resistance and my succumbing to the pain and isolation of Sam's suffering and the depth of his despair. My counter-resistance spoke both of my need to hold out hope for his future happiness and of the overwhelming sense of hopelessness that he evoked in me. In the midst of this tension, Jan's direction to "stay in my chair" and Levinas's words helped me to travel the psychological distance between "my own chair" and Sam's couch, and to traverse the expanse of my counter-resistance while continuing to hold onto hope for his becoming.

In his conversation with Philippe Nemo, *Ethics and Infinity*, Levinas (1985) describes the "there is" or *"Il y a"* experience of being alone in his bedroom as a child and feeling the "rumbling silence" of the "absolute emptiness" before creation (47–49). He describes the horror and panic of the "it" devoid of subjectivity and being, as a something rather than nothing (47–49). I was drawn to this image for Sam because it was, in fact, his reality of sitting alone in his basement bedroom, night after night, waiting for sleep to overtake him. It was and had been his experience since childhood: the "rumbling silence" that was nothing and something all at once—a reality that, by its very nature, was forgetful of itself. He did not remember his childhood or the passage of time, week to week, between sessions. The pain and horror of his "rumbling silence" was pervasive and, at the same time, preservative and sustaining in its forgetfulness. What was left for him was only the dull gnawing ache of lifelong consuming depression. I was haunted by, and often dreamed about, this image of Sam alone in his room with the simultaneous presence and amnesia of his "rumbling silence."

Part of the brilliance of Levinas is that his words "fatigue," "solitude," and "the face" describe not only the metaphysical and ontological foundations of existence but also visceral, bodily experienced phenomenon. Almost weekly, I would leave my sessions with Sam feeling a level of fatigue and psychological draining that was unlike any other I had felt. Levinas (2001) describes the weariness of fatigue of existence itself, in terms of both physical muscular exhaustion as the result of inordinate effort and "weariness of everything and everyone, and above all a weariness of oneself" (11). It was this weariness and fatigue that came to be the focal point of my counter-resistance to Sam's despair. I often dreaded our sessions. My exhaustion actively mirrored his lifelong weariness and the labor of his solitude.

We developed several metaphors in our work together that came to symbolize both his effort and mine. An early metaphor was one of a cat poised and taut, rigid with fear, above a bathtub full of water. A later metaphor was of himself as a spider in the bathtub, scrambling to crawl out, only to slip continuously back down toward the drain. The metaphor of the bathtub was one that allowed containment of the experience of descent into unknown and shadowy depths. Because Sam's orientation to the world and himself was primarily visual and spatial, as an observer and spectator, the significance to him of being in the tub was profound. The importance of feeling that he was not alone in that tub being observed by me was also imperative. What this required, however, was that I be able to be there with him in his effort to climb out of the tub, all the while knowing that we both could go down the drain at any time.

The real crux of most therapeutic work is in finding the delicate and exquisite balance between holding onto faith in a future "getting better," whatever that might mean, and letting go of all hope and joining in the pain and horror of the *Right Now,* in the absolutely present moment of suffering, as Levinas (2001) described it, the condition of the ego being "riveted to its own being" (84). This cannot be done superficially or intellectually. For each moment of horror, there must be presence. The power and potency of therapy is necessarily the opportunity not to be alone in these moments. For Sam, he was gradually able to internalize my presence to him, to the extent that he was ever so slowly able to take me home with him, to experience and begin to remember at least fragments of his pain and surrender to them for himself. I, in turn, carried the presence of Jan with me each time I entered the room with Sam. Her presence allowed me to let go of my own fear and counter-resistance enough to join with Sam in his despair, while holding on firmly to my own tethering of her love and hope for us both.

In *Totality and Infinity,* Levinas (1969) consistently uses the word "apology" with regard to the movement of conscience in the act of being called into question by the Other. As with many of Levinas's terms, it is easy to misconstrue this word in a literal sense as communicated apology or an expression of regret and acknowledgment of a failure of some sort. The word "apology" comes from the Latin *apo* or "away" and *logia* or "word" or "speech." From Plato to modern usage, the word "apology" has come to mean a form of defense, regret, or self-justification for injury or wrongdoing. Levinas, however, uses the word "apology" to indicate, rather, a movement away from self toward the Other in discourse. Ethics, for Levinas, is founded on this movement away from the solipsistic enclosure of my reason and my word. This is not a defensive posture but, rather, a "calling into question my spontaneity" or "a calling into question of the same by the other, that is, as the ethics that accomplishes the critical essence of knowledge" (1969, 43). With Sam, the movement of apology was essential for me in meeting him where he was. This movement required that I let go of my need for him to "get better" and "be happy," because those were my ideas, my reasons, my motivations, and not his. This required that I both identify these ideas as my own and surrender them. It required that I allow myself to be called into question and that I let go of what I wanted for him.

Letting go or surrendering is an act of love. It is also an act or an action that is never complete or finished. In "Peace and Proximity," Levinas writes: "The proximity of the neighbor—the peace of proximity—is the responsibility of the ego for an other, the impossibility of letting the other alone faced with the mystery of death. Concretely, this is the susception of dying for the other. Peace with the other goes that far. It is the whole gravity of love of the neighbor, of love without concupiscence" (1996, 167).

In some of the darkest and most immobile moments with Sam, when he had been unemployed for over eight months, selling his worldly possessions to have money for food and just enough rent money to keep his landlord from evicting him, not leaving his room except to come to our weekly sessions, our therapeutic impasse became more pronounced than ever. For more than a few sessions, we sat together in silence, each waiting for the other to begin. He looked at me through eyes that both beseeched and challenged me to break the silence, to do something. I waited and tried to gently hold him in my gaze, trying to keep my mind, my intentions, and my heart soft and welcoming. My prior attempts to problem solve, intervene, and rescue were ineffective, merely reinforcing his solitude. He was angry with me. My futile attempts to guide and bolster his spirit were resisted and rejected. So I held on and let go at the same time. Jan had said, "He needs you to know how bad it is." In those moments of silence, I let myself know. I felt the tears come and tasted the fear and despair with every pore of my being. No more, "I'll take your word for it."

When he broke the silence, he said he felt abandoned by me. He said it scared him that I did not try to convince him to hope anymore. Then I told him that I had been afraid to really let myself feel how bad it was for him and to admit to myself how afraid I was for him. At this, his eyes filled with tears and he smiled. His smile filled the room. He said, "I really matter to you."

I would love to say that this moment changed everything but, of course, it did not. Some things changed, however. For instance, we began to be able to joke about our familiar parting phrase. "I'll take your word for it" became something he did not need to count on me for. My word did not constitute the experience or possibility of hope for him anymore. He began to imagine it genuinely for himself. He began to be able to feel the "peace of proximity" that Levinas (1996, 161–70) describes.

Although Levinas embraces Buber's notion of the dialogical relationship of the I-Thou, he questions reciprocity and reversibility of this exchange (Smith 2005, 40). In "Meaning and Sense," Levinas writes, "As an absolute orientation toward the Other, as sense, a work is possible only in patience, which pushed to the limit, means the Agent to renounce being the contemporary of its outcome, to act without entering into the Promised Land" (1996, 49–50). This experience of acting without promise of redemption is a central theme in therapy. It is true, as Levinas writes, "I did not know I was so rich, but I no longer have the right to keep anything for myself" (1996, 52). Everything is always on-the-way and never here. Yet, I am deepened and strengthened by the Other as we continue to strive. In the midst of profound impasse and hopelessness, Sam's face called me out of my complacency, invested me with freedom, and commanded me to keep looking in and through our impasse in order to discover a depth and a significance in his own pain that he had never felt before. For him, the significance meant that he mattered enough to me for me to struggle inside of his despair. For me, the significance meant that I needed to surrender hope, in the active sense, in order to keep looking and to discover a new kind of hope in passivity.

LEVINAS ANSWERS PERLS

There is seduction in the "Gestalt Therapy Prayer" that Fritz Perls elevated to mantra status. It is comforting to imagine that I am simply doing the best I can, and for the most part, I do a pretty good job. As a therapist, I accept and acknowledge his primary thesis in *Gestalt Therapy Verbatim* that our primary charge is to "become real, to learn to take a stand, to develop one's center." He writes that "I am what I am, and at this moment I cannot possibly be different from what I am" (Perls 1969, 3). That is true, but for Levinas, it is not enough to stay there. In each moment, I must reach and stretch to be more than I am now. I must not stop. Self is not for self; there only can be self-for-Other. Levinas is relentless and inexhaustible in his return to the Other. The Other is infinite, and ethics is the first philosophy. The standard is set and the ideal stands out in sharp relief. The Gestalt Therapy Prayer is put to shame. Levinas (1989) denounces Humanism because "it is not sufficiently human" (117).

At first glance it seems contrasting Levinas with Perls is almost like comparing apples to oranges. Yet, there is still something in impasse that engages us to be present on deeper levels than can be readily articulated. I am finite, and I resist the call of the Other. I turn away and hide from this call. I struggle against the endless depths of my client's pain and despair. Impasse locks me into this struggle, and much of the time I want to admit defeat. Yet, I cannot look away, for the face of the Other remains. My subjectivity is an "irreplaceable hostage" and my responsibility is "undeclinable" (Levinas 1989, 113). If we are stuck, we are stuck together; but it can be helped. Levinas offers a vision where the work is never done but the struggle has meaning and significance. I cannot *not* resist. In many ways it is, in fact, important to resist. Yet, I must also allow myself to engage fully in the struggle, and to let the Other matter to me—to the point, as Levinas (1996, 79–95) says, of substitution. Sometimes, that means just "staying in my chair."

CONCLUSION

Ultimately, everyone is finite. There is only so much we can do at any given moment and within any given lifetime. That is why Perls's "Gestalt Therapy Prayer" makes sense to us. In the end, I left Sam to continue my own journey of learning. Yet, it is the striving and the loving and the surrendering that we do within our limitation that holds out the paradigm of hope for a Promised Land that is always on the way. Jan believed in me always, and I in turn was able to let go and allow myself to believe in Sam. Paradoxically, this letting go of hope is what allowed for a new hope to begin. Levinas does not outline the specifics of the path to responsibility or even the responsibility for the Other's responsibility. Yet, he holds us to task in the unwavering imperative to strive for the Other, to always keep looking. We cannot necessarily know the outcome of our efforts or the extent to which our looking will matter. Yet, neither fatigue nor death can eclipse the immense power and potency of that movement in faith.

TWELVE

Face of the Other in Motherhood

Kathleen M. Pape

INTRODUCTION

I gave birth to my first and only child after a three-day intense labor that allowed me only brief and uncomfortable moments of sleep. By the time the labor nurse placed my newborn son on my chest, I was less drawn to the beauty of my child as I was relieved that the whole thing was over (little did I know the whole thing was just beginning). My first day into motherhood was what one might call anticlimactic. There was no great pull toward my son, no ecstatic empowerment from birthing, none of the maternal fireworks I was led to expect during my expecting. Mildly concerned about my attitude on becoming "mother," I concluded that I was just tired and might be more enamored of my son after I had a little nap.

As soon as I was moved to the postpartum ward, I fell asleep. Yet nurses work 24/7 and I kept being awakened to follow the newborn take-home instructions delivered by the nurses in a rushed, staccato fashion, often seemingly while I was yet again drifting off to sleep. As the day unfolded, and I slipped in and out of sleep, I began to become aware of my son as a human being in this world, for the first time physically separate from me. Feeling an uncomfortable gulf between me and my son in his hospital bassinet at the foot of my bed, I began placing him in my hospital bed with me. I was concerned with his basic needs and well-being, but still I seemed not wholly taken with him. Everyone said that he was beautiful, and of course I thought he was quite wonderful. It wasn't that I didn't want him. I was quite happy I had him. I just didn't feel any of the unrestrained, mama-bear love for him that I had expected. "I will be fine, we will both be fine," I thought to myself in the daylight. I felt it was all okay, with the full mediocrity that word implied.

RESPONDING TO THE CALL

Our first night out of the hospital and in our own home changed all of that for me, forever. Being a modern, reputable birthing hospital, they had discharged me approximately thirty hours after my son was born. I was not rested when I left the hospital; maybe slightly less tired than I was during my three-day haul toward giving birth. Even so, secured in his NASA-level five-point restraint car seat, our newborn was tenuously transported home. While I settled in to nurse my son and assess the damage to my body from giving birth, my husband finished the last of our nesting preparations by securing our homemade co-sleeper onto the side of our bed. We ate a quiet meal while our son lay on a blanket in the middle of the floor. My husband and I naively proclaimed, "This parenting thing isn't so hard." With daylight fading, we inefficiently changed our son's diaper, wiped him down with a warm, damp cotton ball, put him in an adorable little sleep suit, nursed him, undressed him, changed his diaper again, dressed him again, nursed him again, then swaddled him and laid him next to me in a little co-sleeper measuring one foot by two feet, a few inches to the right of my pillow. He fell asleep, and I, feeling the warmth and comfort of my own bed, drifted off to a well-earned rest.

I was awakened approximately 30 seconds later, or so it felt, by my son's wailing cries. I was lying on my left side, facing away from him. Before I even opened my eyes, before I had even registered a physical response, the thought went through my head, "Oh, this is not going to work for me. I cannot do this"; by which I think I meant parenting, going without sleep, caring for him. Some desire to at least *seem* like a good mother compelled me to roll over in his direction and demanded that I pick him up and address his needs. I felt about as motivated as an adolescent forced to clean her room because of bad grades at school.

But when I lifted my son and brought him to me, I was immediately shot awake by his intense blue eyes locking onto mine with what looked like anguish and terror. Whatever was wrong, he was clearly suffering immensely. Fortunately, it was not immense by our adult standards, just the usual cold, scared, hunger that must be near intolerable for a little baby freshly out of the womb. In the seconds after our eyes locked, I felt a visceral shift in my being. My resistance and fatigue evaporated. I was completely awake, wholly ready, and willing to respond.

This shift manifested as the thought, "Of course I can, and will, do this." Further, that statement was an acknowledgment of something that had already happened inside of me and maybe in spite of me. It did not need repetition or absorption the way a mantra or an aphorism would. It was an epiphany.

In that moment I witnessed his unveiled suffering and felt compelled to respond, not because he was my son, not because I thought of myself as a good person, though both of these things were true. Those were the reasons I turned over. But my response, once we were face to face, was beyond and not subject to any learned ideal or moral code. It was obvious, as though I had always felt this way about him. He was the smaller, more vulnerable one. I became what Levinas (1985) calls a "first person"—she who found the resources to respond to the call, or in my case, the cry (89). Of course I can and will take care of him. Though Cohen (2001) in describing Levinas's ethics was not speaking literally, his description of "the inspired self, maternal psyche, concerned for others in its very being" (214), matches my experience of that night. This was the first moment after his birth that I truly felt like the mother of my child.

THE FACE OF THE OTHER

I had read Emmanuel Levinas a decade before I became a mother, but my understanding of his philosophical ethic settled in me after this experience. I remember thinking in that moment, "Oh, this is what Levinas meant," as I drew my son close to me to nurse him and comfort him. Levinas (1985) noted that "access to the face is straightaway ethical" (85). Levinas was speaking about more than the facial features or expressions of the individual person. The face is the presence of the Other before me, the Other's being and vulnerability.

He also asserted that "the best way of encountering the Other is not even to notice the color of his eyes!" (85). Levinas asks us to enter fully and completely into the encounter with the Other. Interestingly, for me, I remember the bright blue of my son's eyes that night even now. However, the memory stays with me not because I was objectively recording his eye color and facial features but, rather, because I was witnessing the unhinged and raw experience of fear and pain that his eyes conveyed. As Levinas (1985) noted, "before the face I do not simply remain there contemplating it, I respond to it" (88). I had to respond, and I would respond. My fatigue and pain and discomfort were dwarfed by his immediate needs. In fact, they vanished. I felt an endless supply of nurturance and care within me. I was all at once, in Levinas's paradoxical description, "bound and free" (1985, 88). Or, as Cohen (2001) described, in the transcendence that enveloped both me and my infant son, his material needs became my spiritual needs (7).

IN THE THERAPY ROOM

One of the tremendous benefits of being a parent and a psychotherapist is that in watching my son grow I have developed a clearer sense of the developmental wounds that many of my adult clients are trying to heal. Most of my clients arrive in my office having survived horrific childhoods of physical abuse, neglect, mistreatment, and terrifying confusion. Sensitized to my own child's vulnerabilities, attempts and successes at mastery, and simple needs, I now see how much the interaction with those on whom we are dependent influences how we develop. As I move with my child through developments and changes (for the most part successfully, if not always elegantly), I gain a clearer understanding of where my own clients are asking for support, guidance, freedom, space, and holding.

I have since realized that this moment with my son on our first night home was one of his first experiences of hunger, coldness, and aloneness. What I think I witnessed was an unguarded experience of being human in the world. This is something that I notice in my therapy clients, who express their hunger for meaning, describe the pain of living in a fragile human body, and confess their isolation and loneliness. Sometimes they seem terrified that no one, ever, will pick them up and draw them close.

When I am careful and notice that look of human frailty, the response that is called forth from within me is the same: "Of course I can do this, and will do this." Even if, as their therapist, the "doing" is simply staying with and remaining connected to the suffering Other and not letting them fall into insignificance, dying over and over again, alone.

In the darkness and quiet of our little home, my son and I created a sort of "sacred history"—a transcendent event witnessed by no one but him and me, inaugurated by the face-to-face experience of mother and child (Levinas 1990a, 160). My sense is that the best parenting happens in these private moments. My own sweetest memories of being cared for as a child have a uniquely private nature to them, an intimacy that is larger than the scene that seems to contain it. Maybe this is true for most people. It certainly seems true for my psychotherapy clients. When they remember any tenderness from their otherwise painful childhoods, it is often in the form of closeness, quiet, and intimate responses to their needs. It is in the quiet gestures of a mother placing warm food before their child, of the tearful face buried deeply in the father's warm, rough coat, of the large and gentle hands softly rubbing small backs, gently wiping away the pains of the day. These intimate interactions model a Levinasian ethic that calls us to be responsible to one another. Cohen (2001) noted that Levinas "is...pointing to the piercing responsibilities and obligations that link one human to another, demanding that each be attentive, alert, and awake to the other" (23). This basic living in responsibility to one another is our purpose as humans.

THE UNIQUENESS OF THE OTHER

I could not respond to the Other in my son until he was actually other than me. That may seem obvious, but I believe that the negotiation of connectedness and otherness between parents and their children (and in an embodied way between biological mothers and their now physically separate child) is one of the most tricky aspects of parenting. When first introduced to my son, friends and colleagues almost always say, "Oh, he looks just like you." We are quick to seek the familiarity in children to their parents. Though our children may share our physical features or gestures, they are uniquely themselves. Nowhere is this more obvious than in the almost universal experience of the exhausted parent and the child who will not sleep. Levinas (1985) articulated the complexity of this connectedness and uniqueness by describing the relation between fathers and sons. He stated, "filiality is still more mysterious: it is a relationship with the Other where the Other is radically other, and where nevertheless it is in some way me; the father's ego has to do with an alterity which is his, without being a possession or property" (69). Halling (1975) clarified that "Levinas wants to emphasize…that ethics is a relationship with someone exterior to me, in other words, ethics arises in a genuine relationship, not in a pseudo-relationship where there is a meeting of two parts already belonging to a larger whole, where I meet my own image or reflection" (216).

During my pregnancy, about a month before my due date, I awoke in the middle of the night, as had become typical, needing to use the bathroom. Somewhere between the doorway of my bedroom and the bathroom, in my half-asleep state, I suddenly remembered that my condition was only temporary. "This baby is going to come out of me!" I realized with a start. I had grown accustomed to going about my days with this child nestled in my belly, but at some point in the not too distant future, this child would be outside of my body, physically separate from me. Just to be clear, I always knew how pregnancy was supposed to proceed—40 weeks, more or less, and then you give birth. What was so startling about the epiphany was the realization that I was carrying a child inside of me to allow it to eventually become separate from me. Ultimately, my baby couldn't stay physically connected to me if he was to have his own life. On the way back from the bathroom, I realized that this impending delivery would be the first of hundreds of separations he and I would navigate with each other.

As Levinas proposed, my response to my son instantly led me beyond my own limits, my own hesitation. In describing Levinas's philosophical ethics, Cohen (2002) noted that "selfhood emerges as the bearer of obligation and responsibilities for the other" (41).

I emerged as a mother when I responded to the needs of my son. His inconvenient, desperate need of me allowed me to become a mother. This could not have happened had he not in his otherness made the demand upon me.

Another aspect of Levinas's philosophy that is illustrated by parenthood is the idea that the Other can never be fully grasped. My son continually exceeds my understanding, in part because of the speed at which he, like all children, is developing. When he was in my belly, there was no way for me to really predict the being that now 11 years later sits next to me at the table. For that matter, there are some days where the child who snuggled with me on Monday seems a wholly different being on Tuesday. Though I might think I empathize with my son or believe that I understand theories of human development, I cannot fully comprehend what my son — or my client — is experiencing. As Levinas (1969) warned: "The Other remains infinitely transcendent, infinitely foreign; his face in which his epiphany is produced and which appeals to me breaks with the world that can be common to us, whose virtualities are inscribed in our *nature* and developed by our existence. Speech proceeds from absolute difference" (194).

An Ethic of Motherhood and Parenting

Parents come to their role within a particular cultural context or, more often, within several cultural contexts, such as the one in which they currently live, the families in which they were raised, and the ethical and moral ideas to which they have been exposed. Scholars of American history have described the rise of the parenting expert over the past century and in particular the promotion of scientifically informed mothering (Apple and Golden 1997; Blackwell 1997; Ferrara 1995). In scanning bookshelves and searching Amazon, it becomes apparent that many of the current parenting manuals are written by seeming experts (e.g., pediatricians, neuroscientists, clinical psychologists, social workers). These texts present clear, reasonable, "proven" methods for effectively raising children. Yet few, if any of them, inform us in how to actually encounter our child's humanness. These texts give us generalized and totalized solutions to the "problems" of parenthood. In so doing, they carry us away from recognizing the uniqueness of our children. No matter how inundated the current generation of mothers are with websites, books, and La Leche League hotlines, there remains a human encounter that drives our development as mothers that is beyond what we understand as fact or information. Because our infant's needs take moral and physical priority over all else, they challenge the control or dominating influence of knowing, what Cohen (2001) described as the "hegemony of knowledge" (5). A Levinasian ethics upends this hierarchy. As Cohen (2001) stated regarding Levinas's philosophy, "In defending ethics *ethically,* insisting on an excellence rather than yet another truth or untruth, Levinas surpasses the entire enterprise of philosophy hitherto conceived. Herein lies his importance, his genuine postmodernity" (6). Unlike the parenting manuals, an ethical philosophy provides the moral imperative to look, see, and respond to a unique other being.

As a woman who became a mother during one of the most heated and deranged eras of expectations on mothers, it often seemed that simply paying attention to and tending to my child was somehow not enough. Instead, every parenting decision seemed burdened by the judgment of whether it was right, was wrong, or would someday collapse my son's SAT scores.

Similarly, as a practicing psychotherapist, I am constantly being asked to defend my presence and care for my clients as "effective," or supported by "evidence" and research. It seems not enough to assume that humans in pain and suffering would benefit from a gentle presence—the tenderness and care that meets their unique needs.

Halling (1975) noted that "for many psychiatrists and psychologists theoretical considerations seem to have overshadowed considerations about the Other, and the emphasis is placed on comprehension and expertise rather than attentiveness" (222). An over-reliance on diagnostic labels for my clients can distract me from coming to know the complex and undefined person in front of me. In the same way, a quest for expertise in my parenting takes me away from the unpredictable, unknowable Other and limits the creativity and generativity in my response. When I am quick to apply totalizing descriptions to my clients or my child, I miss a great deal of their becoming in the process. A Levinasian ethic calls us to be open to the Other in all of our interactions. It is a radical stance in an era that almost demands totalization of the Other. However, if we can and do remain open, especially in those encounters that call for care, healing, and nurturing, then this stance might guide us in unconventional, yet deep and meaningful ways of knowing.

CONCLUSION

Levinas (1994) clarified: "I would say that philosophy allows man to question himself about what he says and what one says to oneself when thinking…opening oneself to the uniqueness of the unique in the real, that is, the uniqueness of the others. Which is to say, finally, to love….The encounter with the other is the great experience, the grand event. The encounter with the other is awakening" (128). I believe this is what parents are trying to tell us when, for all the challenges, disappointments, and weekend-killing athletic tournaments, they say they are glad they have children. Many parents have experienced that grand event of opening to their unpredictable, unique child. It is what makes parenting such an incredible vocation. This is what saves us from the annoyance, indifference, and general feelings of being overwhelmed as a parent in the modern era in the Western world.

When people find out what I do professionally—psychotherapy—they often ask some variation of this question, "Don't you get tired and sick to death of just sitting there listening to people complain?" After an initial pause of confusion, I always respond, "No." In truth it is not tiring, or deadening, unless I am deadened to my clients' uniqueness, suffering, and vulnerability. My encounters with my clients, when we both discover something of who they really are as irreplaceable persons in the world, is a grand event, a great and wondrous experience.

My awakening to my son that night became "the grand event" that brought me into motherhood. It transformed me into a mother and my son into a being in the world. Since that time that awakening has been repeated thousands of times over and over again as he calls and I respond to love him as he runs, stumbles, and soars through his precious life.

THIRTEEN

When Therapy Wounds

Trevor Slocum

INTRODUCTION

In my psychotherapy practice in Seattle, I have worked with a number of gay men. Some of these men were deeply traumatized by their time with a counselor who tried to guide them toward giving up homosexuality. It is heartbreaking that—in the vulnerability of seeking outside support and help, hoping to be heard, accepted, and understood, perhaps for the first time—these men report having felt pressured to turn against themselves, the pressure coming from seemingly well-meaning and warm counselors. These authority figures who appeared to know all the answers, with an air of certainty about life and relationships, failed to see through their cultural biases and continued the abuse these clients had already experienced at home and in the community. In most cases, these men didn't seek out a counselor to work on the issue of being gay but instead were asked to see a particular counselor by a parent who was worried about their child's sexual preference. Yet despite the counselor's wish to be helpful (which I sincerely believe is present in the hearts of most counselors), what I hear reported by survivors of ex-gay counseling experiences is that they felt, at a deep level, violence was being done to a core part of themselves. A part that feels deeply woven into the pattern of their mind—unalterable and unchosen.

It is to the counselors who sincerely want to create a healing environment for gay clients that I am addressing this chapter. I hope that even counselors from more conservative communities will realize a desire to be authentically healing toward the homosexuals they counsel and will read this chapter with a friendly ear. I offer an invitation to think deeply about the ethical dimensions of our work as counselors and therapists, especially as it pertains to the work with gay men. In order to avoid unintentionally transmitting the sometimes damaging preconceptions of our culture, we need a method to help us see through our acculturated beliefs to the more fundamental experience of being human. Emmanuel Levinas's phenomenology of ethics and the human experience, as well as some of the scholars of his work, offer a perspective that is useful. Levinas's work invites and challenges us to examine our assumptions about what we can know as counselors and examine how to remain helpful to the mystery that is another human being.

BACKGROUND

Gay men[1] won a significant battle in the arena of psychology when homosexuality was finally removed from the *DSM* in 1973, not long after the Stonewall riots marked a turning point in the gay rights movement. Western psychology, with its roots in Judeo-Christian culture, succeeded in shaking off some of its assumptions, allowing that having same sex desire did not make one pathological. However, the vestiges of discrimination remain. The *DSM-IV-TR* (APA 2000) enumerates disorder 302.9 Sexual Disorder Not Otherwise Specified, admittedly a final catchall, but still maintains the language "Persistent and marked distress about sexual orientation" (582).

The practice of psychology, indeed all manner of relating, is not a neutral act. We bring to it all of our assumptions and beliefs. Given the situation of therapy, the prevailing view is that the clients will also have assumptions and beliefs arising from their experience that are causing them suffering and need to be worked through. But this view is lopsided in that it leaves out a focus on the therapist's inherent assumptions and beliefs. According to Heidegger (1996), we are all, both clients and therapists, thrown beings. As thrown we have a situated freedom, a situated-ness that affects how we see the world and also how the world views us. Cushman (1995) reminds us that a therapist's "help" cannot be divorced from the cultural assumptions he holds. Drawing on hermeneutics and social constructivism, Cushman shows how psychotherapy is a cultural product embedded in a historical context: "Psychotherapy is a cultural product and, like all cultural products, it both REFLECTS and REPRODUCES its cultural context. Because the cultural context is in part composed of moral traditions embedded in political structure, psychotherapy is unavoidably a moral practice with political consequences" (quoted in Gantt 2002, 65).

Many explicitly Christian counseling centers use prayer and teachings from the Bible to "pray away the gay." Psychologically these techniques are relatively unsophisticated and basically amount to social influence through cultural teachings. Therapists with advanced training, using powerful psychological methods to attempt change, do more damage. The National Association for Research and Therapy of Homosexuality (NARTH) is staffed by trained psychologists and therapists who seek to treat people who are dissatisfied with their homosexuality. However, because such unexamined beliefs can do great harm, I would like to encourage NARTH therapists and other ex-gay counselors to examine the therapy situation from a perspective informed by Levinas. Levinas's thought offers an alternative to a certainty-of-belief and knowing-what-is-best in favor of a radical openness to what the Other brings. Levinas's ethics are predicated on the singularity of the Other and not on abstract culturally specific beliefs.

Influenced by conservative Judeo-Christian beliefs, NARTH's stated goal is to help gay men and women to become straight, or "ex-gay" through psychotherapy often utilizing a specific set of ideas called reorientation therapy. It would seem unrealistically optimistic for gay people in today's society not to be, to some degree, dissatisfied with the experience of homosexuality. Perhaps not because they feel it is inherently wrong or have a problem accepting it but, rather, for the social repercussions they face—such as being disowned by their families, feeling uncertain about the wisdom of being out at work, or fearing for their lives if they hold hands in public. What is it about being gay that provokes such rejection from society, especially male-dominated societies?

Gay men are linked to femininity and thus are the pariah of male society in general. Larry Cata Becker (2005), professor of law at the Pennsylvania State University writes: "Women are not incidental to masculinity, but they are not always its central feature, either. At times, it is not women as corporeal beings but the "idea" of women, or femininity—and most especially a perception of effeminacy by other men—that animates men's actions. Femininity, separate from actual women, can become a negative pole against which men define themselves" (12). Becker goes on to describe how heterosexual male society is threatened by femininity and how it seeks to reinforce the traditional masculine roles of men. "Communities enforce the ideal normal standard. Such enforcement affects those gendered "female" consequentially—women's ideal is a composite of idealized culturally positive and negative characteristics other than those belonging to men. But, the consequences fall hard on men. Nonconforming men, perhaps even more than women, appear to threaten the viability of the community. They invert, and thus present the possibility of destroying, or at least subverting, the gender ordering which is a part of the bedrock on which the social order is based" (2005, 14).

Given the state of society, the gay men I counsel come to therapy with the symptoms of complex trauma—often with a long-term low-grade depression and an empty or disordered sense of self. Along with the trauma come numerous ways of coping with overwhelming anxiety and affect: depression, chemical addiction, process addictions, isolation from others considered unsafe, feelings of worthlessness, alienation, and withdrawal from social support systems. In my clinical experience, these symptoms are more profound for gay men traumatized by reorientation counseling.

Case Example

My work with one such client can serve to illustrate. Don was 35 years old, a gay Caucasian male, well-educated, single, a software engineer. Having grown up in rural North Dakota with religious parents, Don experienced his childhood as one of danger and isolation. He had always known he was different from other boys, and the difference was fairly obvious to all who knew him. Over the years he learned to share less of himself with his family and community, expressing the fear of being targeted for harm or disowned permanently. He went to conservative private schools where he was bullied by his classmates for being more gentle and withdrawn than the other boys. His parents watched in distress as Don slowly withdrew from activities in the community and became more and more isolated. They wondered why he never took up sports or hunting. During high school, at the height of his misery, they decided that Don's sexual preference was the cause of his distress and sent him to a counselor who claimed to be able to help Don become ex-gay. Out of desperation to fit in, Don went to counseling for a number of months and even participated in a Christian support group offering fellowship and guidance to other young men trying to prevent themselves from acting on their homosexual impulses.

Don ended up quitting the counseling and moving away from his hometown after one of the support group leaders became romantically interested in him. He could not bear the hypocrisy, and his parents wanted to protect him from himself and the support group leader. Far from getting any relief from his suffering, Don describes the counseling experience as extremely negative and painful. He was trained to think of his same-sex sexual impulses as an abomination—sinful, disgusting, ultimately destined to cause him a life of suffering and an eternity in hell.

Here is where Levinas's ethical phenomenology can educate other morality-based counseling approaches and help them to avoid doing harm to their clients. Levinas (1969) helps us to maintain a responsible approach to dealing with the suffering of gay men—an approach that does not pathologize homosexuality or seek to find a cause for it. Many of Levinas's phenomenological descriptions elucidate the experiences of the gay men I have seen in my practice. His work offers a number of important points to consider:

(1) Levinas's (1969) ethical system of *Totality and Infinity* gives us a frame for working constructively with gay men in a validating way. He makes a distinction between *totality* and *infinity*. *Totality* is a process by which we make the things and people of our lived-world a nothing-more-than. *Infinity*, in contrast, is how we experience an other. The Other's experience is mysterious to us, being an always-more-than-I-can-know, an infinity of possibility. By totalizing the world, representing it to ourselves by reducing the things and people around us to objects of knowledge, we make what we totalize an extension of ourselves—it is a nothing-more-than for me.

(2) I will explore the implications of *same* and *other*. By representing people to ourselves we make them the same. The same brings us to the distinction between the self and the Other. The ipseity, the "I-ness," of the self, with its essentially egocentric character, is what Levinas calls the same. By trying to represent the world to itself, the self totalizes the world around it, making the world for-it and more of the same. If everything for a self is the same, there is nothing left but the will to mastery and, finally, war. Thankfully, the Other, being *infinite*, always already breaks into our psyches with its *face*, which says, "here I am." The call of the face of the Other, the call of "don't hurt me, but help me," awakens us to our responsibility to the Other; a responsibility not to harm but, rather, to help the Other.

(3) Levinas's description of *enjoyment* provides a ground for understanding the inherent structure of a gay identity. For Levinas, the very I-ness of the self has enjoyment as its basis. Enjoyment is how we know the boundary of the self, as only I can experience my enjoyment, and it cannot be directly shared by an other.

(4) Levinas's idea of *paternity* and his distinction between *need* and *desire* shed light on the early lives of gay men, especially in relation to their fathers. Needs can be (temporarily) satisfied, like filling the stomach. Through the fulfillment of our needs, we have a sense of our egocentric autonomy and mastery, as when we find food when we are hungry. We experience a need as a lack accompanied by suffering, and we feel better temporarily when we receive what is perceived as missing. In Levinas's radical duality—where the absolute Other is higher than the same (or the egocentric self) and infinite (or always-more-than-we-can-know)—we desire that which we cannot have or fully encompass (Levinas 1969).

We desire the Other, precisely because of his radical difference, his not-same-ness, his strange impenetrable existence beyond my knowing. Desire is never fulfilled, because we can never have the Other, we are never able to make the Other about the self; he always escapes our attempts at reductionist totalizing. He is always both separate from us and more than we can know. Even the face of the Other eludes us to some degree. As Levinas points out, the face is not just the physical face of the being before me but also his invisible presence behind the face, which shines through the face with its saying, its "here I am," its looking-back-at-me.

Desire is a way of transcending the egocentric self for the good of the Other. Desire is the need of someone who lacks nothing; or better, the hunger of a desire for the Other is nourishing in that it calls us to goodness and generosity. In desire, we are asked to give, even our very lives, while not looking to the Other for fulfillment in a consuming way. Our fulfillment in terms of the Other is always an attempt to figure out how to improve the Other's life experience. Working for the good of the Other is the difference between need and desire.

(5) Finally, to better understand the therapist role, we explore some ideas presented by the scholars of Levinas, specifically Cohen's notions of the *maternal psyche* and Kunz's *simplicity, humility,* and *patience.* Cohen explains that the psyche is the part of self that is the "I" as an irreplaceable moral agent, called by the Other, before reasoning and willing, to be self-for-Other (2002). The psyche is the denucleated self, whose wholeness is found in the Other. It is a maternal psyche, the Other is within the self, and the self is *called* to tend the Other. Kunz (2002) defines *simplicity* as the "disposition of consciousness to know by being responsibly opened by the Other to be taught about reality" (120). Instead of approaching the client with preconceived ideas about what the client needs or what would be best for him, simplicity reminds us to clear our minds and truly listen to what the Other is bringing to the encounter. Kunz goes on to define *humility* as the humble service of acting responsibly toward the Other, not manipulating the Other out of our own self-interest but responding to the face of the Other with its saying. It is an acting that is a nonacting, being humble enough to hold back clever interventions in favor of a deeper listening to what is there and what is needed. *Patience* Kunz defines as the willing enduring of the Other's distress with a spirit of generosity and compassion. Often the therapeutic act is simply to be present to the suffering of an Other, to witness it and help to bear it.

Making Homosexuals the Same

Gay men are in a number of clear ways different, or other,[2] from the society in which they find themselves. They are men, and yet they are often excluded, by association with femininity, from the wider community of men. Many gay men flock to cities to find gay communities where they can live in larger numbers and have a sense of belonging. The fact that gay men seek out alternative communities speaks to their exclusion from the male community at large. The descriptions of exclusion and separate communities of belonging point to a word we use to label this phenomenon—homophobia.

Homophobic men[3] totalize gay men by assigning insulting labels to them and dismissively associating them with the feminine. Indeed, the very word "gay," which was once hoped to provide a new positive identity to those who adopted it, is now used by a homophobic culture. Don once described his frustration with his brother for using the phrase "that is so gay." Don found it irritating that the word "gay," which was chosen to provide a positive label of identity for gay men as opposed to clinical labels such as "homosexual," was being used by his brother to express derision and disgust. Don recounted the terms used in school to harass and bully him: "faggot," "queer," "pansy." Homophobic men totalize gay men as nothing-more-than, that is, nothing-more-than-an-effeminate-faggot-to-me, presumably to gain a sense of mastery and somehow protect themselves from a similar fate.

This tendency to totalize is not limited just to the oppressors. Gay men also engage in the temptation to totalize themselves and attempt to make being gay the same as being heterosexual. We see this in the search to find the "gay gene," the hope that genetics might save them from the judgments of God and psychology. As James Hollis (1994) puts it: "This genetic spin of the dice is engineered by the same god worshiped by the fundamentalists who supplant love with fear and oppression" (103). The idea is that, if being gay can be attributed to the genome, homosexuality would be a biological event beyond anyone's personal control. It removes some of the Otherness of being gay by reminding everybody that we are all subject to biological forces beyond our control—we are all made of the same stuff. Again, in this I hear a deep longing to belong, to be seen as a valid part of humanity. But if this search pays off, and gay men are able to make themselves the same in this way, I fear for their collective future. Once becoming biologically same, we open being gay up to the mastery of society.

For an example, I would like to mention another gay client of mine, Roger, who was lucky enough to have open-minded and supportive parents. I was shocked, however, to hear Roger describe an interaction he had with his mother during his college years. Roger is a lover of science, and he remains convinced that one day geneticists will find the genes responsible for determining sexual preference. Over dinner with his well-educated professional mother, he asked her whether she would have chosen to give birth to him if a gene test had been available to indicate that Roger would be gay. "No," she said, "I think I would have had an abortion." Here is a good example of the micro-traumas gay men experience in their relationships, even when those relationships are relatively supportive.

Any mother who decided to get the yet-to-be-discovered "gay gene" test would possibly be open to the temptation to ignore her unborn child's invisible face, his or her very presence, and decide not to have a gay baby. This situation is, perhaps, the model for understanding gay as Other. Regardless to when and where being gay begins, every gay person, even in the womb, has a face begging the world not to hurt him or her.

Organizations such as NARTH also totalize gay men with the label of homosexual. Ironically, they claim to be seeing beyond their homosexuality, to find something more fundamental, their inherent man-ness. NARTH, in seeking to fix a gay man's homosexuality, ultimately totalizes him as having a disorder. They seek to make him the same as straight men, and in their attempts, they totalize all men. They have created a fixed definition of what it means to be a man and are blind to how they presume to make all men fit into this mold. They wish, out of some need to control, to make all men the same. A NARTH therapist sitting with a gay man misses the call of his face, with its "don't hurt me, but help me," and reduces him to an object of knowledge for the NARTH therapist, seeking to fix the gay man into the NARTH idea of a man. If we use the word "fix" in the sense of "neuter," then the NARTH therapists want to, metaphorically, lop off the gay man's otherness. They deny his face and presence as an individual and do violence against him and his enjoyment of other men.

Gay Men Are Passive

For Levinas (1969), enjoyment is fundamental to the ipseity, the I-ness, of the self. It is the place from which we live. We are passive to our enjoyment. We live from our needs, which we enjoy. Enjoyment is not something that is added to the self—that is, we have a self, which enjoys. For Levinas, we are a self *because* we enjoy. Enjoyment is how I know the boundary of myself, as only I can enjoy my enjoyment, and while it can be expressed, it cannot be felt by another. For a gay man, the sight of a beautiful male form is an enjoyment. This is not added to his self later, in that he has a self and then later enjoys the male form. Levinas would say that his enjoyment is primary. This has radical implications for gay sexuality and identity. Levinas, in his phenomenological description of enjoyment, has given us the ground for understanding a gay self as positive. If we take Levinas seriously, being gay cannot be the choice it has sometimes been assumed to be in the past, although we certainly have choice around whether we accept what discloses itself to us. At our deepest level, we are passive to our enjoyment. Following from Levinas, a gay man does not choose to be attracted to men, he finds himself enjoying men at the core of himself, before he can even think or choose. For Levinas, once a taste or need is acquired, we are passive in our having to just enjoy it. An other can break in and question my enjoyment, but its call would be "don't hurt me, but help me." A man's enjoyment of another man's form does not do violence or cause harm. For Levinas, the *caress* is inherently nonviolent.

There is violence and a traumatically destructive impact when enjoyment is shamed or denied. An attack on enjoyment is not just an attack on a particular behavior or emotion. It is an attack on a self. Homophobic society consistently attacks a gay man's enjoyment. In a myriad of subtle ways he is constantly told that his sexual enjoyment is wrong, perverse, inferior, barren, and since the arising of the AIDS crisis in the 1980s, dangerous, even deadly. With each negative message, an attack is fired at the gay man's I-ness, his sense of self. It is no wonder then that often the self-esteem of a gay man is worn away and replaced by a deep rage and sorrow at constantly having to defend himself.

FATHER HUNGER

Robert Bly, an author of the men's movement, writes about the need for initiation into the world of men (1990, 1996). I turn to the poet in Bly to provide a description of the experience of men across time and culture. Although the specifics of male initiation are beyond the scope of this chapter, suffice to say that initiation amounts to an acceptance into manhood after a wounding trial—this belonging to the community is something that only an older, hopefully wiser, man can offer a younger man. Boys do not naturally grow into men in the deepest sense of the word. In a very real way, men are made. Indeed, without initiation, boys remain boys; wild and incapable of true service to the community as a whole. From this perspective, young gay men desperately need their fathers, perhaps more than their heterosexual brothers do, whose struggle for belonging in the world of men is less problematic. The tragic irony is that, despite this need, the fathers of gay sons often pull away and abandon their gay sons from an early age.

Don spoke at length about his relationship with his father and other men. He had more or less written his father off for lack of involvement and interest in his life and, in our sessions, provided a long angry recounting of the injustices he felt he had suffered at the hands of his father. "I found men scary," he remembers. "I was never sure when I would be found out or where the next insult would come." However, despite his angry dismissal of his father, tears of grief burst through unexpectedly when he arrived at the simple statement, "A relationship would have been nice."

It is not hard to find literature on the strange distance between gay sons and their fathers. On the NARTH website you can find articles describing this distance between fathers and gay sons, citing it as one of the causes of same-sex attraction (Hamilton 2013). Alternatively, the psychologist Alan Downs (2005) movingly describes this abandonment from the gay boy's perspective. Due to shame and cultural sanctions around emotional expression, fathers of gay boys are distant and unavailable for the type of relationship the boy needs. We must be careful here, as shame and blame are closely linked and I believe blame—with its fixation on what went wrong and with placing the badness in others—will lead us astray.

Leaving blame aside, Levinas would alert us to both the obligation and the responsibility in the situation. Levinas's descriptions of paternity as well as need and desire help to frame this sad situation. When describing the paradox of paternity Levinas (1969) tells us,

"Paternity is a relation with a stranger who while being Other...*is* me, a relation of the I with a self which yet is not me" (277; italics added). For Levinas, a son is not the work of the father, nor is he the father's property. The son *is* the father and yet is also an absolute other. Fathers have an obligation to their sons, the same as they would have to any other, for the Other always already calls us to be responsible. If the son is the Other, the relation of father toward the son would ideally be one of desire. To desire the Other takes us out of our self-centeredness as we seek to meet the call of the Other. Metaphysical desire, which is insatiable, is an act of love, for we desire the good for the Other.

The son, on the other hand, needs his father. He needs someone to provide for his needs, to teach him and, through love and challenge, make him strong. Don expressed this directly, "I wanted someone to teach me things about being a guy." Ultimately, the son's greatest need from his father is his father's desire. Often, when listening to gay narratives, we hear that the father was remote or not interested—that he had no desire for his son, no openness to his infinite mystery as an other that is always more-than-we-can-know.

Need and desire are never pure but contain aspects of each other. It is not likely the case that gay boys experience no desire from their fathers, but perhaps they experience more the father's need. For Levinas, in paternity, a father is his son, and so a father is his gay son. The father, instead of desiring his son's enjoyment, his son's happiness, needs his son to be different, to be the same as he—not other. His son reflects for him all the negative associations he has about being gay, his fears about his own masculinity and possible banishment from the community of men, and through his son he is tied to homosexuality. The father's subtle, perhaps not fully conscious, perception of his son's homosexuality leaves him humiliated, for he is his son and his son is not as the father would have him be.

Nevertheless, the father is obligated to his son as other and so, for the sake of his son, must learn to turn his humiliation into humility—defined by Kunz as an act of service to the Other. Essentially, the father—or the counselor who would like to be of help to a gay male client—has to be able to transmute his own shame so as not to get stuck in unwittingly shaming his son. If he can manage to do this, he may find that the Other, who is his son, bestows the generous gift of a new world on his father, giving his father what, in his father's limiting sameness, was lacking. If the father can open and tend to his gay son, the father opens to his own maternal psyche.

THERAPY FOR A GAY OTHER

Before I go on to describe an approach to therapy for a gay other, I want to be clear that the healing work with gay men cannot be limited just to individual therapy but, following Cushman (1995), must also include the wider cultural political and moral discourses along with family and societal systems. I believe we need to educate and reduce shame in men around homosexual desire. Gay sons need their fathers. But often, the father will not have managed to do the internal work necessary to turn humiliation into humility. Therefore, the gay son grows up abandoned by a father who doesn't desire him. The gay son needs an other who sees the son as desirable, as belonging, as having something to offer. A gay man needs a therapist who is open to his or her own maternal psyche, who, from the place of moral agency, can tend to gay man as other—even tending to the client's irreplaceable moral agency in relation to his community. Gay men need therapists who can respond to the call of the face of the Other that sits before them, without totalizing the gay man but desiring him in his Otherness.

Kunz (2002), following Levinas, describes the qualities I consider essential to therapists and their maternal psyche. Therapists would have to embody simplicity, in the sense that they are willing to be open to what the gay man, as other, brings to the therapy situation. Therapists with simplicity are passive to the reality brought by the gay man as other and do not seek to impose their own reality. Kunz (2002) writes, "Simplicity comes to the psyche with the revelation that the Otherness of the Other puts them beyond the understanding of the self, that their rights as Others puts them beyond judgments, that their inherent goodness as Other is desirable" (134).

What Don presented to me, as I attempted to sit with him in simplicity, was a man deeply traumatized by the rejection of the men in his community, especially his father. Our work together involved allowing him to bring up the pain of his shame around this rejection, and together we would step out of the shame and attempt to find ways for him to accept himself as good, desirable, whole. By accepting what is there—by validating the right to be, that which discloses itself—we act with simplicity and humility when faced by the Other.

Far from this ideal approach of simplicity, ex-gay counselors approach the gay client with a complexity of already-knowing based in their beliefs. This already-knowing consists of the belief that, if homosexuality is causing him pain, a man should seek to renounce homosexual feelings and behavior. However, to my mind, when a gay man in his shame seeks reorientation therapy, this situation is an enactment in the clinical sense. The act of stepping out of enactments and making their implicit content explicit is widely considered to be healing in psychotherapy. When enactments carry on, however, the result is at best that healing is stalled and at worst that the client will be further traumatized.

Donnell Stern (2010), a psychoanalyst who works from the phenomenological and hermeneutic perspective, describes the complex phenomena of enactments. He describes enactments as inner conflicts that cannot be fully borne and thought about due to trauma and dissociation, and so the conflict is externalized and acted out between two people. For example, a man dissatisfied with his homosexuality, an inner conflict too painful to be solved by himself, externalizes the conflict and plays it out in the relationship with an ex-gay counselor. The ex-gay therapist plays the role of a shaming and rejecting other, while the homosexual man lives from the shamed and self-hating self. An ex-gay therapist's beliefs are too good of fit with the dissatisfied homosexual man's inner tormentor, and so the ex-gay therapist takes on this role of the disapproving father unconsciously, and without the necessary self-examination to break out of the enacted conflict. From this perspective, an ex-gay therapist may unwittingly be preventing healing through not being able to step out of the enactment. We need humility to step out of an enactment.

Kunz (1998) defines *humility* as the willingness to act responsibly toward the Other—to be of service. It is an acting that is a not-acting, allowing the Other to inform us how to act. Humility garners a person's strengths but helps to avoid potential weaknesses. Kunz writes, "It is the opposite of my tendency toward both control by manipulation and the cowardice of the riskless avoidance" (121). One clear way of belonging and being of service to community is to humbly seek *justice*. For Levinas, justice is that we are asked to be responsible for our brother's responsibility. Because we live in a community of *thirds,* the other Others, we are called to concern for others beyond the Other immediately before us. We need to protect the needs of third others as well as provide for our loved ones in face of the demands of others. To do so, we need justice, which is a balancing, a measuring, that allows us to be responsible for the Other's responsibility, thus protecting all of humanity while preserving the fundamental inequality of the psyche before the Other.

Don spent months wading through the injustices done to him over the years. Together, we would seek to find who was responsible for the situation. By naming the others who failed in their responsibilities, slowly but surely, Don began to shake off the profound shame he carried. He began to feel stronger and more at ease with himself. A powerful moment in Don's therapy revolved around his decision to confront his former ex-gay counselor about the abuses of their relationship. He stated clearly what the counselor had done to hurt him, and how he no longer believed he needed to feel ashamed or to change anything about himself. The counselor, of course, did not share Don's perspective, but Don no longer cared. In reflecting on others who had failed in their responsibilities, Don began to question his own responsibilities. He began to consider his agency, reflecting on his choices about how he wanted to live, who mattered to him, and what political and social causes he wanted to support.

For Kunz (1998), *patience* is a suffering for the Other that redeems suffering: "Patience is expressed in compassion and generosity.... *Patience* offers the gift of *self-sacrifice.* The Other's needs command me to restrain my tendency for selfish satisfaction, especially my haughty disgust, to put myself in the place of the Other in order to help her enjoy the satisfaction of her needs" (137). Gay men often internalize their father's rejecting attitude toward their enjoyment. It will take a therapist with great patience to help a gay man process the negative messages he received growing up. By sitting with the pain the gay man brings, the therapist's patience creates the necessary space for the gay man to find meaning in his suffering.

I found myself sitting with patience around how Don related to me in sessions. At first I suffered patiently as Don held himself aloof from me, barely allowing there to be a relationship of any warmth or support. I learned quickly that Don needed me to receive his descriptions of suffering with a compassionate look but without my saying much, for when I did he would react as if I was threatening him, almost as if anything I said might point to some failing of his. Slowly, over time, he came to trust me in my compassion for him, and my desire to never buy into his shaming self-critique. From there, I found myself sitting with patience as Don longed for me to be the father he never had, and he feared that any signs of his autonomy or disagreement between us might threaten my caring about him. I suffered with him, with patience, his terrible fear that I might suddenly change and become like his father, once more confirming the beliefs about relationships with men that had kept him safe earlier in life. I suffered with him in his grief about the limitations of our relationship, and how I couldn't undo the pain he had suffered but could only help him understand himself more clearly through speaking his story, grieve the pain as having been real, and take action in the face of it. Ultimately, he learned to have patience with himself and his pain.

One of the things I learned from working with Don was the importance of the Other in undoing someone's sense of isolation. As Don let go of his shame, he discovered he had much to offer the younger generation of gay men. I am happy to report that toward the end of our work together, no longer trapped by shame about himself and fear of other men, Don allowed himself to get close to and start a relationship with a loving and supportive man. In his free time, he volunteers at a local outreach organization for gay kids living on the street.

CONCLUSION

As therapists we are called to be aware of the Other as other, that he is an infinity, a more-than-I-can-know. Levinas's phenomenology allows us to develop a psychology for the Other that side-steps the pitfalls of psychology's totalizing past and commits us to act responsibly toward our clients. We are called to help our clients return to their own responsibility for the Others in their lives. This entails encouraging our clients, when appropriate, to continue to risk working for justice—working to change the totalizing tendencies of certain aspects of psychology and religion as well as discriminatory practices of society at large.

FOURTEEN

Weak Enough

George Kunz

We want students tough enough for this difficult profession; then we watch to see if they can become *weak* enough.[1] We help them develop knowledge, skill, and emotional stability and hope they allow their sophisticated knowledge, practiced techniques, and emotional sturdiness to be vulnerable enough to be called into question by clients—Levinas would say "*traumatized*" (1981, 56). The weakness and closeness of the client does not place the therapist into a position of power but, rather, one of open sensibility. The proximity of the one hurting is the call for the therapist to be responsible. Responsibility paradoxically demands a certain weakness: an openness to be taught rather than a strong self-conviction, obedient behavior rather than stubborn determination, and suffering rather than emotional restraint.[2] With her responsibility, the therapist seeks understanding, helps with decisions, and feels for her clients in pain. Her understanding is not a measure of knowledge but of *standing-under;* her help is not control but, rather, supports his freedom; her suffering is not restrained neutrality but suffering because he suffers. The more she knows, the more he is a mystery beyond her common diagnostic category. The more she supports him, the more he makes decisions independent of her standard technique. The more she suffers him, the more his suffering reveals his unique singular pain. The therapist's subjectivity is subjected to the client's enigmatic otherness. But this widening gap does not undo his proximity and her infinite responsibility (Levinas 1969, 1981). The more the Other is other and responded to, the more therapy can heal.

215

The Gratuitous Burden and Increase of Responsibility

Levinas writes that "The infinity of responsibility denotes not its actual immensity, but a responsibility increasing in the measure that it is assumed; duties become greater in the measure that they are accomplished" (1969, 244). In therapy the client is dependent on the responsibility of the therapist; she is not responsibility for his life, but for his responsibility. While her responsibility is never complete, she helps him become less dependent and more responsible toward others.

Levinas inspires us to acknowledge the impossibility for the therapist to fulfill the demand to "be there" for the client who is always beyond her "there." Eric Severson confesses that therapists lament their weakness: "The therapist is usurped in the very attempt to provide therapy. This usurpation is not, however, the end of therapy but its most primary condition. So the possibility and necessity of therapy is built on its own ironic incapacity to be enough, to be on time" (2010). The client is always infinitely *close*, demanding responsibility, and infinitely *far away*, beyond her grasp.

One might read Levinas as an intellectual grouch warning about the pathogenic quicksand of trying to serve another who always needs more. No doubt about it, his hyperbolic descriptions from *Otherwise than Being* (1981) could push the helper into despondent frustration:[3]

> For under accusation by everyone, the responsibility for everyone (especially the client) goes to the point of substitution. A subject [therapist] is a hostage. Obsessed with responsibilities which did not arise in decisions taken by the subject [therapist], consequently accused in innocence, subjectivity in itself is being thrown back on oneself. This means concretely: [as therapist] I am accused of what the other [client] does or suffers...The uniqueness of the self is the very fact of bearing the fault of another....The more I return to myself, the more I divest myself, under the traumatic effect of persecution, of my freedom as a constituted, willful, imperialist subject, the more I discover myself to be responsible; the more just I am, the more guilty I am. (112)

This kind of responsible weakness—in the forms of *simplicity, humility,* and *patience*—is the paradoxical strength we hope for in our student therapists.

Too much to ask? Probably. We are all human. But Levinas inspires us to see how this radical *subjection to* the service of others—holding us *hostage,* which offers the path beyond ourselves—pulls us from our self-sabotaging selfishness to the freedom of responsible obedience. Better than others, Levinas tells us we get the good life enjoying filled needs, but he also reminds us that we are given fuller life by ethically sacrificing for others when their needs command.

Neither a grouch nor an ascetic, Levinas is more of an aesthetic. Note his descriptions of the beautiful world in *Otherwise than Being* (1981): "Rather qualities become vibrant and promote themselves as more than added presence; they perform for us: reds redden; green greens; contours open with vacuity. Musical sounds resound, poetic language become sonorous. Beautiful buildings invite and chant" (38–40).

Good stuff delights before it fills needs. Sensation does not, first, record for cognition in order to calculate needs that would fill them and, only then, offer an added layer of affect. Sensitivity before contact is already susceptible to enjoyment. We do not simply fuel up to energize movement but are invaded by goodness through enjoying the fulfilling of our own needs. From this comes responsibility. Only because enjoyment is good can it be worth giving to others.

Here are two powerful but seemingly conflicting quotes: "Life is the love of life, a relation with contents that are not my being but more dear than my being" (1969, 112), and from twelve years later, "the psyche [is] in the form of a hand that gives even the bread taken from its own mouth" (1981, 67). On the one hand, Levinas offers poetic descriptions of the psyche bathing in goodness. For its own self-interest, the psyche takes up the materiality of the world as its milieu, its medium, its home, its place in the sun, that from which it lives. It freely gropes into the prime matter of elemental stuff, grasps, fashions things, buys and sells, carries them off, stores and enjoyably consumes to maintain its happy existence. The psyche "ingests" good stuff with *jouissance* (what a lovely French word for *enjoyment*). Levinas writes, "The identity of the person...is based on...the happiness of enjoyment [*jouissance*]. To be at home with oneself, is 'to live from...its things'" (1969, 147). On the other hand, he has harsh poetry about the burden of the psyche: "The subject,...tight in its skin, encumbered and as it were stuffed with itself, suffocating under itself, insufficiently open, forced to detach itself from itself, to breathe more deeply, all the way, forced to dispossess itself to the point of losing itself" (1981, 110).

Early on when he was only 29, before the Shoah and before his internment, Levinas wrote in *On Escape* (2003b) that by oneself there is no escaping oneself. The rest of his writing tells us that escape from the burden of oneself comes only by responding to being called outside oneself and responding ethically to others. Service gives release to enjoy life.

There is a mix of trouble and redemption in this gift. There appears a kind of dualism here. Alongside beautiful descriptions of enjoyment, Levinas discloses the tragic flaw of self-interest and its self-sabotaging vulnerability to pathology. This two-way push-pull is the burden of humanity. From this conflict he points out an alternative path for escape—neither through indulgent hedonism (sweetness eventually sours), nor sacrificial asceticism (self-righteous vanity self-sabotages), nor meditative contemplation (thinking slips into disconnected, dispassionate rationality), but by being called to give one's material goods and oneself for the real needs of others. Because of others, the psyche is both susceptible to psychosis and available for holiness. He reminds us of what is most difficult but expected of us: "All men are not saints, neither are saints always saints. But all men understand the value of holiness" (Levinas 2001, 111).

SIX REVOLUTIONARY DISTINCTIONS

Here is a quick review of Levinas's distinctions before showing their importance for understanding pathology and therapy. He first distinguishes *totality* from *infinity* (1969). *Totality* is the experience of reducing others to "nothing more than" a category, with a label removing them from their uniqueness into commonality. *Infinity* is to experience the Other revealing herself as "always more than" what the self can reach to know. The Other reveals her *infinite otherness*.

His second distinction is between *need* and *desire* (1969). A *need* wants a good in order to fill a lack in the self. *Desire* wants the good for the Other, for the sake of that Other, without expecting reciprocal benefit. The self, with no self-interest, may receive a return good as a happy side effect—feeling good about oneself that comes from wanting the Other's good—even when the intention is *desire* not *need*.

A third distinction is between *freedom* that is *self-initiated/self-directed* and *freedom* that is *invested* in the self (1969). *Self-freedom* is immediately experienced and enjoyed. To be able to do what one wants is good. *But, freedom is only freedom.* It is never unattached. It is first and always invested with responsibility, commanded by others for the good of others. Spontaneous freedom can be fun and productive but can sabotage the responsible freedom invested in the self by the needs of others and, therefore, sabotage the self. Self-freedom can imprison the self in narcissism.

A fourth distinction is between *social equality* and *ethical inequality* (1981). Even as I am a citizen with rights, the Other has rights over me. Levinas carefully inspires us to recognize that responsibility for others has priority over freedom, and to respect and serve before my needs purely for myself are met. Because the Other holds a higher ethical place, I must serve my skills and energy to make myself ready and able to serve. Remember the onboard airplane warning "Place the oxygen mask on yourself first before you help your dependent other."

A fifth distinction is between the *said* and *saying* (1981). The *said* is the content exchanged in conversation. *Saying* is the presence of the Other revealing, "Here I am." Without needing to verbalize, the Other says, "I am here; I am the one before you revealing my presence. It is me here, not a representative of a group with commonalities." The *said* can be contested; the *saying* of the Other cannot be denied. The Other is a subjectivity who commands recognition, inviolability and service, "Do not do me harm. Respect and care for me."

Finally, the *there is…* is distinguished from the *welcoming of the face* of the Other (1981). The *there is…* is experienced as the weightiness of being the ones we are in this given place and at this specific time. At its extreme, this distinction is between the *horror* of isolation and the testimony of *goodness* expressed as an invitation from another. The haunting presence of being burdened by one's own self—trapped in one's skin, separated from others, without an escape—leads to torturous loneliness. But the Other can draw the self out of its imprisoned isolation.

These Distinctions Are Relevant for Psychotherapy

With this review of Levinas's six philosophical distinctions we can prepare to shift our interest to a psychology of a responsible self (Kunz 1998).

First, *totality* and *infinity*. *Totalizing* conveniently *reduces* a client and his symptoms to general categories. *Infinitizing* recognizes the exasperating distinctive otherness of each other. This compromised relationship expresses the deep paradox of simultaneous *closeness* and *distance:* each one's singular identity *here* in this place and *now* at this time and each one's infinite otherness *there* in that place and time, just beyond grasp, provides the individuality for the therapeutic encounter. As a therapist, each client is "in my face" and "alien to me." As a client, the therapist is simultaneously "in my face" and "alien." Only in a face-to-face encounter between two independent others can a meeting for dialogue happen, rather than a mutual reduction of the Other by totalizing.

Second, *need* (self-wanting) and *desire* (wanting the good for the Other). The therapist desires the good of the client above the filling of her own needs. She should not only desire the good of the client but also want him to not be *nothing more than* a needy other. She wants him to *desire* the good for others in his life. She wants him to be responsible. She wants him to be free of his obsessions, compulsions, and addictions in order to be responsibly free.

Third, freedom *from* and *for the self* and freedom *invested*. The egoism of self-freedom can sabotage the good of invested freedom. The therapist does not want her client in a self-enclosed bunker attending only to his needs but to be *obedient*, that is, responsibly open to others. Obedience is not *obeisance*. To be obeisant is an uncalled-for deference to the Other—cowardly bowing—that is a form of violence toward that Other. Obeisance is submitting to another to protect the self without real regard for the good of the Other. The word "obedience" etymologically comes from the Latin, *oboedire* (to harken), from *ob-* (near) and *audīre* (to hear); hence it means to listen closely. To effectively listen to the Other is to be responsible. Cohen writes, "One can suffer mental anguish because one can be morally responsible! The road from mental illness to mental health is not to create from a shattered ego a fortress ego, but to regain one's obligations, one's responsibilities to and for the other" (2002, 48). Obedience serves the good of the Other and allows the self-centered self to get out of itself to find its truer self-for-others.

Fourth, *social equality* (rights of citizens), from an original *ethical inequality* (rights of the Other before the self). The power structure in therapy is paradoxical. While the therapist may have the power of being the official with credentials, scheduling, payment, location, and so on, the client has the ethical power to call the therapist into question. The client comes first. The therapist is responsible for the client's responsibility. While the client should not act unethically toward the therapist, he is not responsible for the therapist in the manner that she is for him.

Fifth, the *said* (the content exchanged), made meaningful by the *saying*. The Other reveals himself *saying*, "Here I am. It's me here expressing my presence." Without even the need to verbalize, saying is the presentation of the client before the therapist. The client reveals himself and witnesses the therapist experiencing his revealed *hereness* with infinite dignity and worth, despite whatever flaws and hurt he has committed. He is a human subjectivity that commands inviolability and service. "Do not violate me, respect my otherness, my goodness, do not reduce me to a diagnostic label; help me." The saying, "Here I am," by the client to the therapist and therapist to client is the fundamental peaceable dialogue. Therapy is primarily *speaking to* before it is *speaking about*.

Sixth, the *there is*. . . the irremovable burden of being in this place at this time. That I am the one here can be transcended by the *welcoming face* of the Other (calling me out), escaping my absolute isolation through responsibility to others. Everyone experiences loneliness, the inescapable weight of being only oneself. Clients speak of the crushing weight of the isolation of their existence with their anxiety from obsessions, compulsions, delusions, perhaps haunted by hallucinations. They would like to be other than who they are. They also tell about the freeing salvation from the faces of others inviting them out. Therapy is an invitation by the therapist for the client to "come out." It is an invitation by the client for the therapist to "enter in" to the depth of his psyche.

The Paradox of Power and Weakness

These six distinctions provide the bases for two corresponding paradoxes: the *weakness* of *power,* in that power sabotages itself, and the *power* of *weakness,* in that weakness commands attention and help (Kunz 1998).

The weakness of power. The powers of *cognition, behavior,* and *affectivity* are susceptible to undoing themselves by their own power. While knowledge is power, independent cognition can be self-deceptive, thus leading to arrogant illusions of comprehension and certainty. While practiced behavior serves us better than ineptitude, laziness, and cowardice, self-attributed success can be seductive, leading to illusions of control through compulsive manipulation and abuse. While affective enjoyment is better than suffering, self-indulgent consumption can be seductive, leading to self-destructive addictions.

The paradox of the weakness of power is fundamental for psychotherapy. The abuses received by clients and their hurting others call for singular therapeutic approaches. Unlike the medical doctor, the therapist faces an individual whose *singularity* is unique in every way. The power of her expertise must be weakened by the radical otherness of the client. The good therapist is present to the client's distinctiveness. The client's cognitive understanding may be *like* others, but it is his alone. His behavior may be *analogous* to others, but it is unique. His affectivity may be *similar* to others, but his pain and pleasure are singular.

The power of weakness. The therapist is subjected to the power of the client's weakness. Her power of *disclosing* who she thinks he is cannot match his *revealing* who he is. The client's meanings cannot be disclosed by the therapist through her knowledge. The client reveals himself. To *disclose* is to search and find the meaning sought. To *reveal* is to show oneself, to expose one's vulnerability and trust the Other to be open and respectful of what is exposed. To "disclose" is an active verb. To have the Other revealed to the self is a passive experience. The coal miner with his headlight and the therapist with her theory both disclose. They do not just look for what is there; their illumination highlights the ore and the symptoms structured by the lamps of their insights and skills. Their lights disclose what they look for, and then the miner and the therapist choose from their equipment just the right technique to extract *the mother lode*. Their lights' *brilliance* shines on the *reality* they already anticipate to be there. They see what they want to see.

In contrast, the client's *revelation* is like a *prophetic manifestation,* or as Levinas says, an *epiphany* (1981). This *manifestation* is a *religious* event. The client's life is sacred. The revelation of lived pain and confusion manifests this sacredness. The word "religion" is not primarily a theological term. It comes from the Latin: *re* (repeatedly) and *ligare* (to bind). Religious acts bind us again and again to those to whom we are already bound but bind us more dearly, to the widow, the orphan, the stranger, and to God by way of others. Trust of the client to reveal himself is a religious event asking for contact closer than presence; the therapist hopes for sacred susceptibility to his request for a presence that is responsible. The client must bond uniquely and continuously in trust to the therapist. The good therapist must bond uniquely and continuously with trust in return. In the deepest sense, it is a religious event. The proximity of the suffering client is a *closeness* closer than being present, being nearby. His suffering is a vulnerability that invites bonding of responsibility.

Trapped in his skin, the client asks for the graciousness of the therapist to be open to his story, respect his efforts to change, and be patient with him. To listen to his revelation is to accept his trust to bond in return. No profession is more concentrated in the event of the face-to-face than psychotherapy. The essential work of therapy is to endure this facing face revealing itself for bonding. When the client understands that the therapist's weakness cannot penetrate his subjectivity, cannot fix his life, cannot relieve his pain, yet cares for him enough to *listen*, to *stand-under*, and to *suffer* him, then he knows that he can reveal himself to her—and to himself—from his hiding places. He can be welcomed out of solitude into responsible behavior. He can own his pain and choose to suffer for others, all within this ethical arena of the singular concern of the therapist. Alone, the client is not alone. Unlovable for what he has done, he is loved for who he is. Troubled, he is worth troubling his therapist. He can be for others and discover who he is: the isolated one who's self-constraining and self-sabotaging *being-for-himself* can be transformed into his singular *being-for-others*.

Levinas and Responsibility

Levinas takes this notion of responsibility further than we may want. In *Otherwise than Being* (1981), he offers an extraordinary description of the enigma of the burden of being human:

> The psyche [of both the client and therapist] is the form of a peculiar dephasing, a loosening up or unclamping of identity: the same [self] prevented from coinciding with itself, at odds, torn up from its rest, between sleep and insomnia, panting, shivering. It is not an abdication of the self, not alienated and slave to the other, but an abnegation of oneself fully responsible for the other. This identity is brought out by responsibility and is at the service of the other. In the form of responsibility, the *psyche in the soul is the other in me,* a malady of identity, both accused and self, the same for the other, the same by the other. (68–69)

Therapists see dephasing, tearing apart, panting and shivering in clients, what they call de-compensation. The psyche for the Other is a malady of being accused by the Other. However, the Other's commands do not physically restrain nor are his demands to do forced labor. They are mandatory *moral* directives, authoritative obligations, *ethical* imperatives given by the presence of the face of the Other. Therapists experience their own dephasing, tearing apart, panting, shivering, not only from secondary trauma listening to painful stories but from the weight of responsibility for clients. Levinas challenges the traditional Socratic command to "know thyself," *on your own,* with the paradoxical command from the Other to "reveal thyself" as responsible and in this way come to know thyself. Despite the tendency toward self-absorption and avoidance of suffering, the psyche of the therapist can be (note the passive voice) transformed: "from the start, the other effects us despite ourselves" (1981, 129). The client's suffering hurts the therapist and calls her out of herself. When the therapist places the client's suffering before her own, she heals herself.

The client's escape from self-sabotaging existence can be helped by the therapist's transcending her own self-sabotaging *obsessive, compulsive,* and *addictive* existence by means of her incarnate, embodied *simple, humble,* and *patient* existence. These are the exasperating gifts of the singularity (Bozga) of both client and therapist.

The Client's Isolation

Before examining *simplicity, humility,* and *patience,* let's turn to the client's isolation. In *A Different Existence,* J. H. van den Berg defines the study of psychopathology as "the science of loneliness" (1972, 103). The pathological individual is alone, isolated from the world while rooted in it. He is disconnected from *things,* his own *body, others,* his *past* and *future,* while also chained to them. He suffers *cognitive, behavioral,* and *affective* isolation.

Cognitive isolation. Haunted by *obsessions,* the disturbed person denies himself openness. He narrows his attention to guard against surprise. Fearing the coming of anything new and unpredictable, he is held in the isolation of either tranquilized *undisturbance* or chaotic *disturbance* of thoughts, flashbacks, fears, the threatening closeness of others. He is trapped in his disturbed self.

Behavioral isolation. Constricted by *compulsive* habits, he limits any efficient, creative, and generous movements in encounters with others. The stuff of the world is the infrastructure of things for *furnishings, tools,* and *gifts.* His rituals limit work and play with others across this horizon of stuff. He cannot grope into the mysterious "there is..." that stretches beyond the familiar, in search of the possibly scary unknown, in order to reconnect with *things,* his own *body, others,* and *time.*

Affective isolation. Gripped by *addictions* to escape suffering, he suffers more self-destruction. Victimized by his own suffering, he is insensitive to the suffering of others and therefore restricts his possibilities for love and joy. His narcissism conspires to sabotage his freedom and condemns him to paranoid fear.

The Therapist's Isolation

The therapist suffers isolation because her client suffers isolation. His suffering "traumatizes" (Levinas 1981) her. Not unlike her client, the therapist suffers confusion, impotent futility, and numbing apathy.

The therapist suffers *cognitive* isolation. The client's resistance to her efforts to disclose him leaves her in the dark. Jan Rowe—beloved faculty member and supervisor of our students, who died in

2007—described therapy as "working in the dark." The client may try to open himself, while the therapist struggles to find some meaning to be *understood* but never understands *enough*. She cannot prompt him with speculations. She must be responsibly available to her client in this dark place. When she speaks to him with merely *said* words without *saying* "Here I am, I am listening," her talk is only rhetoric. Frustrated about what he has *said*, she struggles to listen, to encounter him in face-to-face conversation. He needs her to attend to his *saying*, "Here I am." But her attention is *never* quite *enough*.

The therapist suffers *behavioral* isolation. She is impotent to change the client's habits. She cannot change the violence and indifference he has received from family, friends, coworkers. She can change neither his situation nor him, but neither can she be paralyzed and do nothing. Just sitting seems like detaching and isolating, like *not enough*. But sitting there—at more than spatial closeness, but there, revealing her responsibility for him—may be enough to start. It can be the *standing-under* he needs for support. He needs her responsible presence of her face facing him.

She suffers *affective* isolation. She is unable to suffer his suffering. She knows she cannot suffer his pain. She may even feel she is *apathetic*, insufficiently compassionate. She suffers because he suffers; but her suffering feels *not enough*. She deserves to suffer as he, but she can't. She suffers paralysis similar to a survivor's guilt. But he needs her to suffer being there for him.

Questioned and Exposed, the Therapist Confesses Responsibility

Levinas writes, "Finding the guilt in ourselves and taking responsibility for the Other is the most profound experience of subjectivity" (1981, 87). Developmentally, a subject forms identity by fulfilling needs and by enjoying stuff. "Life is love of life" (Levinas 1969, 112). The existentialist has called *authenticity* knowing one will die and taking a stand toward one's death. But for Levinas, deeper subjectivity is being present as the one before the Other, called to individual responsibility, aware of being *subjected* as hostage to the Other, with no escape but finding openness, service, and love. Levinas finds *authenticity* in knowing oneself to be responsible for the Other, even for the death of the Other.

The therapist is called to responsibility, but whatever her response it is *never enough*. There is no response able to reduce the needs of the client to what she can provide. For the therapist, psychotherapy is not a personal act of altruism but a response of responsibility. To recognize one's own guilt for *not knowing enough, not being skilled enough, falling short on compassion* is the ground for doing *good enough* therapy.

Levinas evokes this experience of responsibility with extravagant images: "We are traumatized, persecuted, pained, held hostage" (1981, 87). He adds, "In a sense nothing is more burdensome than a neighbor" (88). Maybe nothing is more burdensome than a client, because of the weight of responsibility. "Burden," "trauma," and "persecution" are strong words to describe the effect on us brought about by the presence of the Other, but Levinas uses them deliberately, to describe the interpersonal, as always an "undergoing." Allowing herself to be burdened, held hostage, and persecuted is commanded of the therapist undergoing her client.

Acknowledging her *ignorance* and her *clumsy groping to* do something can be the therapist's "useful suffering." Levinas (1998a) describes in his powerful article "Useless Suffering" that all suffering is useless except that which is suffered for the good of another. The commitment of responsibility without promise of success, without expectation of reward are the therapist's nonuseless suffering. We are not called to be successful—only to be faithful (Mother Theresa, quoted in *The Promises of God* [Warner 2005, 124]).

What Does the Client Ask of the Therapist?

He asks for therapy to be therapeutic, for her weakness to be vulnerable, to accept responsibility, to listen, to serve, and to suffer him. He asks for *simplicity,* for her to *know him by not knowing,* to be open to him by not obsessing about what theories and labels she can make him fit into, holding back knowledge in order to listen to the meanings he reveals. He asks for *humility,* for her to *act by not acting,* being present without practicing techniques, without manipulating him. He asks for *patience,* to not try to suffer his suffering, but to suffer him because he suffers. These experiences of taking hold of herself to support her client originate neither from her virtuous *dispositions,* nor from her practiced *habits* for self-improved techniques, nor from her self-acquired styles of *moral excellence*. One cannot willfully decide to be *simple, humble,* and *patient*. These are the exasperating gifts (Bozga 2009) of scandalous obligation (Severson 2011), painfully inspired by one in the Other, by the client in the therapist, and hopefully by the therapist in the client.

Client and therapist sit together not as experts but as two persons responding to each other. He lives his story; she *undergoes* his telling it. Their unprotected openness inspires both to *simplicity,* to honesty deeper than each could imagine. They listen. Even without speaking, the client asks the therapist to use the freedom he has invested in her to attend to him. The therapist asks the client to use the freedom invested in him to listen to others.

They sit together, *impotent* with inadequate technical skills. He asks her to do something about his confusion and suffering; he cannot do it alone. She cannot change him but can help him choose to change. Neither is a mechanic or a miracle worker, nor are they disabled klutzes. They talk to each other. Their talk is primarily speaking *to* each other, and secondarily speaking *about* anything. They dialogue in an arena of trust. Choices get made when trust is laid.

They often sit in a kind of stunned *numbness,* unable to feel the Other's suffering. Their faces say "I hurt; be *patient;* don't dismiss or abandon me; suffer my unworthiness because I am worthy." Listening and suffering in psychotherapy is saying, "Here I am committed to you." Their suffering is redemptive.

What Does the Therapist Ask of the Client?

She asks him to live a good life by being *weak enough* to be responsible toward others. Of course, she wants him to be free—but free to be open to others without obsessive pre-judging. She must help the client learn to "know others by not knowing them." She wants him to be *simple,* to be available to see and hear the concerns of others, and therefore to be vulnerable to pain and joy. She wants him to welcome surprise, to live situations and face others, "as if for the first time" (Halling 1975). She wants him to be curious but not voyeuristic. She wants him to expect puzzles and confusions and laughter at his own clumsiness as he tests himself in work, play, and love. She wants him free from isolation.

She wants him to be able to chat. "Chatter" is too quickly dismissed as mindless distraction. "Idle talk" may indeed be used to escape facing reality, but it is generally healthy. Casual conversation about the weather, sports, TV can be topics for responsible facing. It need not be heavy discussion but a kind of play, testing that the same world is available and enjoyed by both. Sharing commonalities bond people. Even some gossip can connect one to another as a kind of solicitation to be alike and acceptance to join the way we think. Talking is first talking *to* before it is talking *about*. It is *between* them as Buber and Gadamer point out.

The therapist wants her client to be *humble*, "to act by not acting," to be free of compulsive behavior in order to begin each moment as new, in order to encounter others, released from the sedimented rituals that have dominated his life. She wants her client to recognize the vulnerability of others, asking to not be manipulated by him. The therapist wants him to be helpful—not in slavish servitude, not obeisance, not bowing and groveling, but with obedience to the real needs of others. She wants him to play with things, to hold and caress objects as lovely pieces of nature or things fashioned by others as gifts for enjoyment. Common tools and furnishings are the meeting ground, the infrastructure that supports his encounters with others. She wants him to be grateful toward others. Gratitude is the heart of a healthy psyche.

She wants him to test his body, to stretch beyond his stilted postures, to have the courage to extend beyond his comfort zone. She wants him to learn to *grope,* to risk searching in the dark for what can be surprisingly enjoyable and/or painfully learnable. She wants him to interact with others in the back-and-forth play of dialogue and joking, giving and receiving.

She wants him to be whimsical but not so *capricious* that he victimizes others and himself with foolishness. She does not want him to hurt others and sabotage himself. She is given responsibility for his responsibility from his request, "Help me regain responsible freedom." She is not responsible for his behaviors, but she has the responsibility to help him deepen his sense of obligation. She does not want to take away his freedom but wants for him to open himself to allow others to invest responsible freedom in him. She wants him to care, to be responsible for the responsibility of others. The client serves his own responsible freedom by serving the freedom of others.

The therapist does not want the client to take upon the suffering of others but wants him to suffer *because* they suffer. She models genuine compassion by suffering because he suffers, so he can suffer others because they suffer. The psychotherapist suffers the client because she values his infinite goodness within his suffering. Neither his suffering nor his inflicting of suffering on others is good. He learns that ethical behavior is good because others are good and their suffering is not good and he wants them to not suffer. When clients suffer others with vulnerable *simplicity, humility, and patience,* healing happens. She wants to enjoy his company so he can enjoy the company of others.

How to conclude? Pathology is isolation from ethical responsibility. Health is getting outside oneself in responsibility to others. Therapy comes when the client becomes responsibly responsible toward others in his life.

Emilie's Poem

Halfway down my street I recognize instantly,
my house stands out amongst the many,
yet is held in place by its neighbors.

It has a "street front" but also its secrecy.

My facade, the word ties itself
back to the face. The face of my building,
my home, my structure that holds and contains
all of me, to my very core. The skin I carry,
protects and presents.

The face of my building, marks the outside,
the very boundary of me,
covered in a coat of paint,
sturdy and steadfast but not impenetrable.

We're not made a fortress. Our windows,
let in light, greet the world outside.
Growing up, an Indian family came to stay.
Unnerved by such construction,
the father simply wished to let in some air,
blind to the handle, he unhinged
the entire frame instead. Unpredictably,
a window landed in the garden,
right in front of my feet.

We're not solitary but nestled in. The weeds anchor
the earth, strengthen our foundation. The concrete
covers over and it's easy to forget.

Each day the Other beckons me out.
Tantalizingly, calls down the street, leads me

out of my familiarity. Each day I venture too,
to work and gather things for my enjoyment.

In need of a return, a home to digest,
this is where I dwell. The key fits without question.
Unloading my goods I scan my living room.
My reflection, my expression surrounding me
but *recollection refers to a welcome.*
It's a chance to catch up, while secretly
I eat my soup, curled up on top of the stove.

This is all my own, and yet who is it for?
For who, do I string little lanterns onto lights?

My decoration, my music and my story,
I collect. In the absence of an audience
it might pass unnoticed, yet it offers

an entry into my interior domain.

There must be — I believe —
a reason inside and out,
are separated by skin, a facade or a coat. On
different sides, there's only a step in-between.

By this split,
all that I have, and know and collect,
the little spinning universe I call my own,
the random relics I have come to hold,
are questioned, by the stranger welcomed
onto the doorstep. With a single suspicious
glance, with a chiropractical subtle move,
my bone structure is revealed.

In that split second,
of recognition coming forth,
I stand the chance to find
more than I can give.

With all that I hold on to, I lose.
With all that I loose, I gain some more.

Or so I hope. The space once carved,
bears its purpose and my own.

In the private practice more room is unfilled.

The stories told and unfold, demand all that I've
got, inside and out. Halfway down his street, I
see only his facade. How easy to strip him from
his walls, blast open this defense, dismantle his
guard.

In a position of power, why not push our way
in?

But what would we find, exposed, uncovered
and unwelcomed? Who might withstand such
invasion?

Therein falls the stranger, expelled
from his home. I am left roaming
through his hull. Herein too
lies the danger of our collapse.

A house without walls is not a house.
A stranger, without a face may not exist,
but rather we find a door in both.
Rather, we trust and await a way in.

                                        Emilie Zuckerman

Notable Events, Works, and Personal Characteristics of Emmanuel Levinas

George Kunz

Levinas gave us only eleven sentences as a biography. He began with "The Hebrew Bible from the childhood years in Lithuania, Pushkin and Tolstoy, the Russian Revolution of 1917 experienced at eleven years of age in the Ukraine." He ended with "This disparate inventory is a biography." He added another sentence, "It is dominated by the presentiment and the memory of the Nazi horror" (Levinas 1990a, 291). There followed four more pages of the development of his thought. Biographers have found more in interviews. The remainder of this chapter is taken from those biographies.[1]

The deepest and longest influence on Levinas was that he was born into a traditionally observant Jewish family on December 30, 1905, in Kovno (Kaunas), Lithuania. They read the Bible, attended synagogue, ate kosher, observed Shabbat (Malka 2002, 6). He inherited thousands of years of religious bonding. In 1914, after the German invasion, the family emigrated to Kiev, Ukraine. In an interview in 1986 he recalled, "I learned to read Russian from the label on the cocoa in the morning" (Robbins 2001, 26), and having a Russian speaking mother may have helped. He went on to read "Pushkin, Lermontov, Gogol, Turgenev, Tolstoy, and Dostoyevsky, above all, Dostoyevsky" (26). Their stories were preoccupied with fundamental things, shot through with anxiety and the search for the meaning of life (28). Their characters were self-destructively trapped in their own *being-for-the-self,* and some escaped when they behaved as a *being-for-the-other.*

The family returned to Kovno when he was 15. Two years later he went to the University of Strasbourg, France, to major in philosophy. He took sociology and a class from Charles Blondel, "a psychology professor who was very anti-Freudian . . . and very quickly became a man to whom I could say anything" (Malka, 2002, 29). In 1928 he went to the University of Freiburg to study with Edmund Husserl. He later said, "I went to see Husserl and found Heidegger. The way in which he practiced phenomenology in *Being and Time*—I knew immediately that this was one of the greatest philosophers in history" (32).

During the 1930s in Paris he became enthralled by the Enlightenment and the revolutionary spirit of Western Europe. He drifted from Jewish to Greek thinking until the Holocaust betrayed the spirit of the Enlightenment. In 1932 he began to write and then abandoned a book on Heidegger. He came to regret his earlier enthusiasm not only because he could never forgive Heidegger's Nazism but also for his placing *ontology* before *ethics,* that is, placing the *being-for-oneself* of Dasein (Heidegger's term for the human, the being who is there for himself) before *being-for-others.*

He also inherited the Western philosophical tradition. As Michael Kigel described in his translator's notes for *Emmanuel Levinas,* for centuries, ethics had been based on the metaphysics of theology, with blind faith toward the moral authority of an Infinite Being. Then, with the Enlightenment, Immanuel Kant established authority on the autonomy of the moral law, which was basically an internalized theology that equated itself with morality. Reason crowded out a distant deity. But this new authority was destroyed by Hitler. "Nothing was official anymore. Nothing was objective" (Malka 2002, xx). Nothing was sacred. "The face of the Other was exposed in its utter nakedness and vulnerability, abandoned and unprotected, open to any unanchored phenomenology that could now interpret the weakness of the face as a license to violate" (xx–xxi). "The Nazi horror belongs to the order of catastrophe and trauma" (xviii). He admitted that this "wound in memory" dominated all his writing.

So how are humans to decide on ethical behavior after the collapse of both metaphysical and rational authority? God was dead for those who were "enlightened," and reason could no longer be trusted. Given a first premise that select others were less than human, only objects in the way, both a God and reason could justify violence. Levinas described a radically new authority in the *face-of-the-other-person* showing itself to be a nonauthoritative moral authority. Of course, many believers kept faith in *divine justice;* many others in *reason;* many do not believe in ethics: for them, "homo homini Lupus est."[2] Levinas reestablishes ethics in an epi-phenomenological way. His approach is not a theology, not a philosophy, not even a method of logical thinking. It inspires looking and listening in order to get a glimpse of the infinite otherness and goodness of the Other always just out of phenomenal reach, yet "always already" commanding respect and service. This strange philosophy elevates the phenomenological task for an openness of *sensibility,* not of cognition but of *sense,* to the revelation of what is beyond *what shows itself,* the face of the Other calling for responsibility.

Where had the *face* been all these centuries? Did it only show up for Levinas? Of course not. The face "always already" has been *there* in the accusative, demanding the self to not kill, to not harm, to not reduce to an object. God has been there, not as a big manipulating metaphysical being imagined by the pious to be directly communicating messages that must be blindly believed. Rather, God reveals morality through the faces of others. Reason has always been evoked, not by itself out of itself but by the command of others. Reason is called forth to "figure it out" with its repertoire of cognitive, behavioral, affective powers to find the proper response to protect and serve the needs of the Other. The face was the *trace* of God saying, "Thou shalt not kill. Thou shalt not harm. Thou shalt not reduce me to an object to be known." Levinas reminds us that we have no choice whether to *be* responsible or not but only in *how* to respond. That is the task of reason and will to these unchosen commands. This ambiguity, "I must, but I'm not sure how," is the source of our anxiety and *insomnia.*

From 1930 to 1979, interrupted by the war, Levinas taught at the École Normale Orientale (ENIO), attached to the Alliance Israelite Universelle in Paris, a school for mostly North African students to teach Judaism in their home country. The students remembered him as a small energetic man, like a tight ball of nerves pacing the hallways (Malka 2002).

He had extensive, rather routine and trying responsibilities for the day-to-day welfare of ENIO students. He could lose his temper with the unruly but was remembered as paternal, at times a humorous teasing grown-up. They all admired him (Malka 2002). Because he did not have the *agregation* (the civil service examination for teaching in the public school system) in philosophy, he could not apply for a university position. Why? He admitted that he did not know Greek (Critchley and Bernasconi 2002, xviii). With his thesis, *The Theory of Intuition in Husserl's Phenomenology,* he received a doctorate from the Institut de France. He became a naturalized citizen and, with a new passport, returned in 1932 to Lithuania to betroth Raissa Levy, his neighbor's daughter, and brought her back to Paris. Sartre credited him for bringing the phenomenology of Husserl and Heidegger to Paris with his publications and translations in the 1930s (Critchley and Bernasconi 2002, 1).

In 1934, before Hitler became chancellor, Levinas wrote a prescient article, "Reflections on the Philosophy of Hitlerism" (Levinas 1990c), which prefigured themes yet to come. Shortly after that, he published his first original thematic essay, "De l'évasion" (1935).[3] Its English translator, Bettina Bergo (*On Escape*) attended our first Psychology for the Other seminar at Seattle University, in 2003. *On Escape* is short and packed with sociological and psychological insights on how we try to escape being who we are. Jacques Roland as editor of the 1981 edition wrote that Levinas's project in 1935 was to renew the problem of *being* (Levinas 2003b, 110). Heidegger in 1928 had said all there was to be said about *being* (*Zein und Zeit*). But Levinas, already challenging Heidegger, reveals in *being* a *defect* or *taint* (2003b, 10). He finds the human riveted to its being and struggling to get out. "Thus, escape is the need to get out of oneself, that is, to break that most radical and unalterable binding of chains, the fact that the 'I' is oneself" (55). He unfolds psychological experiences of inner disturbances—*unmet needs, disappointments when met, malaise, shame,* and *nausea,* all experienced as embodied (29). Psychotherapists face these in the room. They should ask Levinas to scrub up and assist them.

Need is not simply a negative, a lack in the self. Positively, needs allow us to seek from the outside what will fill us inside for satisfaction and the enjoyment of its pleasures. We are happy to have needs so long as they do not develop into suffering. But pleasure is concentrated in the instant because the satisfaction of a need does not destroy it. Need returns, always reborn, sometimes addictive. Unsatisfied needs bring *disappointment* and *discouragement*. Satisfied needs often bring disappointment—their pleasures are not quite what was anticipated—and when they do, they can bring *shame*. Ordinarily we take shame to be from an immoral act: ashamed for failing to be responsible. Levinas, however, relates shame to being incapable of escaping. We do not want others to see us for who we are: ashamed of being caught in "intimacy with itself," always too self-concerned, exposed as selfish. We want to hide or cover over our egoism. Shame discovers an existence that seeks excuses. *Malaise* is the effort to escape but without a clear goal. We just get tired of our needy selves, and tired of being tired. *Nausea* is malaise in pure form: desperate to get out, powerless to leave, revolted from the inside, we feel like *heaving, vomiting* out those shameful pleasures, even our innards. Take note, therapists; his word choices may be more extravagant than you would use, but they fit. There is plenty of indigestion in *On Escape* (2003b) to digest.

Totality and Infinity (Levinas 1969) first appeared in 1961. It is filled with valuable psychological distinctions that I can only list here: between *totalizing* and *infinitizing; needing* and *desiring; initiating* freedom *for-ourselves* and finding freedom *invested-by-and-for-others;* being socially *equal* and ethically *unequal,* as the Other has rights over me; behaving *actively* and receiving *passively;* the *saying* and the *said; suffering* the horror of the *there is*. . .and *being welcomed* by others. These distinctions are often used by the authors of this collection.

In "Useless Suffering,"[4] he describes the effort to find meaning in what is utterly meaningless: *suffering.* "Pain is an undiluted malignity; it is suffering for nothing and every effort to try to make the other's suffering make sense is odious" (98). Levinas would recommend psychotherapists pause in their attempts to make theoretical meaning out of what is inherently meaningless, especially that pain that absorbs the rest of consciousness. Therapists add violence in trying to comfort clients by positing causes, especially hidden causes that evade challenge

(93). Psychological theories are ideologies: explanations that serve the vested interest of the ideologue but not the sufferer's. Levinas calls for the end of theodicy—justifying God by making meaning out of suffering. Psychologists should call for the end of theory and of justifying themselves by insisting on meanings for suffering. They should get back to describing its uselessness so clients can get back to living a useful life. Suffering is meaningful only when suffered for the good of others.

Levinas is a *behaviorist*. He urges us to attend to our behavior directed toward others. It is our responsibility for others that we derive our consciousness of others (Malka 2002, 280). Every action is ethical. Psychology could be the science of responsible behavior, including its excuses. Psychotherapy is the art of helping others face their excuses and discover how their *intended* service to others offers unintended escape for their healing.

Returning to biographical events: his daughter, Simone Levinas, was born in 1935. (Hosting the North American Levinas Society conference in 2008 at Seattle University, we were deeply honored by her attendance at our Psychology for the Other seminar along with her family.[5]) Then in 1939 Levinas reported for military duty as a translator of German and Russian. His Jewish unit, quickly forced to surrender on June 18, 1940, spent the next five years as military prisoners. His uniform saved him from the death camps. Enduring hunger, separation from his wife and daughter, back-breaking labor, submission to the arbitrary, and also the kindness and sacrifices of fellow prisoners deepened his thinking about ethical behavior. Returning each day to camp from chopping wood, the prisoners were met by a stray dog they named Bobby, "the only one who treated us as humans, the last Kantian in Nazi Germany" (Malka 2002, 71). Only after liberation did he hear that his father, mother, two younger brothers, and both maternal and paternal grandparents were all murdered in Lithuania by Nazi collaborators. His friend since Freiburg days, Maurice Blanchot, helped his wife, Raissa, and daughter, Simone, hide in a Catholic monastery in Orleans, France. After the war Levinas vowed never to set foot again on German soil.

Returning in 1945 he regularly attended lectures at the Sorbonne, the Saturday soirees of Gabriel Marcel, and the regular conferences at the Collège Philosophique founded by Jean Wahl in 1947. His dear

friend Dr. Nerson introduced him to the mysterious peripatetic vaga-
bond called M. Chouchani (nobody knew his real name, where he
was from, where educated), the prestigious and merciless teacher of
exegesis and Talmud. This strange and brilliant man helped Levinas
reengage his Judaism.

Time and the Other (1987), a collection of four lectures for which
he had also jotted down notes in the German camp, was published
two years after his liberation, in 1947. The next year, in 1948, he published his first original book, *Existence and Existents* (2001). It offers
powerful psychological descriptions of everyday phenomena: *insomnia, fatigue, effort, sensuous enjoyment, erotic life, birth,* and *the relation to death.* He introduced the term *hypostasis*—*hypo* (under) and
stasis (stand)—to indicate the showing up of the self standing under
itself to move from simply *existing* to being an *existent*, a responsible person (Levinas 2001). This is a helpful notion for therapeutic
change—for clients' coming out of themselves to take possession of
themselves. In this book he tended to use the male point of view. In
her preface to *The Second Sex* (2009), Simone de Beauvoir justifiably
criticized his description of the feminine as the Other to the masculine. Recently there has been renewed interest among feminist philosophers who still take issue with his language but find a strong support
for gender equality (see Atterton and Calarco 2010). Also in 1948,
Levinas published "Reality and Its Shadow" (Levinas 1989, 129–43),
a critique of art published in *Les Temps Modernes* with a critical note
attached by either Merleau-Ponty or Sartre, co-editors.

Back to his daughter, Simone, who remembers him while writing
"sleeping only six hours a night; he had insomnia struggling to *get
it right* with multiple erasures, tearing up, starting over, losing his
temper with himself because it was forever not ready" (Malka 2002,
230). (Some solace for those insecure in writing.) Michael, his son,
remembers his father nearly tearing up the manuscript of *Totality
and Infinity* when it was first refused publication. Jean Wahl urged
him to try again and Fr. Herman van Breda, from Louvain, Belgium,
came and took the book to be published by Martinus Nijhoff in 1961
(Malka 2002, 267).

In 1964 Jacques Derrida published "Violence and Metaphysics"
(1978) in French, the first extensive and critical essay on *Totality
and Infinity* (Malka 2002, 172). Derrida thought Levinas used too

much ontological language while criticizing the ontology of Western philosophy. Levinas responded to Derrida's critique: "Basically, you reproach me for taking the Greek *logos* in the same way one takes a bus, in order to get off" (176). Derrida was a devoted student of Levinas and expressed this so warmly in his funeral oration, *Adieu to Emmanuel Levinas* (1999): "to someone whose thought, friendship, trust, and 'goodness'...will have been for me a living source" (quoted in Malka 2002, 185). Derrida's critique likely urged Levinas to write *Otherwise than Being, or Beyond Essence* (1981) where he did get off the Greek logos bus. He turned up the intensity, moving from the language of *ontology* and toward the language of *substitution* and stressed even more the responsibility of *subjectivity* (Malka 2002, 172). "To be oneself, the state of being as hostage, is always to have one degree of responsibility more, the responsibility for the responsibility of the other" (Levinas 1981, 117).

That he wrote brilliantly beginning in the 1930s but did not get much notice until the 1970s was explained by Jean Luc Marion: "No one understood what he was saying. His phenomenology was in its purest form" (Malka 2002, 275). Levinas challenged the defenses of philosophers in his use of both difficult language and the hyperbolic accusative form. Levinas did not accuse but described the face of the Other as accusative. Psychotherapists could well notice his rich psychological insights. Psychotherapists could also consult the many secondary authors like the psychoanalyst Paul Marcus (2008) who understand what he was saying and who write accessible and inspiring expositions.

In 1974, *Otherwise than Being, or Beyond Essence* appeared. We can only list without context some of his dramatic terms that are helpful to therapists who witness these dramas in the room: *trauma of accusation, exposure to outrage, wounding, hostage, coring out of the ego, obsession, persecution, expiation,* but also *forgiveness, nourishment, maternity, obedience, appeal, sanctity, here-I-am.* Rich in psychological insights, this was to become his most important work and the most difficult to read. In the 1970s, Edith Wyschogrod published *Emmanuel Levinas: The Problem of Ethical Metaphysics* (1974), the first book-length study of Levinas in English. She visited us here at Seattle University in 1983.

In 1980 Levinas met John Paul II. The pope then invited him to his gathering of philosophers at his summer retreat in 1983 and again in 1985. Reminding them of the Crusades, the pogroms, and the Holocaust, Levinas had a circle of Christian friends. When asked what Christians could learn from Levinas, Adriaan Peperzak, a priest from Holland, responded that it was his critique of the mystical, that whenever charity is missing mysticism is led astray (Malka 2002, 249). Psychologists could analogously ask what they could learn from Levinas. While some accuse him of being too abstract, too disconnected from life, perhaps too religious, too spiritual, too mystical, Levinas was critical of both mysticism and abstract theory. He could be called a philosopher of the concrete: he describes the here-and-now face of the Other in her or his here-and-now situation, calling the "I" in its here-and-now presence, unable to escape its own skin. The "I" must not only be inspired to awe, it must act. Turning away, to not act, is to act. The proximity in the face-to-face event is radically objective, that is, it is given without choice and subjective interpretation. Nothing is more "objectively" *there* than the face-of-the-Other resisting any interpretative reduction by an "objectively" *here* subject, rooted in itself.

Roger Burggraeve, a priest from the Catholic University of Louvain, Belgium, helped set up Levinas's archives there alongside Husserl's. He declared that Levinas brought to Christian thought an inspiration, a reference point, more than a path to follow. He claimed he "become a better Christian thanks to Levinas" (Malka 2002, 208). Peperzak, however, responding to the same question replied that he had perhaps become less a Christian. "He made me rethink the basis for theology. I perhaps become more of a believer in humanity, because Levinas was not only a master who taught thinking but also a model for how to live life" (Malka 2002, 208). Levinas could help psychotherapists become better believers in the infinite goodness and otherness of clients, in their vulnerability and command to be helped, and in the goodness and command of the other Others in their lives to be helped by clients.

Ethics and Infinity: Conversations with Philippe Nemo first appeared on French radio in 1982 and then were collected and translated by Richard Cohen in 1985. (Cohen has provided us a penetrating and generous preface for this collection.) These conversations, covering a wide range of topics, are probably the most accessible for unprepared readers. I have often assigned students three of my favorite chapters, "The Face" (Levinas 1985, 83–92), "Responsibility for the Other" (95–101), and "The Glory of Testimony" (103–10). Also in 1982, Michael, his son, traveled to Heidelberg to accept the Karl Jaspers Prize for his father, because of Levinas's vow never to return to Germany (Malka 2002, 261).

Almost hidden from psychologists are articles by and about Levinas. Alphonso Lingis translated into English the *Collected Philosophical Papers* in 1987 (Levinas 1997). *Outside the Subject,* a collection of late philosophical papers, was also published in 1987. A very important collection of his papers and interviews, *Entre Nous: Thinking of the Other,* came out in 1991 (Levinas 1998a); *Alterity and Transcendence* (2000), a collection of occasional texts, encyclopedia entries, and interviews, came out in 1995; then *Basic Philosophical Writings* came out in 1996. He was a very busy man, barely keeping ahead of his translators. There are many excellent secondary sources: *Face to Face with Levinas,* an important collection of articles by several scholars edited by Cohen (1986); *The Provocation of Levinas,* edited by Robert Bernasconi and David Wood (1988); *Re-Reading Levinas,* articles edited by Robert Bernasconi and Simon Critchley (1991). Don't forget Atterton and Calarco's *Radicalizing Levinas* (2010).

His beloved "Rainka," from whom he could not be separated according to his children (Malka 2002, 241) died in 1994. Levinas missed his wife terribly, became increasingly ill, and died on December 25, a year later. Jacques Derrida read his eulogy "Adieu," at the cemetery to several groups of mourners. First was his family, Simone and husband, Georges, their children and grandchildren, and Michael. Another group was made up of the neighbors from their synagogue. Without a rabbi, Emmanuel, son of Yokhiel the Levite, was the center of this community, holding the post of teacher and spiritual guide, always insightful, always reserved and discrete, always in control, never coming across as warm. A third group was his former students at ENIO, once the boys and girls for whom he was principal, teacher, and mentor, the one who had remembered every face, name, wedding, birth of children and those who died. A fourth group were friends, colleagues, former university students, rabbis, representatives from Jewish institutions, the Catholic priests, and a collection of disciples, readers whose lives had been changed by one or more of his books. Conspicuous by their absence were any official university or cultural representatives; there were no TV, radio, newspaper, or political bigwigs; there were no French dignitaries, those who honor their philosophers and to whom he often spoke publicly about many topics. Found later were numerous notes on the speeches he gave to the European Parliament and elsewhere (Malka 2002, 284). Simone and Michael, however, were not unhappy with the absence of officials at his burial. His death was reported on TV, and obituaries were printed in *Liberation* and a lengthy one in the *New York Times*.

He often said that, while philosophy is the love of wisdom, it is more truly "the wisdom of love at the service of love" (Levinas 1981, 163), and he began his classes with the announcement that philosophy is the science of naiveties. Along with too many philosophers, psychologists remain naive about his inspirational question, not *How shall we know?* but *How shall we live* with our neighbor, the widow, the stranger, the orphan?

Psychotherapy is dialogue, where *speaking to*...is its central characteristic, more important than whatever is *spoken about*. There is no profession where dialogue with another should be more pronounced in its sincerity, its responsibility; where the topic of *being-for-the-other* must arise over *being-for-oneself,* where *self-transcendence* should be achieved over *self-imminence,* where psychotherapy should be for the Other.

NOTES TO CHAPTER 2 / SEVERSON

1. See, for instance, Levinas 2003a, 63, 76. Many authors who have utilized the work of Levinas to influence psychotherapy have done so with the open admission that there are difficulties in this alignment. Alford (2002) seems to be particularly aware of this.

2. Details altered to protect his privacy.

3. Levinas (1996) wrote concerning the trace of the other person: "But then is not the trace the weight of being itself outside of its acts and its language, weighing not through its presence, which fits into the world, but by its very irreversibility, its absoluteness?" (62)

4. Pausanias 1900, 264 (Paus. 24.1). True self-knowledge, for Plato, would be the ultimate knowledge, however evasive such wisdom might be. Teaching, Socrates tells us in *The Meno* (1961), is recovering knowledge for oneself. To know the truth for the self would be to know the truth for *every* self. And in this regard, Platonic philosophy tilts away from the Sophistic division of knowledge and toward the primacy of the *same*.

5. Jolley 1995, 224–69. Socrates might have demonstrated some skepticism and the hope of Leibniz in the development of a language without any misunderstanding, but we can certainly see that the journey that leads to Leibniz begins with the Platonic rejection of Sophistry.

6. It is thought that Freud made this comment in a discussion with Ernest Becker in Berlin. For a discussion of the history of this remark, see Trilling 1950, 34.

7. This is an important theme in Freud's pivotal essay *The Interpretation of Dreams* (1972). Through a decoding process, Freud suggests that the content of dreams can be interpreted in consistent fashion. The key would be to avoid arbitrary and divergent interpretations by developing a common lexicon of symbolic elements and their correlations in reality.

8. Freud (1975) wrote: "So it comes about that psycho-analysis derives nothing but disadvantages from its middle position between medicine and philosophy. Doctors regard it as a speculative system and refuse to believe that, like every other natural science, it is based on a patient and tireless elaboration of facts from the world of perception; philosophers, measuring it by the standard of their own artificially constructed systems, find that it starts from impossible premises and reproach it because its most general concepts (which are only now in process of evolution) lack clarity and precision. This state of affairs is enough to account

for the reluctant and hesitant reception of analysis in scientific quarters" (Freud 1975, 217).

9. Henriques (2011) wrote: "the absence of a general foundation has been hugely problematic for psychology, especially from the pragmatic standpoint of the field's capacity to effectively impact society. Some psychologists have seen the lack of a coherent foundation as being so significant that it threatens the core integrity of the field" (4–5).

10. I suspect that several scholars in the psychological disciplines have long been working on the identification of language at this register, even if their work has not been incorporated into the canons of mainstream psychology. The movements of relational psychology seem fruitful in this direction. Philip Cushman, for example, turns to the linguistic configurations of Jewish midrash for a model for considering language in psychoanalysis (Cushman 2009).

11. Levinas, in *Entre Nous,* wrote: "'Swifter than eagles, stronger than lions'—a surpassing of the *conatus essendi* of life—an opening of the *human* through the living being: of the human, the newness of which would not be reduced to a more intense effort in its 'persevering in being'; would awaken in the guise of responsibility for the other man; the human in which the 'for the other' goes beyond the simple *Fürsorge* exercising itself in a world where others, gathered round about things, *are* what they do; the human, in which worry over the death of the other comes before care for the self. The humanness of dying for the other would be the very meaning of love in its responsibility for one's fellow man and, perhaps, the primordial inflection of the affective as such." Levinas, "Dying For…" This was a 1987 lecture first published in *Heidegger: Questions ouvertes,* ed. E. Escoubas (Paris: Editions Osiris, 1988), 255–64 (Levinas 1998a, 216).

12. In an interview, Levinas was asked about his criticism of "Western philosophy as egology." He responded: "The various relations that can exist in man and in being are always judged according to their proximity or distance from unity. What is relation? What is time? A fall from unity, a fall from eternity." See "Philosophy, Justice, and Love," remarks recorded by R. Fornet and A. Goez, October 3, 8, 1981 (Levinas 1998a, 112).

13. I am thinking particularly here of the work of Martin Heidegger and Hans-Georg Gadamer.

14. For Levinas, the anarchy of the other person refers to the fact that the relationship is established before any *arche* that could organize the relation into themes. He wrote: "Proximity appears as the relationship with the other, who cannot be resolved into 'images' or be exposed in a theme" (1998a, 100–01).

Notes to Chapter 4 / Adame

1. I will follow Levinas's convention of capitalizing the "Other" throughout this essay, in order to denote the hierarchal relationship of responsibility to other people that his philosophy describes.

2. It is important to note that Buber says an authentic I-Thou meeting characterized by full mutuality is limited by the unequal power hierarchy in relationships such as that between therapist and client or between teacher and student. However, he does advocate that both psychotherapists and educators follow the same principles of immediacy and reverence with their clients and students so that the latter groups may in turn carry forth those relational experiences in their interactions with others.

Notes to Chapter 9 / Goodman and Becker

1. People living in these residences are caught in the web of memories and regrets, living and reliving experiences without escape from some claustrophobic circuit. For instance, out of curiosity, two characters ventured out to find the home of Napoleon and upon looking at him through one of the windows discovered him: "Walking up and down—up and down all the time—left-right, left-right—never stopping for a moment…he never rested. And muttering to himself all the time. "It was Soult's fault. It was Ney's fault. It was Josephine's fault. It was the fault of the Russians. It was the fault of the English." Like that all the time. Never stopped for a moment. A little, fat man and he looked kind of tired. But he didn't seem able to stop it" (Lewis 2001, 12).

2. Levinas writes about two different forms of insomnia. First, the vacuousness of being and its brute lack of subjectivity (see Alford 2002 and Marcus 2008 for a clearer picture of this), what Levinas terms the "there is" (*il y a*), which generates a terror that keeps one from sleep. This terror dominated Levinas's early works, particularly *On Escape* and *Existence and Existents*. Some have argued that this early emphasis was informed by Levinas's experience of imprisonment and catastrophic familial losses during World War II (Alford 2002; Cohen 1994). The second form of insomnia described by Levinas gives an account of the violent awakening that the self experiences when its egoist slumber is disrupted in proximity to the Other. It is this second account that will be the focus of this piece.

3. Mitchell (2003) states, "It is the very otherness of the other that defines the limits to one's own omnipotence and creates the vulnerability, often the experience of helplessness, that accompanies desire. Thus romantic longing skates always on the edge of humiliation" (141).

4. As Levinas describes it, "The shock of the divine, the rupture of the immanent order…of the order which can become mine" (Robbins 2001, 48).

5. If the ego is naturally lived *for-itself*, with its inherent smallness and over-determined narratives, then Levinas calls for a "reversal of the natural order of things" (Robbins 2001, 47–48), a reversal of the natural progression of egoist fantasies. This reversal takes place in proximity to the Otherness of the Other.

6. Critchley (1999) writes that "Trauma is a 'non-intentional affectivity,' it tears into my subjectivity like an explosion, like a bomb that detonates without

warning, like a bullet that hits me in the dark, fired from an unseen gun and by an unknown assailant" (190).

7. Critchley (1999) refers to Levinas's logic as "masochistic" and "self-lacerating" (189).

8. Levinas and Kearney (2004) further state: "Ethical subjectivity dispenses with the idealizing subjectivity of ontology which reduces everything to itself. The ethical 'I' is subjectivity precisely insofar as it kneels before the other, sacrificing its own liberty to the more primordial call of the other. For me, the freedom of the subject is not the highest or primary value. The heteronomy of our response to the human other, or to God as the absolutely Other, precedes the autonomy of our subjective freedom. As soon as I acknowledge that it is 'I' who am responsible, I accept that my freedom is anteceded by an obligation to the other. Ethics redefines subjectivity as this heteronymous responsibility in contrast to autonomous freedom" (78).

9. Hutchens (2004) writes, "The opposition between freedom and responsibility, then, does not pose a question of exclusive alternatives, an 'either/or,' but rather a question of privilege and subordination" (18). Levinas states, "This is the most profound paradox in the concept of freedom: its synthetic bond with its own negation. A free being alone is responsible, that is, already not free. A being capable of beginning in the present is alone encumbered with itself" (Robbins 2001, 78–79).

10. The self is without rest in proximity to the Other. Levinas (1998c) writes that, "The identity of the subject is here brought out, not by a rest on itself, but by a restlessness that drives me outside of the nucleus of my substantiality" (142). Instead of the ego calling its surroundings into question, the ego is called into question. The face of the Other creates this violent inversion.

11. Emerging from his Jewish sensibilities, Levinas claimed that freedom can come only from sacrificial love and recognition of and moral responsibility for the Other.

12. Levinas writes, "[Ethics] is the original awakening of an I responsible for the other; the accession of my person to the uniqueness of the I called and elected to responsibility for the other" (Robbins 2001, 182).

13. R. D. Laing (1969a) and Erich Fromm (1955), among many other social theorists, consider the sociopolitical forces that entrap the self in alienation. Phillip Cushman (1995) draws out how economic infrastructures exert significant influence on the configuration of selves into consumptive and inward-facing orientations. Ernest Becker (1973) views the narcissism inherent in being organisms as contributing to the formation of self-centering myths we tell ourselves. Social context provides much of the terrain and landscape upon which we build our residences in Hell. This is rarely attended to adequately in psychotherapeutic theories and practices.

14. See Bromberg (2006) and Davies and Frawley (1991) for more recent engagement with the link between trauma and dissociation.

Notes to Chapter 13 / Slocum

1. By using the terminology "gay man," I run the risk of totalizing the very group of people for whom I wish to advocate. Gay men, as individuals, are other and therefore always-more-than-I-can-know.

2. When referring to being gay as "other," I am using analogy. For Levinas, the Other was always a living being with a face.

3. When writing about homophobic men, I realize that each of these men is an individual other and, therefore, a more-than-I-can-know. In representing them as homophobic men, I have totalized them, and out of justice I feel I owe an acknowledgment of my totalizing gesture and its potential violence.

Notes to Chapter 14 / Kunz

1. This chapter was originally a paper presented at the tenth annual Psychology for the Other seminar, November 2012, Seattle University.

2. Feminine pronouns for therapist and masculine for client will be used throughout the chapter.

3. Although awkward, I have inserted "therapist" and "client" in brackets.

Notes to Appendix B / Kunz

1. Malka 2002; Critchley and Bernasconi 2002; Robbins 2001.

2. "Man is a wolf to man" (Plautus, circa 194 BC). This aphorism is drawn on by Thomas Hobbes in the dedication of his work *De Cive* (1651).

3. This was first an essay published in *Recherches Philosophiques* as "De l'évasion" in 1935, then a book introduced by Jacques Rolland in 1981, and finally translated into English (Levinas 2003b).

4. This appeared first in *Giornale di Medatisca* (January–April 1982) and was collected in *Entre Nous: Thinking about the Other* (Levinas 1998a).

5. Husband, Georges Hansel, a talmudic scholar; son, David, a neuroscientist; and daughter-in-law, Joelle, a philosopher.

Adame, Alexandra L., and Roger M. Knudson. 2007. "Beyond the Counter-Narrative: Exploring Alternative Narratives of Recovery from the Psychiatric Survivor Movement." *Narrative Inquiry* 17:157–78.

———. 2008. "Recovery and the Good Life: How Psychiatric Survivors Are Revisioning the Healing Process." *Journal of Humanistic Psychology* 48:142–64.

Adame, Alexandra L., and Larry M. Leitner. 2011. "Dialogical Constructivism: Martin Buber's Enduring Relevance to Psychotherapy." *Journal of Humanistic Psychology* 51:41–60.

Alford, C. F. 2002. *Levinas, the Frankfurt School, and Psychoanalysis.* Middletown, CT: Wesleyan University Press.

American Psychiatric Association (APA). 1994. *Diagnostic and Statistical Manual of Mental Disorders (DSM-IV).* 4th ed. Washington, DC: American Psychiatric Association.

———. 2000. *Diagnostic and Statistical Manual of Mental Disorders (DSM-IV-TR).* 4th ed., text revision. Washington, DC: American Psychiatric Association.

———. 2013. *Diagnostic and Statistical Manual of Mental Disorders (DSM-V).* 5th ed. Washington, DC: American Psychiatric Association.

Apple, Rima D., and Janet L. Golden. 1997. *Mothers and Motherhood: Reading in American History.* Columbus: Ohio State University Press.

Aristotle. 1984. *The Complete Works of Aristotle.* Vol. 2. Edited by Jonathan Barnes. Princeton: Princeton University Press.

Atterton, Peter. 2010. "'The Talking Cure': The Ethics of Psychoanalysis." In *Radicalizing Levinas,* edited by Peter Atterton and Matthew Calarco, 185–203. Albany: State University of New York Press.

Atterton, Peter, and Matthew Calarco, eds. 2010. *Radicalizing Levinas.* Albany: State University of New York Press.

Atterton, Peter, Matthew Calarco, and Maurice S. Friedman. 2004. *Levinas and Buber: Dialogue and Difference.* Pittsburgh: Duquesne University Press.

Atwood, George E., and Robert D. Stolorow. 1984. *Structures of Subjectivity: Explorations in Psychoanalytic Phenomenology*. Hillsdale, NJ: Analytic Press.

August, Peter. 2010. *Is There a Language to Logos? The End of Metaphor and the Beginning of Time*. Unpublished paper.

Bachelard, Gaston. 1969. *The Poetics of Reverie*. New York: Orion Press.

Baird, M. 2007. "Whose Kenosis? An Analysis of Levinas, Derrida, and Vattimo on God's Self-Emptying and the Secularization of the West." *Heythrop Journal* 48:423–37.

Beals, Corey. 2007. *Levinas and the Wisdom of Love: The Question of Invisibility*. Waco, TX: Baylor University Press.

Becker, E. 1973. *The Denial of Death*. New York: Free Press Paperback, Simon and Schuster.

Becker, Larry C. 2005. "Emasculated Men, Effeminate Law in the United States, Zimbabwe, and Malaysia." *Yale Journal of Law and Feminism* 17.1. ssrn.com/abstract=618863 (accessed May 21, 2006).

Bernasconi, Robert, and Simon Critchley. 1991. *Re-Reading Levinas*. Bloomington: Indiana University Press.

Bernasconi, Robert, and David Wood. 1988. *The Provocation of Levinas: Rethinking the Other*. London: Routledge.

Binswanger, Ludwig. 1963. *Being-in-the-World: Selected Papers of Ludwig Binswanger*. Translated and edited by Jacob Needleman. New York: Basic Books.

Blackwell, Marylin S. 1997. "The Republican Vision of Mary Palmer Tyler." In *Mothers and Motherhood: Reading in American History,* edited by Rima D. Apple and Janet L. Golden, 31–51. Columbus: Ohio State University Press.

Bly, Robert. 1990. *Iron John: Men and Masculinity*. London: Rider.

———. 1996. *The Sibling Society*. New York: Vintage Books.

Bohart, Arthur, Maureen O'Hara, Larry M. Leitner, Fred J. Wertz, E. Mark Stern, and Kirk Schneider. 1997. "Guidelines for the Provision of Humanistic Services." *Humanistic Psychologist* 24:64–107.

———. 2001. "Recommended Principles and Practices for the Provision of Humanistic Psychosocial Services: Alternative to Mandated Practice and Treatment Guidelines." In *Task Force for the Development of Practice Recommendations for the Provision of Humanistic Psychosocial Services,* edited by Arthur Bohart. American Psychological Association Division 32, Humanistic Psychology.

Boszormenyi-Nagy, Ivan. 1987. *Foundations of Contextual Therapy: Collected Papers of Ivan Boszormenyi-Nagy MD.* New York: Brunner/Mazel.

Bozga, Adina. 2009. *The Exasperating Gift of Singularity.* Bucharest: Zeta Books.

Bromberg, P. 2006. *Awakening the Dreamer: Clinical Journeys.* New York: Routledge.

Buber, Martin. 1957. *Pointing the Way: Collected Essays.* New York: Harper and Brothers.

———. 1958. *I and Thou.* 2nd ed. Translated by Ronald Gregor Smith. New York: Scribner.

———. 1965. *Between Man and Man.* New York: Macmillan.

———. 1966. *The Way of Man: According to the Teaching of Hasidism.* Secaucus, NJ: Citadel Press.

———. 1988. *The Knowledge of Man: Selected Essays.* New York: Harper and Row.

Bugental, James F. T. 1987. *The Art of the Psychotherapist.* New York: W. W. Norton.

Burggraeve, Roger. 1985. *From Self-Development to Solidarity: An Ethical Reading of Human Desire in Its Socio-Political Relevance according to Emmanuel Levinas.* Translated by C. Vanhove-Romanik. Leuven: Centre for Metaphysics and Philosophy of God.

Butcher, J. N., W. G. Dahlstrom, J. R. Graham, A. Tellegan, B. Kaemmer. 1992. *MMPI-A: Minnesota Multiphasic Personality Inventory-A: Manual for Administration and Scoring.* Minneapolis: University of Minnesota Press.

Cohen, Richard A. 1994. *Elevations: The Height of the Good in Rosenzweig and Levinas.* Chicago: University of Chicago Press.

———. 2001. *Ethics, Exegesis, and Philosophy: Interpretation after Levinas.* Cambridge: Cambridge University Press.

———. 2002. "Maternal Psyche." In *Psychology for the Other: Levinas, Ethics, and the Practice of Psychology,* edited by Edwin E. Gantt and Richard N. Williams, 32–64. Pittsburgh: Duquesne University Press.

Cohen, Richard A., ed. 1986. *Face to Face with Levinas.* Albany: State University of New York Press.

Collins, Anthony. 2004. "Critical Psychology: The Basic Coordinates." In *Introduction to Critical Psychology,* edited by D. Hook, 10–24. Cape Town, South Africa: University of Cape Town Press.

Critchley, Simon. 1999. *Ethics-Politics-Subjectivity: Essays on Derrida, Levinas, and Contemporary French Thought.* Brooklyn: Verso.

———. 2007. *Infinitely Demanding: Ethics of Commitment, Politics of Resistance.* New York: Verso.

Critchley, Simon, and Robert Bernasconi. 2002. *The Cambridge Companion to Levinas.* Cambridge: Cambridge University Press.

Cushman, Philip. 1990. "Why the Self Is Empty: Toward a Historically Situated Psychology." *American Psychologist* 45:599–611.

———. 1995. *Constructing the Self, Constructing America: A Cultural History of Psychotherapy.* Cambridge, MA: Perseus Publishing.

———. 2009. "A Burning World, an Absent God: Midrash, Hermeneutics, and Relational Psychoanalysis." In *Answering a Question with a Question: Contemporary Psychoanalysis and Jewish Thought,* edited by Lewis Aron and L. Henik, 47–88. New York: Academic Studies Press.

Dana, Richard H. 1998. *Understanding Cultural Identity in Intervention and Assessment.* Thousand Oaks, CA: Sage.

Davies, J. M., and M. G. Frawley. 1991. "Dissociative Processes and Transference-Countertransference Paradigms in the Psychoanalytically Oriented Treatment of Adult Survivors of Childhood Sexual Abuse." In *Relational Psychoanalysis: The Emergence of a Tradition,* edited by S. Mitchell and L. Aron, 269–304. New York: Analytic Press.

de Beauvoir, Simone. 2009. *The Second Sex.* Translated by Constance Borde and Sheila Malovany-Chevallier. New York: Random House. First published 1949.

Derrida, Jacques. 1978. "Violence and Metaphysics." *Writing and Difference.* Chicago: University of Chicago Press. First published in French 1964.

———. 1999. *Adieu to Emmanuel Levinas.* Translated by Pascale-Anne Brault and Michael Naas. Stanford, CA: Stanford University Press. Speech given at Levinas's funeral in 1995, first published in French 1997.

Diprose, Rosalyn. 2009. "Nietzsche, Levinas, and the Meaning of Responsibility." In *Nietzsche and Levinas: "After the Death of a Certain God,"* edited by J. Stauffer and B. Bergo, 116–33. New York: Columbia University Press.

Downs, Alan. 2005. *The Velvet Rage: Overcoming the Pain of Growing Up Gay in a Straight Man's World.* Cambridge: Da Capo Lifelong Books.

Ehrenberg, Darlene B. 1992. *The Intimate Edge: Extending the Reach of Psychoanalytic Interaction.* New York: W. W. Norton.

Elliott, Robert, Leslie Greenburg, and Germain Lietaer. 2004. "Research on Experiential Psychotherapies." In *Bergin and Garfield's Handbook of Psychotherapy and Behavior Change*, 5th ed., edited by Michael J. Lambert, 493–539. New York: Wiley.

Farber, Leslie H. 1966. *The Ways of the Will: Essays toward a Psychology and a Psychopathology of the Will*. New York: Basic Books.

Ferrara, Leonard. 1995. "The Meaning of Mother-Infant Bonding: A Constructionist Analysis." California School of Professional Psychology–Berkeley/Alameda. Available at search.proquest.com/docview/304188 395?accountid=28598.

Finn, Stephen. 2007. *In Our Client's Shoes: Theory and Techniques of Therapeutic Assessment*. Mahwah, NJ: Erlbaum.

Fischer, Constance. 1994. *Individualizing Psychological Assessment*. Mahwah, NJ: Erlbaum. First published 1985.

Fiumara, Gemma Corradi. 1995. *The Other Side of Language*. New York: Routledge.

———. 2001. *The Mind's Affective Life: A Psychoanalytic and Philosophical Inquiry*. East Sussex: Brunner-Routledge.

Freire, Paulo. 1998. "Cultural Action and Conscientization." *Harvard Educational Review* 68:499–521.

Freud, Sigmund. 1972. *The Interpretation of Dreams*. Translated by James Strachey. New York: Harper and Row.

———. 1975. "The Resistances to Psychoanalysis." In *The Standard Edition of the Complete Psychological Works of Sigmund Freud*, vol. 19, translated by James Strachey. London: Hogarth Press.

———. 1989. "Mourning and Melancholia." Translated by James Strachey. In *The Freud Reader*, edited by Peter Gay, 215–43. New York: W. W. Norton.

———. 2004. *Freud Dictionary of Psychoanalysis*. New York: Barnes and Noble.

Friedman, Maurice. 1960. *Martin Buber: The Life of Dialogue*. New York: Harper and Row.

———. 1992. *Dialogue and the Human Image: Beyond Humanistic Psychology*. Newbury Park, CA: Sage.

———. 1996. *Martin Buber and the Human Sciences*. Albany: State University of New York Press.

Fromm, Erich H. 1955. *The Sane Society*. New York: Henry Holt.

———. 1994. *Escape from Freedom*. New York: Henry Holt. First published 1941.

Fryer, D. R. 2007. "What Levinas and Psychoanalysis Can Teach Each Other, or How to Be a Mensch without Going Meshugah." *Psychoanalytic Review* 94:577–94.

Gadamer, Hans-Georg. 1998. *Truth and Method*. Translated by Joel Weinsheimer and Donald G. Marshall. New York: Continuum. First published 1960.

Gantt, Edwin E. 2002. "Utopia, Psychotherapy, and the Place of Suffering." In *Psychology for the Other: Levinas, Ethics, and the Practice of Psychology*, edited by Edwin E. Gantt and Richard N. Williams, 65–83. Pittsburgh: Duquesne University Press.

Gantt, Edwin E., and Richard N. Williams, eds. 2002. *Psychology for the Other: Levinas, Ethics, and the Practice of Psychology*. Pittsburgh: Duquesne University Press.

Gendlin, Eugene T. 1996. *Focusing-Oriented Psychotherapy: A Manual of the Experiential Method*. New York: Guilford Press.

Ginzberg, Louis. 2010. *Die Haggada bei den Kirchenvätern*. Charleston, SC: Nabu Press.

Goldberg, Carl. 2000. "Healing Madness and Despair through Meeting." *American Journal of Psychotherapy* 54:560–73.

Goodman, D., and S. Grover. 2008. "Hineni and Transference: The Remembering and Forgetting of the Other. *Pastoral Psychology* 56:561–71.

Graf-Taylor, Rose. 1996. "Philosophy of Dialogue and Feminist Psychology." In *Martin Buber and the Human Sciences,* edited by M. Friedman, 327–34. Albany: State University of New York Press.

Guthrie, William K. C. 1971. *The Sophists.* Cambridge: Cambridge University Press.

Haidt, J. 2003. "The Moral Emotions." In *Handbook of Affective Sciences,* edited by R. J. Davidson, K. R. Scherer, and H. H. Goldsmith, 852–70. Oxford: Oxford University Press.

Halling, Steen. 1975. "The Implications of Emmanuel Levinas' *Totality and Infinity* for Therapy." In *Duquesne Studies in Phenomenological Psychology,* vol. 2, edited by Amedeo Giorgi, Constance T. Fischer, and Edward L. Murray, 206–23. Pittsburgh: Duquesne University Press.

Hamilton, J. 2013. "Homosexuality 101: What Every Therapist, Parent, and Homosexual Should Know." Available at narth.com/2011/11/

homosexuality-101-what-every-therapist-parent-and-homosexual-should-know-2. Retrieved May 20, 2013, from National Association of Research and Therapy of Homosexuality.

Hand, Seán. 1996. *Facing the Other: The Ethics of Emmanuel Levinas.* Richmond, Surrey: Curzon.

Heaton, John. 1988. "The Other and Psychotherapy." In *The Provocation of Levinas,* edited by Robert D. Bernasconi, 5–14. London: Routledge.

Hegel, Georg F. W. 2009. *Phenomenology of Spirit.* Translated by J. B. Baillie. Lawrence, KS: Digireads.

Heidegger, Martin. 1962. *Being and Time.* Translated by John Macquarrie and Edward Robinson. New York: Harper and Row. First published 1927.

———. 1996. *Being and Time.* Translated by Joan Stambaugh. Albany: State University of New York Press. First published 1927.

Henriques, Gregg. 2011. *A New Unified Theory of Psychology.* New York: Springer.

Hillman, James, and Michael Ventura. 1992. *We've Had a Hundred Years of Psychotherapy and the World Is Getting Worse.* San Francisco: Harper.

Hobbes, Thomas. 1904. *Leviathan.* Cambridge: Cambridge University Press.

Hollis, James. 1994. *Under Saturn's Shadow: The Wounding and Healing of Men.* Toronto: Inner City Books.

Huskinson, L. 2002. "The Self as Violent Other: The Problem of Defining the Self." *Journal of Analytical Psychology* 47:437–58.

Hutchens, B. 2004. *Levinas: A Guide for the Perplexed.* London: Continuum International.

Hycner, Richard H. 1991. *Between Person and Person: Toward a Dialogical Psychotherapy.* Highland, NY: Gestalt Journal Press.

Irigaray, L. 1991. "Questions to Emmanuel Levinas: On the Divinity of Love." In *Re-Reading Levinas,* edited by R. Bernasconi and S. Critchley, 109–18. Bloomington: Indiana University Press.

Jolley, Nicholas. 1995. *The Cambridge Companion to Leibniz.* Cambridge: Cambridge University Press.

Jourard, Sidney M. 1971. *The Transparent Self.* New York: D. Van Nostrand.

Kaiser, Hellmuth. 1965. *Effective Psychotherapy: The Contribution of Hellmuth Kaiser.* Edited by L. B. Fireman. New York: Free Press.

King, B. B. 1996. *Blues All around Me.* New York: Avon Books.

Kohut, Heinz. 1971. *The Analysis of the Self.* New York: International University Press.

———. 1977. *The Restoration of the Self.* New York: International University Press.

Kunz, George. 1998. *The Paradox of Power and Weakness: Levinas and an Alternative Paradigm for Psychology.* Albany: State University of New York Press.

———. 2002. "Simplicity, Humility, Patience." In *Psychology for the Other: Levinas, Ethics, and the Practice of Psychology,* edited by Edwin E. Gantt and Richard N. Williams, 118–42. Pittsburgh: Duquesne University Press.

———. 2006a. "Interruptions: Levinas." *Journal of Phenomenological Psychology* 37:241–66.

———. 2006b. "Levinas Psychoanalysis." Paper presented at the Psychology for the Other Seminar, Seattle, WA. October.

Laing, Ronald D. 1969a. *The Divided Self.* New York: Penguin Books.

———. 1969b. *Self and Others.* New York: Penguin Books.

La Leche League of Seattle AM. www.lllofwa.org/la-leche-league-seattle-am.

Levinas, Emmanuel. 1969. *Totality and Infinity: An Essay on Exteriority.* Translated by Alfonso Lingis. Pittsburgh: Duquesne University Press. First published 1961.

———. 1981. *Otherwise than Being, or Beyond Essence.* Translated by Alphonso Lingis. The Hague: Martinus Nijhoff. First published 1974.

———. 1985. *Ethics and Infinity: Conversations with Philippe Nemo.* Translated by Richard A. Cohen. Pittsburgh: Duquesne University Press. First published 1982.

———. 1987. *Time and the Other.* Pittsburgh: Duquesne University Press. First published 1947.

———. 1989. *The Levinas Reader.* Edited by Seán Hand. Cambridge: Basil Blackwell.

———. 1990a. *Difficult Freedom: Essays on Judaism.* Translated by Seán Hand. Baltimore: Johns Hopkins University Press. First published 1963.

———. 1990b. *Nine Talmudic Readings.* Translated by A. Aronowicz. Bloomington: Indiana University Press. First published 1968.

———. 1990c. "Reflections on the Philosophy of Hitlerism." Translated by Seán Hand. *Critical Inquiry* 17.1:63–71. First published 1934.

———. 1993. *Outside the Subject.* Translated by Michael B. Smith. Stanford, CA: Stanford University Press. First published 1987.

———. 1994. "On the Utility of Insomnia." In *Unforeseen History,* translated by Nidra Poller, 127–29. Chicago: University of Illinois Press. First published 1987.

———. 1996. *Emmanuel Levinas: Basic Philosophical Writings.* Edited by Adriaan T. Peperzak, Simon Critchley, and Robert Bernasconi. Bloomington: Indiana University Press.

———. 1997. *Collected Philosophical Papers.* Translated by Alphonso Lingis. Dordrecht, Netherlands: Martinus Nijhoff Publishers. First published 1987.

———. 1998a. *Entre Nous: Thinking of the Other.* Translated by Michael B. Smith and Barbara Harshav. New York: Columbia University Press. First published 1988.

———. 1998b. *Of God Who Comes to Mind.* Translated by B. Bergo. Stanford, CA: Meridian Press. First published 1982.

———. 2000. *Alterity and Transcendence.* Translated by Michael B. Smith. New York: Columbia University Press. First published 1995.

———. 2001. *Existence and Existents.* Translated by Alphonso Lingis. Pittsburgh: Duquesne University Press. First published 1978.

———. 2003a. *Humanism of the Other.* Translated by Nidra Poller. Chicago: University of Illinois Press. First published 1972.

———. 2003b. *On Escape.* Translated by Bettina Bergo. Stanford, CA: Stanford University Press. First published 1935.

Levinas, Emmanuel, and Richard Kearney. 1986. "Dialogue with Emmanuel Levinas." Interview by Richard Kearney. In *Face to Face with Levinas,* edited by Richard Cohen. Albany: State University of New York Press.

———. 2004. "Emmanuel Levinas: Ethics of the Infinite." In *Debates in Continental Philosophy: Conversations with Contemporary Thinkers,* edited by R. Kearney, 65–84. New York: Fordham University Press.

Lewis, C. S. 2001. *The Great Divorce.* New York: HarperCollins. First published 1946.

Malka, Salomon. 2002. *Emmanuel Levinas: His Life and Legacy.* Translated by Michael Kigel. Pittsburgh: Duquesne University Press.

Marcus, Paul. 2008. *Being for the Other: Emmanuel Levinas, Ethical Living, and Psychoanalysis*. Milwaukee, WI: Marquette University Press.

Marcuse, Herbert. 1962. *Eros and Civilization*. New York: Vintage Books.

May, Rollo. 1967. *Psychology and the Human Dilemma*. Princeton, NJ: D. Van Nostrand.

McCann, Lisa, and Laurie A. Pearlman. 1990. "Vicarious Traumatization: A Framework for Understanding the Psychological Effects of Working with Victims." *Journal of Traumatic Stress* 3(1):131–49.

Mitchell, S. 2003. *Can Love Last? The Fate of Romance over Time*. New York: W. W. Norton.

Oppenheim, M. 2006. *Jewish Philosophy and Psychoanalysis: Narrating the Interhuman*. New York: Lexington Books.

Pausanias. 1900. *Description of Greece*. London: George Bell and Sons.

Perls, Fritz. 1969. *Gestalt Therapy Verbatim*. Lafayette, IN: Real People Press.

Plato. 1961. *The Meno*. Edited by R. S. Bluck. Cambridge: Cambridge University Press.

———. 1990. *The Theaetetus*. Translated by M. J. Levett. Indianapolis: Hackett.

———. 1992. *Republic*. Translated by G. M. A. Grube and C. D. C. Reeve. Indianapolis: Hackett.

———. 2009. *Plato's Protagoras*. Translated by Benjamin Jowett. Rockville, MD: Serenity Publishers.

Praglin, Laura. 2006. "The Nature of the 'In-Between' in D. W. Winnicott's Concept of Transitional Space and in Martin Buber's *das Zwischenmenschliche*." *Universitas* 2:1–9.

Prilleltensky, Isaac. 1997. "Values, Assumptions, and Practices: Assessing the Moral Implications of Psychological Discourse and Action." *American Psychologist* 5:517–35.

Ricoeur, P. 1992. *Oneself as Another*. Translated by K. Blamey. Chicago: University of Chicago Press. First published 1990.

Robbins, J. 1991. *Prodigal Son / Elder Brother: Interpretation and Alterity in Augustine, Petrarch, Kafka, Levinas*. Chicago: University of Chicago Press.

Robbins, Jill, ed. 2001. *Is It Righteous to Be? Interviews with Emmanuel Levinas*. Stanford, CA: Stanford University Press. First published 1987.

Rogers, Carl. 1959. "A Theory of Therapy, Personality Relationships as Developed in the Client-Centered Framework." In *Psychology: A Study of a Science*, vol. 3, *Formulations of the Person and the Social Context*, edited by Sigmund Koch. New York: McGraw Hill.

———. 1970. *Carl Rogers on Encounter Groups*. New York: Harper and Row.

———. 1979. "Being in Relationship: Voices." *Art and Science of Psychotherapy* 6.2:11–19.

Sartre, Jean-Paul. 1947. *No Exit, and Three Other Plays*. Translated by S. Gilbert. New York: Knopf. First published 1944.

———. 1977. *Existentialism and Humanism*. Translated by Philip Mairet. Brooklyn: Haskell House.

Sayre, G. 2005. Toward a Therapy for the Other. *European Journal of Psychotherapy, Counseling, and Health* 7:37–47.

Severson, Eric. 2010. "Time, Lament, and Testimony: Levinas' Late Work and the Impossible Possibility of Therapy." Paper presented at the 8th annual Psychology for the Other Seminar, Seattle University, WA. October.

———. 2011. *Scandalous Obligation: Rethinking Christian Responsibility*. Kansas City, MO: Beacon Hill Press of Kansas City.

Siegel, R. 2009. *This Very Moment: Mindfulness in Psychotherapy*. Grand Rounds presentation at Cambridge Health Alliance/Harvard Medical School. Cambridge, MA.

Smith, Michael B. 2005. *Toward the Outside: Concepts and Themes in Emmanuel Levinas*. Pittsburgh: Duquesne University Press.

Spinoza, de Baruch. 2000. *Ethics*. Edited and translated by George H. R. Parkinson. Oxford: Oxford University Press.

Steiner, H., and Z. Matthews. 1996. "Psychiatric Trauma and Related Psychopathologies." In *Treating Adolescents*, edited by Hans Steiner and Irvin Yalom, 345–95. San Francisco: John Wiley and Sons.

Stern, Donnell. 2003. *Unformulated Experience: From Dissociation to Imagination in Psychoanalysis*. Hillsdale, NJ: Analytic Press.

———. 2010. *Partners in Thought: Working with Unformulated Experience, Dissociation, and Enactment*. New York: Routledge.

Sternberg, Robert, and Elena L. Grigorenko. 2001. "Unified Psychology." *American Psychology* 12:1069–79.

Stewart, David, and Algis Mickunas. 1990. *Exploring Phenomenology: A Guide to the Field and Its Literature*. Athens: Ohio University Press.

Stone, I. F. 1998. *Reading Levinas / Reading Talmud: An Introduction*. Philadelphia: Jewish Publication Society.

Strean, Herbert S. 1993. *Resolving Counterresistances in Psychotherapy*. London: Routledge.

Sue, Derald, and David Sue. 1990. *Counseling the Culturally Different: Theory and Practice*. New York: Wiley.

Taylor, C. 2007. *A Secular Age*. Cambridge, MA: Belknap Press.

Trilling, Lionel. 1950. *The Liberal Imagination*. New York: New York Review of Books.

Unamuno, Miguel de. 1985. *San Manuel Bueno, Martir*. Madrid: Alhambra.

Valle, Ronald S., Mark King, and Steen Halling. 1989. "An Introduction to Existential-Phenomenological Thought in Psychology." In *Existential-Phenomenological Perspectives in Psychology*, edited by Ronald S. Valle and Steen Halling, 3–16. New York: Plenum Press.

van den Berg, Jan Hendrick. 1972. *A Different Existence*. Pittsburgh: Duquesne University Press.

Vanier, Jean. 1992. *From Brokenness to Community*. Mahwah, NJ: Paulist Press.

Visker, R. 2000. "The Price of Being Dispossessed: Levinas's God and Freud's Trauma." In *The Face of the Other and The Trace of God: Essays on the Philosophy of Emmanuel Levinas*, edited by J. Bloechl, 243–75. New York: Fordham University Press.

Waddington, Miriam. 1968. *Call Them Canadians*, ed. L. Monk. Ottawa: Queen's Printer.

Walker, Lenore E. 1979. *The Battered Woman*. New York: Harper and Row.

Walters, James W. 2003. *Martin Buber and Feminist Ethics: The Priority of the Personal*. Syracuse: Syracuse University Press.

Warner, C. Terry. 2001. *Bonds That Make Us Free: Healing Our Relationships, Coming to Ourselves*. Salt Lake City, UT: Shadow Mountain.

Warner, Clarence. 2005. *The Promises of God*. Camarillo, CA: Xulon Press.

Wayne, L. 2008. *Lollipop*. Available at www.metrolyrics.com. Retrieved September 20, 2010.

Wertz, Frederick J. 1983. "Some Components of Descriptive Psychological Reflection." *Human Studies* 6:35–51.

Wiesel, E. 1990. *The Night Trilogy*. New York: Hill and Wang. First published 1960.

Williams, R. N. 2002. "On Being for the Other: Freedom as Investiture." In *Psychology for the Other: Levinas, Ethics, and the Practice of Psychology*, edited by Edwin E. Gantt and Richard N. Williams, 143–59. Pittsburgh: Duquesne University Press.

———. 2003. "Psychology in the Breach: The Importance of Being Earnest." In *Theoretical Psychology: Critical Contributions*, edited by N. Stephenson, H. L. Radtke, R. J. Jorna, and H. J. Stam, 2–10. Concord, Ontario: Captus University Publications.

———. 2005. "Self-Betraying Emotions and the Psychology of Heteronomy." *European Journal of Psychotherapy, Counselling, and Health* 7.1–2:7–16.

Williams, R. N., and E. E. Gantt. 1998. "Intimacy and Heteronomy: On Grounding Psychology in the Ethical." *Theory and Psychology* 8.2:253–67.

———. 2002. "Pursuing Psychology as Science of the Ethical: Contributions of the Work of Emmanuel Levinas." In *Psychology for the Other: Levinas, Ethics, and the Practice of Psychology*, edited by Edwin E. Gantt and Richard N. Williams, 1–31. Pittsburgh: Duquesne University Press.

Wyschogrod, Edith. 1974. *Emmanuel Levinas: The Problem of Ethical Metaphysics*. The Hague: Martinus Nijhoff.

Alexandra L. Adame is an assistant professor of psychology at Seattle University, where she both teaches undergraduate classes and works with graduate students in the master of arts in existential phenomenological psychology program. Her scholarly interests include social activism movements, Martin Buber, researcher reflexivity, and first-person madness narratives. She has published in various scholarly journals, most recently coauthoring with N. Zerubavel a manuscript on the importance of dialogue between qualitative and quantitative approaches in psychology.

Brian Becker is an assistant professor of neuropsychology in the Division of Psychology and Applied Therapies at Lesley University and a research fellow at the Psychology and the Other Institute. Along with his research in the neuropsychology of aging and HIV, he has written on topics related to phenomenology and psychological theory. His most recent work, to be published in the *Journal of Theoretical and Philosophical Psychology,* is an exploration of the phenomenology of gift-giving as an alternative to economic models that define contemporary psychology. Becker is a licensed psychologist and practicing neuropsychologist at Integrative Assessment Services located in Cambridge, Massachusetts.

Richard A. Cohen is professor of philosophy and director of the Institute of Jewish Thought and Heritage at the University of Buffalo and director of the annual Levinas Philosophy Summer seminar. His scholarly interests include modern and contemporary European thought. He is author of three volumes on the philosophy of Emmanuel Levinas: *Elevations: The Height of the Good in Rosenzweig and Levinas; Ethics, Exegesis and Philosophy: Interpretation after Levinas;* and *Levinasian Meditations: Ethics, Philosophy, and Religion.* A fourth volume, *Levinas and Spinoza: Ethics, Politics, Science, and Religion,* is forthcoming. He is also translator of four books by Levinas and author of many articles in modern and contemporary philosophy.

David Goodman is interim associate dean at the Woods College of Advancing Studies at Boston College and a teaching associate at Harvard Medical School/Cambridge Hospital. He has written articles on continental philosophy, Jewish thought, social justice, and psychotherapy, and his book *The Demanded Self: Levinasian Ethics and Identity in Psychology* considers the intersection of psychology, philosophy, and theology. Goodman also co-directs an interdisciplinary and interinstitutional theoretical, historical, and philosophical psychology research lab, working with students and colleagues on topics related to critical psychology, moral development theory, intersubjectivity, and relational psychoanalysis, hermeneutical and dialogical psychologies, and the interfacing of religious/theological and psychological theories of selfhood. He is also a licensed clinical psychologist and has a private practice in Cambridge, Massachusetts.

Jackie Grimesey Szarka is a licensed clinical psychologist in private practice. She is also a program manager with the Department of Veterans' Affairs division of Health Services Research and Development. The focus of her clinical work and research is on the experiences of trauma survivors and their significant others and on health services delivery in the U.S. Department of Veterans' Affairs.

Steen Halling is a licensed psychologist and professor emeritus of psychology at Seattle University, where he has taught since 1976 the master of arts program in existential-phenomenological psychology as well as in the undergraduate program. His research and publications have focused on topics such as psychology of forgiveness, phenomenological study of psychopathology, psychology of hopelessness, interpersonal relations, and qualitative research methods. He is editor of the *International Human Science Research Conference Newsletter;* co-editor with Ronald S. Valle of *Existential-Phenomenological Perspectives in Psychology;* and author of *Intimacy, Transcendence, and Psychology.* Since 1996 he has been involved with the Psychotherapy Cooperative, a nonprofit counseling service for low-income clients in Seattle.

Kevin C. Krycka is professor of psychology and director of the Master of Arts in Existential-Phenomenological Therapeutic Psychology at Seattle University. Since joining the faculty in 1989, he has taught both graduate and undergraduate courses in the area of abnormal psychology and the preparation of psychotherapists from an ethical foundation. Krycka's scholarship utilizes phenomenological research methods used toward developing a deep understanding of how human beings experience and respond to change. His theoretical writings bring the works of Emmanuel Levinas and Eugene Gendlin into dialogue. Currently he is developing a model for peace-building that helps bring the felt-sensing process of Focusing into social change theory and practice. He was appointed to the Focusing Institute Board of Directors in July 2014.

George Kunz received his B.A. from Gonzaga University in 1960, his M.A. from Marquette University in 1964, and his Ph.D. from Duquesne University in 1975. His dissertation title is "Perceived Behavior as a Subject Matter for a Phenomenologically Based Psychology." He taught psychology in the Department of Psychology at Seattle University from 1971 to 2011, when he retired. During his career, he helped establish the dialogal research method and wrote an important book that applied Levinas's philosophy to psychotherapy, *The Paradox of Power and Weakness: Levinas and an Alternative Paradigm for Psychology*.

Claire Steele LeBeau is an assistant professor in psychology, teaching undergraduate and graduate courses in the existential-phenomenological foundations of continental philosophy to psychology. Her scholarly interests include the interpersonal origins of ethics as seen through the philosophy of Emmanuel Levinas, the therapeutic application of existential phenomenology to healing relationships, the use of Genlin's Focusing Technique in therapy and embodied research, and the developmental transition and transformation of new parenthood. Claire also has a small private psychotherapy practice in the Seattle area.

Heather Macdonald is assistant professor in the department of psychology and applied therapies at Lesley University, after working as a clinical psychologist with community outreach, child assessment, individual therapy services to children and families in the foster care system, and youth in the juvenile justice system. Gang resistance initiatives, youth violence prevention, and cultural psychology are long-standing professional interests. Macdonald has undertaken research on the interface between culture, social justice, and psychotherapy, drawing upon ideas and disciplines including cultural phenomenology and theories of embodiment. Her articles include "Issues of Translation, Mistrust, and Co-Collaboration in Therapeutic Assessment" and "The Ghetto Intern: Culture and Memory," and they examine the danger of imposing overarching psychological universals to specific cultural environments.

Marie McNabb is a therapist in private practice in Seattle, Washington. She is a member of the Psychotherapy Cooperative, which provides low-cost therapy services to the underserved, and she is an organizer of the annual Giving Voice to Experience conference at Seattle University, which supports qualitative research in the broader therapeutic community. With a background in financial services, she currently leads qualitative research projects on money as a shared, human symbol.

Kathleen M. Pape has a private practice in Seattle and is an adjunct professor of psychology at Seattle University. Her research has focused on the experience of adult sibling bereavement, feminist maternal theory, and the philosophy of Emmanuel Levinas. Her current scholarly interests include mothering and motherhood, hermeneutics and psychological theory, and perinatal mood and anxiety disorders.

George G. Sayre holds a doctorate in clinical family psychology and has 25 years of experience as a marriage and family therapist. Currently he is a health science researcher and qualitative resources coordinator at the Puget Sound VHA HSR&D Center of Innovation for Veteran-Centered and Value-Driven Care and a clinical assistant professor at the University of Washington Department of Health. Previously he was a visiting assistant professor at Seattle University, department of psychology, and a clinician in private practice in Seattle, Washington.

Eric R. Severson is author of *Scandalous Obligation* and *Levinas's Philosophy of Time*. He lives in Kenmore, Washington, with his wife, Misha, and their three children, and he currently teaches for both Seattle University and Seattle Pacific University.

Trevor J. Slocum is a licensed mental health counselor with a private practice in Seattle. His interests include social justice and the application of Buddhist philosophy and mindfulness practices to therapeutic psychology. He teaches at the Seattle Buddhist Center and is also training in Accelerated Experiential-Dynamic Psychotherapy.

Richard N. Williams is a professor of psychology and currently director of the Wheatley Institution at Brigham Young University. His scholarly interests include the conceptual foundations of psychological theories and the relationship between traditional and postmodern perspectives. Related to this topic, he has written *What's Behind the Research: Discovering Hidden Assumptions in the Social Sciences* (with Brent Slife) and edited (with Edwin Gantt) *Psychology for the Other*. He has published in various scholarly journals, most recently in the *Journal of Moral Education*.

Emilie Zuckerman is a licensed mental health counselor associate with a private practice in Belltown, Seattle. Before receiving her master of arts degree in psychology from Seattle University's existential-phenomenological psychology program, she completed a bachelor of arts degree in film and media studies from Temple University. She continues to explore ways to creatively engage and reconnect her clients with their fuller potential. She interned at Seattle Therapy Alliance, where she worked with women in a low-cost private practice setting.